THE
BUSINESS WRITER'S BOOK OF
LISTS

The all-in-one office companion with lists of . . .

- **TRANSITION WORDS AND PHRASES TO MAKE YOUR WRITING FLOW SMOOTHLY**

- **BUSINESS JARGON THAT SHOULD BE USED CAUTIOUSLY**

- **SEXIST WORDS THAT READERS MAY NOT FORGIVE**

- **COMMON REDUNDANCIES THAT ADD DEADWEIGHT TO YOUR WRITING**

- **COMMONLY MISSPELLED WORDS**

- **LOADED LANGUAGE THAT MAY REVEAL A BIAS**

- **LANGUAGES AND CURRENCIES FOR INTERNATIONAL CORRESPONDENCE**

- **USEFUL DATABASES FOR WRITERS**

- **ACTIVE WORDS FOR LIVELY, EFFECTIVE MESSAGES**

and more

Berkley Books by Mary A. DeVries

The Encyclopedic Dictionary of Business Terms

The Business Writer's Book of Lists

THE
BUSINESS WRITER'S BOOK OF
LISTS

MARY A. DeVRIES

 Message Creation

 Word Choice

 Business English

 Reference Library

  Resources

BERKLEY BOOKS / NEW YORK

This book is an original publication of The Berkley Publishing Group.

THE BUSINESS WRITER'S BOOK OF LISTS

A Berkley Book / published by arrangement with
the author

PRINTING HISTORY
Berkley trade paperback edition / May 1998

The Penguin Putnam Inc. World Wide Web site address is
http://www.penguinputnam.com

ISBN: 0-425-16312-1

BERKLEY®
Berkley Books are published by The Berkley Publishing Group, a member of
Penguin Putnam Inc.,
200 Madison Avenue, New York, New York 10016.
BERKLEY and the "B" design
are trademarks belonging to Berkley Publishing Corporation.

PRINTED IN THE UNITED STATES OF AMERICA
3 5 7 9 10 8 6 4 2

CONTENTS

MESSAGE CREATION

Contents

WORD CHOICE

BUSINESS ENGLISH

IV

REFERENCE LIBRARY

V

RESOURCES

PREFACE

If you were preparing a bad-news message and were concerned that your choice of words might create unnecessary alarm or stress, what would you rather do: (1) read some chapters in a handbook about bad-news messages and word choice or (2) scan an already compiled list of words to avoid in such messages? If you had to write many messages, you might want to do both. A lot of the information in a list book can't be found in a handbook and vice versa. If you were in a hurry, though, scanning word lists would be a quick and easy way to find words to use or avoid.

This is what *The Business Writer's Book of Lists* offers—easy-access, quick-scan lists that dispense with the chitchat and instead provide hundreds of actual examples so that you can go right to work. This is the type of book, then, that you would lay open beside the letter, report, article, or other document that you were preparing. Whenever you felt uneasy about your choice of language, chances are that the book would have a list you could instantly scan to find out whether your choice is okay or whether you need a better substitute.

However, there's more than that: Although the book doesn't have detailed, handbook-style discussion designed for a lengthy, serious reading session, it does have brief, concise hints and tips about message composition and document preparation. If you're worried about making embarrassing grammatical errors, there are also easy-view lists about correct grammar, punctuation, and related matters. Or perhaps research is your main concern. That subject is covered, too, with a wide variety of address lists for both foreign and domestic sources of information, as well as data lists with other useful reference material.

This book is therefore designed to be a practical, hands-on tool for writers. Although it's not designed as a study guide, the lists nevertheless provide valuable information that writers must know to be successful. In fact, most of the lists offer many more choices and examples than can be found in any other type of book for writers. These lists have been arranged in five main parts:

Part I, "Message Creation," has lists of succinct hints and tips about message composition and document preparation, such as tips on composing a successful letter, suggestions for overcoming writer's block, and hints for preparing better E-mail messages.

Part II, "Word Choice," has lists of all kinds of words that writers need and use, such as friendly words when you want to please, dangerous words that can get you in legal trouble, and overused expressions that will make you sound dull and unimaginative.

Part III, "Business English," has lists that make the all-important subject of grammar and related matters relatively painless, including more than two hundred compound terms spelled and punctuated correctly, examples of words that should always be in italics, and more than a hundred difficult-to-remember and commonly misused irregular verbs.

Part IV, "Reference Library," is a large store of new technology, international, and other important reference material for writers, such as commonly abbreviated Internet phrases, widely used E-mail emoticons, and a list of the principal languages used for business and other purposes around the world.

Part V, "Resources," has numerous address lists to help in a variety of research, including lists of large public libraries nationwide, useful business databases for on-line research, and the locations of U.S. embassies in other countries.

If you've never worked with a list book, two things will surprise you. The first thing is the length of the lists. Those of us who have always turned to handbooks for information have grown accustomed to an abundance of text discussion with a limited number of actual examples. In a list book, the opposite is true: The lists are extensive, whereas the discussion is limited.

The second thing that is different about a list book is the extent to which you can actually pluck suitable examples from many of the lists, such as those in Part II, "Word Choice," and incorporate them in a particular document. Handbooks will tell you what, in general, you should do to improve your writing but usually leave it up to you to find the actual words or expressions that are needed for a particular situation. List books do much of the search work for you by providing already compiled and organized lists with numerous suitable selections and alternatives that you can quickly find and use.

In short, handbooks are excellent study and procedural guides. List books are excellent hands-on working tools. Neither type of book should replace the other, and together, they form a powerful desk reference set for a writer.

Having written three list books, as well as many handbooks, I'm especially impressed with the practical quality of the list-book format. In fact, as a writer, I regularly use list books and by now am completely addicted to their easy-access, rapid-scan format. It reminds me of the quick search-and-access characteristics of certain features in my word processing program. I hope you, too, will enjoy using this type of resource.

Acknowledgments

Words and other examples in *The Business Writer's Book of Lists* were compiled from dozens of sources and were checked and verified in both general and specialized dictionaries. In particular, endless checks and comparisons were made in the *Oxford English Dictionary*, *American Heritage Dictionary of the English Language*, *Merriam Webster's Collegiate Dictionary*, *Webster's Third New International Dictionary*, and *Webster's Encyclopedic Unabridged Dictionary of the English Language*. The list book has benefited greatly from the collective wisdom in these and other impressive works. I'm also grateful for the information and many useful suggestions supplied by other writers while the lists were being compiled. In particular, I appreciate the recommendations and careful review of the manuscript by writer-editor-researcher Jean McCormack in Prescott, Arizona.

MESSAGE CREATION

The Most Common Objectives in Business Messages

The reason for sending a particular message may apply only to a specific situation or a certain type of business. Most business communication, however, has one of the objectives listed here. Since each objective may require a different tone, degree of formality, and choice of words (congenial, forceful, persuasive, and so on), it's often unwise to mix several objectives in a single message. The most effective messages, in fact, have only one *predominant* objective, and the more objectives that a message has, the less effective it becomes. Some of the most common objectives are as follows:

To make initial contact with someone

To acquire, provide, or exchange information

To influence or motivate someone to respond as you desire

To instruct someone

To ask or grant a favor

To thank someone

To change someone's behavior or attitude

To praise someone

To reprimand someone

To strengthen a relationship and encourage feelings of goodwill

To build a favorable image of one's self or company (public relations)

To buy or sell something

To begin or end something

2

Five Principal Types of Readers

When you compose a message, your comments are typically directed to the readers (audience) you want to reach. This doesn't mean that no one else will read the message. Several people may see what you've written. Therefore, you may also want to consider whether you need to include information of interest to other readers as well. Here are five ways to classify prospective readers (see list 3 for factors to consider in reader evaluation).

Primary, or main, reader(s): The one(s) you especially want to reach

Secondary, or incidental, reader(s): One or more others who may also read your message

Initial reader: The first person to read your message, whether or not this person is also another type of reader, such as a primary reader

Final reader: The last person to read your message, whether or not this person is another type of reader, such as a secondary reader

Multiple readers: All those who read your message, including all primary, secondary, initial, and final readers.

3

Key Factors to Include in Reader Evaluation

The specific factors you need to consider in analyzing your audience depends on the type of communication you're preparing. However, certain general reader characteristics are important in preparing many types of messages or documents. Although you may not know, or even need to know, all of the following points about your readers, the more you know about them, the easier it will be to tailor your material appropriately so that it will be understood, appreciated, and accepted by the readers (see also list 2 for a description of the basic types of readers).

Educational level

Social status or background

Type and level of employment

Level of income

Geographical location

Marital status

Number and age of children

Knowledge and understanding of your topic

Interest in your message or topic

Possible bias for or against your message or topic

Possible motivation to respond to your message

Doubts or questions that your message or topic may prompt

Requests that your message or topic may generate

Five Basic Steps in Creating a Document

Writers who follow the five basic steps listed here tend to create the most impressive documents. Those who skip a step, or part of it, tend to create inferior documents. It's tempting, for example, to skip some or all of the planning stage and blindly forge ahead with the research. Or it may seem that there isn't time to revise a document, which is often an even greater mistake. Unless you're the exception to the rule, you'll be doing yourself a favor if you take time to complete each of these basic steps (for additional considerations in document creation, refer to the other lists in this part).

Planning: Consulting others (brainstorming); selecting a theme/thesis; setting objectives; analyzing the audience; developing a topic outline; deciding how to proceed

Research: Deciding on sources; estimating costs of research; contacting the sources; collecting and recording information and source data (such as a bibliography); assembling the information

Composition: Revising the preliminary outline; deciding on punctuation and capitalization style, format, formality and tone, and complexity of language; writing a first, unrefined, uncorrected draft

Revision: Reading and evaluating the first draft (see the checklist in list 19); checking for clarity; verifying facts and figures; checking text and illustrations; making additions, deletions, and other corrections and improvements

Printout: Printing the revised document; spell-checking and proofreading the document manually; making final adjustments; printing the finished copy

The Main Goals of a Well-Organized Document

Everyone agrees that a document should be organized clearly and logically, although not all documents fit that description. A surprising number of abuses occur in this respect, suggesting that some writers may be overlooking the benefits of organizing textual and illustrative information in the best possible way. If you've been guilty of paying only lip service to this matter of organization, use the following list to refocus on the objectives of a well-organized document (see also the points about document design in list 6).

To introduce, discuss, and conclude your comments—in that order

To be certain that you've given readers everything they need to know to act or make a decision

To be certain that you've omitted everything irrelevant or nonessential for readers to act or make a decision

To provide useful supporting material (tables, diagrams, and so on) that will enhance the text

To omit supporting material that is only cosmetic and does not make the text clearer or more meaningful

To arrange text paragraphs and sections and the associated illustrations in a logical sequence that makes the information clear and easy to understand

To position the text material and illustrations so that they automatically lead readers, step by step and page by page, from beginning to end

6
Five Reasons You Need Good Document Design

Some writers tend to think only about what they're writing to the exclusion of how the information is arranged and presented on each page. Document design may be the responsibility of another person or department. But if it's the writer's responsibility, he or she needs to keep in mind how an effective design will enhance the text and illustrations. The following points are five reasons that a writer should aim for a well-designed, in addition to well-written, document (see also the points about good organization in list 5).

To ensure that the document has a pleasing and inviting appearance

To make the written text and supporting information easier to read

To encourage readers to read the entire document

To highlight or emphasize certain text or illustrations that you especially want readers to notice

To help readers quickly and easily find text information and illustrations of interest to them

7

Eight Common Qualities
of Successful Communication

Two very different messages—with different objectives, style, audiences, and so on—may both be highly successful, even though they don't have all the same qualities. Nevertheless, certain qualities tend to characterize most successful messages, regardless of other ways in which the messages may differ. Here are eight of the most important of these qualities.

The communication takes into account the specific needs, interests, and other characteristics of the audience (see list 3).

The objective or thesis of the message or document is founded on levelheaded, sound reasoning rather than emotion (see list 1).

The information has been verified as accurate and reliable (see list 8).

The language is clear, grammatically correct, in good taste, and appropriate for the audience (see the lists in Parts II and III).

The tone and degree of formality are appropriate for the audience and the objectives of the message (see lists 1, 2, 3, and 13).

The communication is complete, with all parts and information presented in a logical, appropriate order (see list 5).

The message is ethical and lawful.

The document design and the format enhance the clarity, readability, and overall effectiveness of the message (see list 6).

8

Ten Essential Steps to Ensure Accurate Messages

As writers, people believe it's important to create accurate material; as human beings, they sometimes fail to do so. More is involved than simply watching for a typo. The greatest threats to accuracy are more subtle, involving the difficulties that most people have in controlling a personal bias, hidden agenda, or other insidious influence. This list, therefore, places more emphasis on guarding against such problems than on checking for minor technical errors, although attention to both is necessary.

Conduct thorough research of your subject so that your comments are based on fact rather than on hunches or speculation.

Use reliable, current, and unbiased sources to support your facts.

Use logic and sound reasoning in developing your subject.

Address both sides of a controversial matter objectively.

Deal with essential facts that are in opposition to your view rather than ignore them.

State individual facts clearly and objectively without distortion or exaggeration, either for or against.

Avoid *ad hominem* arguments (emotional appeals).

Do not abuse the message or document by using it to promote other, personal interests aside from the main purpose of the communication.

Proofread each draft slowly and carefully, manually as well as by computer, and correct errors and weaknesses as needed.

Review (criticize) your draft from a reader's perspective and, when practical, ask a *qualified* person (expert) to review it.

Helpful Hints for Using Numbers to Enhance Your Text

In certain material, backing up your comments with statistics can make a presentation much more effective. But using numbers improperly can just as easily weaken a message. Observe the following suggestions to be certain that any numbers you use will strengthen, rather than weaken, your text.

Use statistics to support or strengthen text statements that might otherwise be questioned or contested.

Use only current figures to describe current conditions.

Double-check the accuracy of all numbers.

Avoid overwhelming the reader with too many numbers in one sentence, paragraph, or other limited area (except for a statistical table or list).

Use statistical comparisons when appropriate, such as in comparing population growth this year with that in a previous year.

Use easy-to-remember round numbers when precise figures are not essential, such as using *500* instead of *491.67.*

Confirm the reliability of your sources for any numbers that you use.

Provide the sources of your statistics as a footnote or text statement.

10
Business Material in Which It Is Proper to Abbreviate Words, Names, and Phrases

An abbreviation that is pronounced letter by letter, such as *asap* (as soon as possible), is an *initialism*. One pronounced like an actual word, such as *BASIC* (*Beginners All-Purpose Symbolic Instruction Code*), is an *acronym*. Others, such as *nat'l* or *mgr.,* are shortened forms of words that omit some of the letters. (For examples of abbreviations, see lists 63 and 65 in Part IV.) Two common problems are the failure (1) to spell out an unfamiliar abbreviation on first use—*Internet Relay Chat (IRC)*—and (2) to capitalize or punctuate it consistently. (Follow your company's style or consult an appropriate style guide.) Here are examples of material in which it is proper or even preferred to use abbreviations.

In documents in which a name is repeated many times, provided that the name is identified on first use

In documents that are directed to a technical or scientific audience

In informal rough notes or rough drafts

In invoices, purchase orders, and other such forms

In the source material of footnotes, reference lists, and bibliographies: *Princeton, N.J.: The Book Co., 1998.*

In street addresses containing compass points: *101 Adams Street, NW*

In envelope addresses prepared for automated postal sorting

In electronic mail, such as in designated Web sites or in the use of Internet abbreviations: *FAQ (frequently asked questions)*

In technical instructions, lists, tables, charts, and other such material, such as in the commands *(CTRL—control)* listed in computer documentation

In correspondence and other material addressing a person by a title preceding the name: *Mr. John Dennison*

In correspondence and other material addressing a person with an academic degree following the name: *Nancy Lawson, Ph.D.*

11
Problem Language That May Weaken Your Message

Most writers realize that their language should be clear, appropriate for the audience, and in good taste. But they're surprised to learn that even widely accepted language, such as idioms, can be confusing to certain readers. Someone in another country, for example, might be puzzled by the idiom *day in, day out*. Therefore, writers should be certain that their language is clear, appropriate, and tasteful and that questionable expressions have been deleted or rephrased (see the lists of problem language in Part II).

Cliches: Tired, overworked expressions, such as *the last straw* (one thing too many)

Slang: Figures of speech, such as *kiss off* (dismiss rudely), coined to shock, be different, or be irreverent

Euphemisms: Evasive expressions, such as *verbally deficient* (illiterate), intended to be less blunt or harsh than the original or actual term

Idioms: Expressions peculiar to a language, such as *keep tabs on* (stay informed about), that are not readily understood or defined by the individual words

Jargon, or newspeak: Specialized or technical expressions, such as *decision tree* (a visual aid or flow chart depicting alternative strategies)

Buzzwords: An often sarcastic form of jargon, such as *clip trip* (an official's trip taken at public expense)

Sexism: Expressions appearing to favor men or women, such as *executives and wives* (better: *executives and spouses*)

Portmanteau words: Blended words composed of parts of two words, such as *blandiloquence* (*bland* + *grandiloquence*— smooth or flattering language intended to soothe)

Emotives: Expressions that reveal a bias, as in "He supports the status quo" (he's *against* change) instead of "He supports a *continuation* of present policy" (he's for the current policy)

Doublespeak, or gobbledygook: Generally unintelligible language often used to hide or misrepresent the truth, such as "critical, detailed cerebral formulation" (careful scheming)

Hedges: Words such as *maybe* and *perhaps* that limit and tend to weaken, as in "I *guess* we should proceed."

Tag questions: Useless words such as *right?* that are tacked on to a sentence and tend to weaken it, as in "Most employees prefer a staggered lunch hour, *you know?*"

Inexplicit qualifiers: Descriptive words (adjectives), such as "*improved* detergent," that raise new questions; for example, *how* is it improved?

12

More Than Two Dozen Steps
Toward More Successful Business Letters

Letters can help or hurt your cause, depending on how well they're composed. If a reader is unimpressed or irritated by your letter, you may lose your chances of getting what you want. In spite of this simple truth, well-written business letters are rare. Although certain factors, such as tone, may need to be adjusted for a specific type of letter, all successful letters—conventional and electronic—share certain characteristics, such as accuracy and good grammar. Yet many letter writers overlook not only one but sometimes many of the following basic steps (see also the suggestions in list 7 and the tips specifically about tone in list 13).

Respond promptly to incoming letters.

Mention the date of the other letter in your first paragraph or place a reference line *(Your letter of May 6, 19XX)* under the dateline of your letter.

Highlight, underline, or check off the points you want to answer in an incoming letter.

Write a separate one-sentence summary of what you want to accomplish to help you focus your thoughts.

Prepare a brief list of the main points you want to make, and use this list to guide you in composing your letter.

Keep your letter short, to one page if possible, especially if it is an electronic message (see list 17).

Use the person's name—spelled correctly—one or more times: "Thanks for letting me know about your invention, Mr. Stanos."

Use the opening paragraph—the first one or two sentences—to tell the reader what your letter is about.

Use clear, simple language and avoid long, multisyllable words; unnecessary technical language; and vague expressions that hinder comprehension (see the lists in Part II).

Avoid nonstandard English, such as idioms, slang, or cliches, that certain readers may find unfamiliar or offensive (see the lists in Part II).

Begin a bad-news message with a buffer, something positive to soften the coming blow (see the tips in list 15).

Follow the tips in list 13 for an appealing tone, such as being positive, taking the *you* approach, using humor carefully, writing on the reader's level, and not writing in anger.

Admit it when you've made a mistake or are wrong about something, and apologize to the reader.

Use underlining, italic type, and other potentially distracting forms of emphasis sparingly (but see lists 57 and 58 in Part III).

Use the *active voice*—"We discovered that"—unless you have a good reason for using a *passive voice*—"It was discovered that" (see definitions in list 40 of Part III).

Avoid using adjectives (see definition in list 40 of Part III) that make your comments sound exaggerated (*horrendous* workload), except in certain sales material (*incredible* savings).

Make clear which comments are your *opinions* and which are *facts*.

State only the necessary facts and avoid overstating a problem, making it appear worse than it is.

Offer a solution, recommending ways to correct a problem and prevent it from happening again.

Support your facts with a few statistics but avoid so many that you overwhelm the reader (see list 9).

Don't try to impress the reader with your position or knowledge.

Use correct grammar (see the lists in Part III).

Use a clean, attractive, standard letter or memo format.

Proofread and edit carefully, correcting word choice (see the lists in Part II); spelling, punctuation, and grammar (see the lists in Part III); and other problems.

Make your final paragraph short and simple, saying what you want the reader to do and when: "If you can join us, Helen, call me at 555-2010 by April 11. Hope to see you soon."

13
Practical Suggestions for an Appealing Letter Tone

An appealing tone signals a well-written message that reflects the writer's interest in and concern for the reader. No matter how tempting it may be for a writer to be harsh or cold, and no matter how busy a writer may be, tone is a quality of writing that is too important to sacrifice. As Ralph Waldo Emerson once said, "Life is not so short but that there is always time for courtesy." (See also the general letter-writing suggestions in list 12.)

Begin by saying something nice: "I was delighted to receive your report."

Write laterally—on the reader's comprehension level—but avoid fawning over a superior or talking down to a subordinate.

Avoid writing when distractions, such as feelings of anger or frustration, make it difficult to be levelheaded and pleasant.

Be natural and, except in formal communications, adopt a conversational tone.

Be honest and sincere and avoid phony sweetness or excessive flattery.

Be sensitive to the reader's feelings and concerns, particularly when you're saying no (see the tips on composing a bad-news message in list 15).

Be diplomatic, phrasing your remarks to inform but never to wound, even when a reader is wrong or was previously rude to you.

Adopt a positive attitude and use positive words (see examples in list 24 of Part II), such as *benefit* and *appreciation*.

Avoid a negative attitude and negative words (see the examples in lists 31 and 32 of Part II), such as *demand* and *fail*.

Emphasize the reader and the reader's needs and interests (the *you* approach), not the writer or the writer's needs and interests *(I, we, me)*.

Beware of sarcasm, irony, and humor, which may backfire and sound offensive if readers misunderstand or have a different sense of humor.

Avoid imprecise language, such as *later* instead of *Tuesday, April 14.*

Avoid words with double meanings (*cheap = shoddy* as well as *inexpensive*).

Close with a pleasant remark: "I hope you enjoy your exciting new assignment."

14

Ten Easy Ways to Arouse Reader Interest

When you write to people who haven't asked for the information you're providing, you may need to use special tactics to get them to pay attention. Sometimes it's necessary to use an interest-arousing comment on the envelope just to get the recipient to open it and read what's inside. In the letter itself, other tactics may be necessary to motivate the reader to read the full message. Some of the easiest strategies for capturing reader interest are also the most effective, as, for example, the following proven interest-arousal techniques.

Choose a tantalizing or provocative headline: *The Biggest Money Waster in Your Personal Budget.*

Begin by saying something amazing, fascinating, or surprising: "Tax software may save you time, but it doesn't always save you from making costly mistakes."

Begin with a teaser question: "Can you use an extra $1,000 per week?"

Include an illustrative anecdote, such as bolstering an article about retirement plans with the story of a poor farmer who retired a wealthy man because he chose the right plan.

Use amazing statistics, such as a $5,000 difference in the cost of insuring the family sedan, depending on the state in which you live and the insurer you choose.

Appeal to feelings of pride and social status: "Enjoy the look of a famous timepiece that sells for thousands of dollars—at a fraction of the price!"

Tell readers why they need what you're offering: "Busy executives like you don't have time to pore over investment reports—but financial advisors like us do."

Offer or send the reader a free gift, such as a wallet-sized calendar or a mileage log book.

Say something nice about the reader: "Your company has been a valued part of our community for more than two decades, surpassed only by your capable leadership."

Use testimonials from prominent people, such as an endorsement of a business start-up guide by a successful, well-known CEO.

15
Important Guidelines for Composing a Bad-News Message

Saying no or sending some other type of bad news to a reader can be a challenge. In most cases, the writer wants to retain the goodwill of the recipient. Even in cases of severed associations, it's never helpful to create an enemy. Therefore, this type of message must be composed skillfully, with special concern for the reader's feelings and possible response. The following tips may help to soften an otherwise harmful, hurtful, or disappointing message (see also the tips in lists 12 and 13).

Imagine yourself in the reader's position, receiving instead of writing the message.

Use language that the reader will understand, but avoid any appearance of condescending to the reader.

Use positive words (see the examples in list 24 of Part II), such as *appreciation* and *helpful*.

Avoid negative words (see the examples in list 31 of Part II), such as *absurd* and *misinformed*.

Begin by expressing appreciation for the reader's request or suggestion: "Thank you, Jim, for your very interesting and detailed proposal on refinancing."

Define policies or circumstances that make your bad-news decision necessary: "As much as we like your suggestions, Nancy, our bylaws limit what we can do."

Identify the points (if any) on which you and the reader agree: "I agree that we have to back-order too many items."

Identify any of the reader's valid or useful comments, even if they do not change your decision: "I was happy to learn about the new program you mentioned."

Compliment the reader on previous successes or contributions in related areas: "We're all impressed with the good work you did on the Madison project."

Encourage the reader to continue making contributions: "I hope you'll let us see more of your ideas in the future, Tom."

Close with a pleasant remark: "Thanks, Ellen, for giving us a chance to reconsider our refinancing options. I wish we had more creative thinkers like you."

16

Crucial Factors to Consider in International Messages

International messages are difficult to write. An informal style or language can cause nightmares for readers in other countries. Social, religious, and other customs are often different, with something such as a friendly gesture in the United States—for example, using first names—often considered a sign of disrespect in another country. Therefore, writers should thoroughly research the customs and cultures of their readers. Without understanding their background, one could easily make a serious blunder. (For sources of worldwide country and regional information, see lists 69–71 in Part V.)

Use the accepted business language of the other country, which often is English (see list 61 in Part IV).

Use more formality than you would use for American readers.

Use the personal and professional titles common in the other country (*Ms.,* for example, which is standard in the United States, is not used in most countries).

Observe variations in the arrangement of names (in some Asian countries, for example, the family name is stated first: *Yam Mun Hoh; Mr. Yam*).

Beware of topics that may be forbidden because of religious, social, economic, political, or other customs.

Pay attention, if you're a woman writer, to tone and word choice to avoid sounding bold or pushy, a taboo in Latin American, Arab, and certain other countries.

Use your regular conventional letter or E-mail format, provided that it is simple, clean, and easy for an international reader to follow.

Use your own style of spelling, capitalization, and punctuation *consistently* to avoid confusing and puzzling readers with an unexplained change in style.

Be precise and clear, avoiding trendy words, jargon, cliches, idioms, and other language that a reader may translate literally (see the lists in Part II).

Watch for *misplaced modifiers* (see the definition in list 40 of Part III), misplaced punctuation, and other problems that may be confusing.

Use short words, sentences, and paragraphs to help the reader understand your comments and translate your message without difficulty.

Use more punctuation than is common in domestic messages, such as placing a comma after short introductory phrases, to guide readers through each sentence.

Avoid abbreviations or spell them out on first use: *the American Bar Association (ABA).*

Don't ask international readers to contact you or meet with you on a day that represents a religious or other holiday in their country.

Have the business cards you enclose with your message printed on the reverse side in the language of the other country (avoid abbreviations on cards).

Observe local practices in the conduct of business (in some Asian and Arab areas, for example, it's unacceptable to conduct business in the first letter or meeting).

Compliment or flatter the reader in some way, such as by mentioning a place you admire or once visited in the reader's country.

Show respect by including a phrase that is common in the other country, such as "God willing" in a letter to a Muslim reader.

Commonsense Do's and Don'ts for Sending E-Mail Messages

Many of the guidelines for sending electronic messages are the same as those for sending conventional messages. The lists in this part about accuracy, reader evaluation, and other matters apply to both conventional and electronic messages. Etiquette, for example, is an important concern in all messages. However, with the Internet available to almost anyone who has a computer and a modem, a new collection of rules of etiquette has evolved (called *netiquette*). Most of these rules, like all rules of etiquette, are based on common courtesy and common sense.

Don't waste other users' time with idle comments, unnecessary requests, junk mail, and other time wasters.

Don't send multiple messages to people who may not need or want them.

Do make new users feel welcome in your own messages to them and by introducing them to others in discussion groups.

Do use a pleasant tone (see the hints in list 13) so that you won't be considered unfriendly.

Don't make comments that incite hostile exchanges (called *flames* in Internet jargon).

Don't use nonstandard language, such as jargon, slang, and other trendy words, that users may not understand or may find offensive (see the lists in Part II).

Don't use nonliteral language, such as sarcasm, irony, or humor, that could be misunderstood (but see list 64 in Part IV).

Don't send a message when you're tired, angry, or impatient (see also examples of words to avoid in lists 31–36 of Part II).

Resist the urge to use the immediacy of E-mail to send a hastily composed response to a provocative incoming letter.

Mention the other person's letter by date when you do respond to it.

Don't pass on confidential information or make comments to a reader that would embarrass you if other people should also retrieve the message.

Do review what you've typed before actually transmitting the comment during a conversational exchange.

Do use emotion sparingly and discriminately to be certain that it will be welcomed and understood (but see list 64 in Part IV).

Don't use all capital letters, which represent shouting.

Don't use abbreviations unless you identify them on first use, are certain that the reader will understand them, or previously sent the reader a list of those you commonly use.

Do use accurate, clear, and consistent spelling, punctuation, and capitalization, the same as you would use in a conventional letter.

Do aim for short, single-subject messages that fit on one computer screen.

Do use a clear, specific subject line in a business message: *Revision of Zoning Ordinance Code 3/21790.*

Do use lists and other quick-scan formats that will help the reader.

Do forward messages you receive in error to the intended recipients or return them to the senders, including a cover letter explaining the problem.

Do double-check names and addresses for accuracy before transmission to avoid misdirecting your own messages.

Don't publicly post someone else's message or other information without permission.

Don't misuse discussion groups to sell your products or services or to do anything that might make other users uncomfortable or displeased.

Do wait for someone to recognize you and invite your participation after making yourself known to a discussion group.

18

Fifteen Steps Toward
More Successful Reports and Proposals

Like letters, business reports and proposals differ by type (informative, analytical, and so on), by length and degree of formality, and in many other ways. But to be successful, they all must share certain characteristics, such as usefulness, accuracy, and readability. Some or all of the following steps, therefore, will apply to the preparation of most types of reports and proposals.

Analyze the audience that will read and evaluate the report or proposal (see list 3).

Define, for your own use, the problem, purpose, and scope of the report or proposal.

Make a preliminary outline, with topics arranged in a logical order.

Decide on prospective research sources and methods (electronic or conventional library, personal interviews, and so on).

Gather more material and take more notes than you believe you will need.

Record names and addresses of sources to contact for permission to quote copyrighted material.

Sort and analyze the data you have collected.

Revise your initial outline after you have reviewed the newly organized data.

Decide technical points: punctuation and capitalization style; format; length; tone and formality; tables, charts, and other supplementary material; and method of preparation.

Write a first draft, following the suggestions in other lists in this part.

Use proper language and word choice (see the lists in Part II) and correct grammar (see the lists in Part III).

Use lists, indented or displayed text, and other special features to break up and simplify long, complex, tedious sections of copy.

Arrange the parts of a report in logical order: cover, flyleaf (blank page), title page, authorization letter, transmittal letter, contents page, list of illustrations and tables, abstract or summary, introduction, methodology, background, data analysis, conclusions and recommendations, appendix, notes section, glossary, bibliography, and index.

Arrange the parts of a proposal in logical order: title page, abstract, contents page, introduction, description of problem, objectives of project, procedure for project, plans for postevaluation of methods, equipment needs, personnel needs, budget, and appendix.

Proofread and edit the first draft, correcting errors, inconsistencies, questionable language, and so on (see the checklist in list 19).

A Timesaving Checklist for Reviewing Your Final Draft

It's difficult to remember to check everything in a document. Therefore, when a document is complex, even longtime writers use checklists to be certain they don't forget anything. If you'd rather not trust your memory, use this checklist for a step-by-step review of your final draft. Use the "Other" line at the end to add any points pertinent to a specific type of document you're preparing. (Review other lists in this part and in Parts II and III that address items mentioned in the checklist.)

Yes	No	
❏	❏	Is the general format appropriate?
❏	❏	Are elements of the document (subheads, footnotes, and so on) formatted and styled (punctuated, capitalized, and so on) consistently throughout?
❏	❏	Are all parts of the document—front matter, body, and back matter—complete and positioned in the correct place?
❏	❏	Is the text—language, tone, and so on—appropriate for the intended readers?
❏	❏	Does each part of the document provide the expected information for that part?
❏	❏	Do heads and subheads correctly identify the text that follows?
❏	❏	Does the introduction effectively open the subject?
❏	❏	Does the conclusion effectively end the subject without initiating new thoughts and ideas to be considered or explored?
❏	❏	Are paragraphs short and easy to read?
❏	❏	Does each paragraph begin with a lead (topic) sentence that guides readers into the sentences that follow?
❏	❏	Are sentences short and varied?
❏	❏	Has each sentence been worded clearly, expressing a complete thought?
❏	❏	Are the sentences phrased in a positive way?
❏	❏	Are transition words, such as *however* and *therefore,* used to help sentences and paragraphs flow smoothly from one to another?

Yes	No	
❏	❏	Have long, complex discussions been simplified and made more readable by using lists or other rapid-scan features?
❏	❏	Are illustrations (tables, diagrams, photographs, and so on) complete and positioned properly?
❏	❏	Are footnotes or other note sections and bibliographies complete and positioned properly?
❏	❏	Are special terms, names, and so on capitalized, spelled, and punctuated consistently throughout?
❏	❏	Has the text been proofread carefully for correct grammar?
❏	❏	Have slang, cliches, unnecessary business jargon, and other forms of nonstandard English been eliminated?
❏	❏	Have vague words and undesirable generalities been eliminated?
❏	❏	Is the text written with strong, active verbs rather than weak, passive verbs?
❏	❏	Has a *you* approach—or any other viewpoint selected for the document—been used consistently throughout?
❏	❏	Has the text been edited to eliminate wordiness and redundancies?
❏	❏	Has discriminatory language been eliminated?
❏	❏	Have complex, pretentious words and phrases been restated in simple, natural language?

Yes	No	
❏	❏	Are factual statements backed by reliable, current statistics or other proof?
❏	❏	Have exaggerated statements been eliminated?
❏	❏	Has the document been evaluated for overall effectiveness?
❏	❏	Has the final, corrected version been both spell-checked and proofread manually?
❏	❏	Other _____

20

Thirty-two Common Mistakes That Writers Make

Writers don't all make the same mistakes, but some are so prevalent that most professional writers have made them at some time in their careers. Even when a writer knows better, bad habits can be hard to break. Check the following list to see whether you're still falling into any of these writing traps.

Failing to put yourself in the reader's place (faulty audience analysis) and to be sensitive to educational, cultural, and other important factors (see lists 2 and 3)

Failing to do adequate research or other prewriting preparation (see list 4)

Failing to take time to prepare an initial outline or list of points or topics arranged in a logical order, resulting in a disorganized presentation (see lists 4 and 5)

Using generalities, such as *equipment* instead of *fax machine,* when specifics would be more helpful to the reader

Being too vague and unclear: "Please check if we can get a *professional* to design the brochure, instead of "Please check if we can get a *freelance artist.*"

Digressing to make unnecessary or unrelated statements that don't contribute anything of value to the concise, logical progression of facts in your message

Expressing unconfirmed or unsubstantiated facts or opinions, thinly disguising them as tested or authoritative facts

Failing to supply sources for important data or omitting statistics or other facts that would support your assertions (see list 9)

Leaving out a crucial part of your message, such as a brief introductory hook that will capture the reader's attention

Overcrowding sentences and paragraphs with too many statistics for a reader to absorb and remember (see list 9)

Choosing the wrong format for a document, thereby making the text seem unnecessarily confusing and difficult to follow (see lists 5 and 6)

Writing from an *I, we,* or *me* viewpoint when a *you* approach would be more personal and relevant to the reader (see list 13)

Sounding too preachy or too condescending toward the reader (see list 13)

Using redundancies (see examples in list 38 of Part II): "The office has four *different* [delete] kinds of computers."

Sounding trite and unimaginative by using overworked expressions, such as *tried and true* (see examples in list 39 of Part II)

Using other language that is inappropriate for the audience, such as too complex, too casual, too unfamiliar, too unfriendly, or too crude

Using unnecessary qualifiers, such as "*sort of* exciting," that dilute and weaken a statement

Weakening comments with a *passive voice,* as in "It *was decided,*" instead of an *active voice:* "They *decided*" (see definitions in list 40 of Part III)

Adding misplaced or unnecessary punctuation, such as "He knew the policy prohibited it[,] but did it anyway."

Misplacing phrases, thereby changing the intended meaning: "The man whistled at the dog *holding a camera,*" instead of "The man *holding a camera* whistled at the dog."

Using *dangling modifiers* (see definition in list 40 of Part III): "Like his last *report,* he also made this one too long," instead of "Like his last report, *this one* also is too long."

Using the wrong verb tense (see examples in list 49 of Part III): "By the time you leave, I *will finish* the report," instead of "By the time you leave, I *will have finished* the report."

Splitting verbs unnecessarily and awkwardly: "Mr. Adams *did,* as I recall, *say* that we should wait," instead of "Mr. Adams *did say,* as I recall, that we should wait."

Using a plural verb with a singular noun: "Another *box* of files *are* ready," instead of "Another *box* of files *is* ready" (see lists 41–43 in Part III)

Using a plural verb with a singular pronoun: "*None* [no one] of the employees *are* qualified," instead of "*None* of the employees *is* qualified."

Using an *adjective* when an *adverb* is needed (see definitions in list 40 of Part III): "She worked *slow* to save her energy," instead of "She worked *slowly* to save her energy."

Using *-er* and *-est* forms of adjectives incorrectly in making comparisons (see definition in list 40 of Part III): "Tom is the *slowest* worker of the two," instead of "Tom is the *slower* worker of the two."

Using an *adverb* when an *adjective* is needed (see definitions in list 40 of Part III): "*He* felt *badly* about the error," instead of "*He* felt *bad* about the error."

Using the *objective case* when the *nominative case* is needed (see definitions in list 40 of Part III): "*It* was *him*," instead of "*It* was *he*."

Failing to proofread slowly and carefully enough to catch errors such as the mistakes just listed

Failing to review objectively and to rewrite and revise as many times as necessary until the work is perfect ("Amateurs *write;* professionals *rewrite*")

Showing your writing to friends, relatives, and other "friendly" critics who are not qualified or disposed to give sound, objective advice

21
Ten Ways to Develop Better Writing Habits

Writers lose hours, days, and even more time because of poor writing habits. Often, they wait for inspiration that never comes or delude themselves into thinking that writers should not be encumbered with the annoying rules, goals, and deadlines that affect one in a "regular" job. The most successful writing habits, however, are based on a businesslike approach to an assignment. The following tips suggest that a writer should treat writing like any other job that has established procedures and requires personal discipline.

Set daily goals, such as drafting a section a day, five days a week, starting each day at 8 A.M.

Keep a paper or electronic calendar on which you schedule daily work and assignment deadlines.

Develop schedules that have extra time built in for emergencies and unforeseen delays.

Reward yourself in some way, such as by buying a video you want, for staying on schedule or finishing ahead of schedule.

Discourage unnecessary interruptions, such as chatting with coworkers (tell them you'll visit later when you've finished your present task).

Resume work immediately after being interrupted.

Reduce any noise that you can control and practice tuning out any noise beyond your control.

Work at a comfortable pace when your schedule will permit this.

Schedule periodic breaks, rest periods, and stretching periods throughout the day.

Follow the suggestions in list 22 to help you begin each assignment and start each daily writing session.

22

Proven Strategies for Overcoming Writer's Block

Staring at a blank page or computer screen, unable to begin or continue work, is a common frustration for many writers. Often, all that a writer needs is to improve the physical conditions or to think of routine, easy-to-start preliminary tasks that will unlock the flow of words. The following tips are often overlooked because they seem too simple to be effective. Nevertheless, many professional writers swear by them and insist that strategies don't have to be complex and difficult to be effective.

Choose the most appealing and appropriate time and place to write when circumstances will allow this flexibility.

Write a brief, one-paragraph summary of your proposed message or document (its objective, thesis, and so on).

Prepare a preliminary outline that lists your proposed topics or main points in a tentative order.

Divide large tasks or assignments into manageable goals or blocks, such as drafting one section or topic at a time.

Pick the easiest point, topic, or section to draft first, if it's possible to work on parts of a document out of order.

Don't try to create precise, polished, or finished copy in your first draft (postpone spell-checking, formatting, editing, and so on until later).

Don't punish yourself if, on occasion, you fail to accomplish what you expected or wanted to do (it's okay to fail).

Observe the tips in list 21 for developing better writing habits.

WORD CHOICE

23

Active Words for Lively, Effective Messages

Clear, persuasive, dynamic messages combine the right tone and the right words. Dull, passive prose, such as "We *are of the opinion* that," can dampen and weaken a message, even when everything else in it is perfect. Straightforward, active words, such as "We *believe* that," are needed to make a message strong and effective. If your language sometimes sounds weak, lifeless, or dull, try replacing the passive verbs with appropriate choices from this list of active verbs.

absorb	aid	attend
accelerate	allot	attract
accept	alter	awaken
access	amaze	balance
acclaim	amuse	bargain
accommodate	analyze	beat
accompany	answer	beautify
accomplish	anticipate	begin
achieve	appear	believe
acquire	appoint	benefit
act	appreciate	bill
adapt	approach	bind
add	approve	blend
address	arrange	bolster
adjust	aspire	book
administer	assemble	boost
advance	assess	break
advise	assign	broaden
affect	assist	budget
affirm	assure	build
afford	astonish	buy
agree	attach	call

cancel	consult	develop
capitalize	consume	devise
captivate	continue	diminish
care	contribute	direct
categorize	control	discount
cater	convert	discover
celebrate	cooperate	discuss
challenge	coordinate	display
change	correct	distribute
charge	correlate	divert
charm	cost	do
chart	counsel	document
check	count	double
choose	create	dramatize
circulate	credit	dream
clarify	customize	duplicate
classify	cut	earn
clean	dazzle	economize
collaborate	deal	edit
color	debate	educate
combine	decide	effect
come	declare	elect
compare	dedicate	electrify
compel	defend	eliminate
compete	delegate	emphasize
complete	delight	enact
compose	deliver	encourage
compress	demonstrate	endorse
conceive	depart	endure
condense	depend	energize
conduct	describe	enforce
confer	deserve	engineer
confide	design	engross
confuse	desire	enhance
connect	detail	enjoy
construct	determine	enlighten

enliven	finance	heal
enrich	find	heed
enter	fit	help
entertain	fix	hint
enthrall	flourish	hire
enthuse	focus	honor
entitle	follow	hope
equip	forget	hurry
establish	form	identify
estimate	formalize	ignite
evaluate	formulate	illuminate
evoke	free	imagine
exalt	fulfill	imitate
exceed	function	implement
excel	furnish	impress
exclude	galvanize	improve
execute	gauge	improvise
exercise	gear	increase
exhibit	generate	indicate
exhilarate	get	indict
expand	give	induce
expedite	glamorize	indulge
expend	glorify	inflate
experience	go	influence
explain	govern	inform
explore	graduate	initiate
expose	grant	innovate
express	grow	inquire
extend	guarantee	inspire
facilitate	guard	install
fall	guess	institute
familiarize	guide	instruct
fascinate	handle	insulate
fashion	harmonize	insure
feel	hasten	integrate
figure	head	intensify

interact	mail	orient
intercede	maintain	originate
interpret	make	outclass
intimate	manage	outperform
introduce	maneuver	outrank
invent	manufacture	overcome
invest	mark	oversee
investigate	market	overwhelm
invigorate	marvel	owe
invite	match	own
involve	mediate	pack
join	meet	pamper
judge	merit	participate
jump	mesmerize	pass
justify	minimize	pay
keep	model	penetrate
kindle	modernize	perceive
know	modify	perfect
label	monitor	perform
launch	motivate	permit
lead	move	personalize
learn	multiply	persuade
let	necessitate	pick
license	negotiate	pilot
lift	nominate	pinpoint
lighten	normalize	pioneer
like	object	pique
limit	observe	place
link	obtain	plan
list	offer	play
loan	officiate	please
locate	open	pledge
lock	operate	point
look	oppose	possess
lose	order	power
lower	organize	practice

praise

predict

prefer

prepare

present

preside

pressure

prevent

probe

process

procure

produce

profess

profit

program

project

promote

prompt

pronounce

propel

propose

protect

prove

provide

purchase

pursue

put

qualify

question

quit

quote

raise

rank

rate

reach

realize

reason

reassure

recede

receive

recognize

recommend

reconcile

recruit

redesign

reduce

refer

refine

reform

refresh

regard

regulate

reign

reinforce

rejuvenate

relate

relax

relieve

rely

remark

remodel

remove

renew

reorganize

repeat

report

represent

reproduce

request

require

research

resolve

respond

restore

restructure

revamp

reveal

revel

reverse

review

revise

revitalize

revive

revolutionize

rouse

route

run

rush

satisfy

saturate

save

savor

schedule

screen

seal

search

secure

seem

seize

select

sell

send

sense

serve

service

set

settle

shape

share	talk	uncover
ship	tantalize	understand
shop	taste	unify
show	teach	unleash
simplify	tempt	unlock
solve	tend	unmask
soothe	terminate	upgrade
sound	test	uphold
spark	testify	urge
spread	thank	use
stabilize	think	vacate
stand	thread	value
start	thrill	verify
stimulate	thrive	vindicate
stir	throw	voice
stop	thrust	volunteer
streamline	tie	wait
stretch	tighten	want
strive	tolerate	warm
structure	tower	waste
study	track	watch
stun	trade	weaken
substantiate	train	welcome
succeed	transact	win
suit	transcend	wish
supersede	transfer	witness
supervise	transform	wonder
support	transport	work
suppress	travel	wrestle
surpass	treat	write
surprise	trim	yearn
sweep	trust	yield
tailor	try	
take	turn	

24

Positive Words to Use in All Types of Messages

Certain words, such as *benefit* and *reasonable,* are nice to hear. They may make us feel happy, relieved, assured, or satisfied. Unlike other words, such as *regret* and *substandard,* they don't make us apprehensive or cause our stress level to increase (see lists 31 and 32 for examples of negative words). When you want a reader to relax and feel good or want to motivate someone to respond agreeably and positively to your message, select appropriate choices from the following list. (Commonly used parts of speech follow each term; for other possibilities, consult a current dictionary.)

able, *adj.*	ample, *adj.*
absolutely, *adv.*	appealing, *adj.*
accessible, *adj.*	appreciate, *vb.*
acclaimed, *adj.*	appreciation, *n.*
accommodate, *vb.*	approval, *n.*
accomplished, *adj., vb.*	approve, *vb.*
accurate, *adj.*	assist, *vb.*
achievement, *n.*	assure, *vb.*
adaptable, *adj.*	attractive, *adj.*
adept, *adj.*	bargain, *n., adj.*
admirable, *adj.*	beautiful, *adj.*
admire, *vb.*	benefit, *n., vb.*
adroit, *adj.*	boundless, *adj.*
advantage, *n.*	brilliant, *adj.*
agree, *vb.*	can, *vb.*
agreeable, *adj.*	capable, *adj.*
aid, *n., vb.*	captivating, *adj.*
alert, *adj.*	care, *vb.*
alleviate, *vb.*	carefree, *adj.*
amazing, *adj.*	careful, *adj.*
amicable, *adj.*	caring, *adj.*

celebrated, *adj., vb.*

certain, *adj.*

charming, *adj.*

cheerful, *adj.*

classic, *adj.*

clean, *adj.*

commendable, *adj.*

compassion, *n.*

compassionate, *adj.*

compatible, *adj.*

competent, *adj.*

completely, *adv.*

compliment, *n., vb.*

complimentary, *adj.*

concur, *vb.*

confident, *adj.*

congenial, *adj.*

congratulate, *vb.*

congratulation, *n.*

conscientious, *adj.*

consistent, *adj.*

cooperate, *vb.*

cooperation, *n.*

cooperative, *adj.*

correct, *adj.*

courteous, *adj.*

courtesy, *n.*

cozy, *adj.*

creative, *adj.*

cute, *adj.*

dedicate, *vb.*

dedicated, *adj., vb.*

dedication, *n.*

delight, *n., vb.*

delighted, *adj., vb.*

delightful, *adj.*

depend, *vb.*

dependable, *adj.*

desirable, *adj.*

desire, *vb.*

distinctive, *adj.*

dynamic, *adj.*

eager, *adj.*

easy, *adj., adv.*

educated, *adj.*

educational, *adj.*

effective, *adj.*

efficient, *adj.*

effortless, *adj.*

elated, *adj., vb.*

elegant, *adj.*

enchanting, *adj.*

energetic, *adj.*

engaging, *adj.*

enhance, *vb.*

enhancement, *n.*

enjoy, *vb.*

enrich, *vb.*

enriched, *adj., vb.*

entertaining, *adj.*

enthuse, *vb.*

enthusiasm, *n.*

enthusiastic, *adj.*

established, *adj., vb.*

excellent, *adj.*

exceptional, *adj.*

excite, *vb.*

excitement, *n.*

exciting, *adj.*

experienced, *adj.*

expert, *n.*

extraordinary, *adj.*

facilitate, *vb.*

faithful, *adj.*

famous, *adj.*

fast, *adj.*

favor, *vb.*

favorable, *adj.*

favorite, *adj.*

feasible, *adj.*

festive, *adj.*

fine, *adj.*

first, *adj.*

fit, *adj., vb.*

flair, *n.*

flexible, *adj.*

foolproof, *adj.*

foremost, *adj.*

fortify, *vb.*

fortunate, *adj.*

fortunately, *adv.*

forward, *adj.*

free, *adj.*

freedom, *n.*

fresh, *adj.*

friend, *n.*

friendly, *adj.*

fulfill, *vb.*

functional, *adj.*

future, *n., adj.*

generous, *adj.*

genius, *n.*

genuine, *adj.*

gift, *n.*

glad, *adj.*

glamor, *n.*

glamorous, *adj.*

glorious, *adj.*

goal, *n.*

good, *adj.*

gracious, *adj.*

grand, *adj.*

grateful, *adj.*

great, *adj.*

greet, *vb.*

greetings, *n.*

growth, *n.*

guarantee, *n., vb.*

handsome, *adj.*

happily, *adv.*

happy, *adj.*

hardworking, *adj.*

harmonious, *adj.*

healthy, *adj.*

help, *vb.*

helpful, *adj.*

honest, *adj.*

honesty, *n.*

honor, *n., vb.*

honorable, *adj.*

hope, *vb.*

hopeful, *adj.*

hospitable, *adj.*

humorous, *adj.*

ideal, *n., adj.*

illustrious, *adj.*

imaginative, *adj.*

immaculate, *adj.*

important, *adj.*

improve, *vb.*

improved, *adj., vb.*

improvement, *n.*

incentive, *n.*

increase, *n., vb.*

influential, *adj.*
ingenious, *adj.*
initiative, *n.*
innovative, *adj.*
integrity, *n.*
intelligence, *n.*
intelligent, *adj.*
invaluable, *adj.*
inventive, *adj.*
invigorating, *adj.*
inviting, *adj.*
irresistible, *adj.*
joy, *n.*
joyful, *adj.*
joyous, *adj.*
jubilant, *adj.*
kind, *adj.*
kindness, *n.*
legitimate, *adj.*
liberal, *adj.*
liberate, *vb.*
liberty, *n.*
lifelong, *adj.*
likable, *adj.*
like, *vb.*
live, *adj.*
lively, *adj.*
longevity, *n.*
love, *n., vb.*
lovely, *adj.*
loyal, *adj.*
loyalty, *n.*
luck, *n.*
lucky, *adj.*
lucrative, *adj.*
lustrous, *adj.*

luxurious, *adj.*
luxury, *n., adj.*
magical, *adj.*
magnetic, *adj.*
magnificence, *n.*
magnificent, *adj.*
majestic, *adj.*
majesty, *n.*
manage, *vb.*
manageable, *adj.*
markedly, *adv.*
marvel, *n.*
marvelous, *adj.*
matchless, *adj.*
mellow, *adj.*
memorable, *adj.*
merit, *n.*
meritorious, *adj.*
miracle, *n.*
modern, *adj.*
momentous, *adj.*
monumental, *adj.*
motivated, *vb.*
motivation, *n.*
moving, *adj.*
multitalented, *adj.*
mutual, *adj.*
natural, *adj.*
notable, *adj.*
noted, *adj.*
noteworthy, *adj.*
nurture, *vb.*
oblige, *vb.*
offer, *vb.*
often, *adv.*
opportune, *adj.*

opportunity, *n.*

optimism, *n.*

orderly, *adj.*

organized, *adj., vb.*

original, *adj.*

outgoing, *adj.*

outstanding, *adj.*

palatable, *adj.*

palatial, *adj.*

patient, *adj.*

patronage, *n.*

payment, *n.*

peaceful, *adj.*

perceptive, *adj.*

perfect, *adj.*

perfectly, *adv.*

permanent, *adj.*

perpetual, *adj.*

personable, *adj.*

pertinent, *adj.*

play, *n.*

pleasant, *adj.*

please, *vb., adv.*

pleasing, *adj.*

pleasure, *n.*

plentiful, *adj.*

plenty, *n.*

plus, *n.*

polished, *adj., vb.*

popular, *adj.*

popularity, *n.*

positive, *adj.*

practical, *adj.*

praise, *n., vb.*

prestige, *n.*

prestigious, *adj.*

pretty, *adj.*

principled, *adj.*

prizewinning, *adj.*

productive, *adj.*

professional, *n., adj.*

proficient, *adj.*

progress, *n.*

progressive, *adj.*

prominent, *adj.*

promise, *n.*

prompt, *adj.*

promptly, *adv.*

propitious, *adj.*

protected, *adj., vb.*

protection, *n.*

proven, *adj., vb.*

qualified, *adj., vb.*

quality, *n., adj.*

quick, *adj.*

quickly, *adv.*

ready, *adj.*

reasonable, *adj.*

recommend, *vb.*

refined, *adj.*

regular, *adj.*

regularity, *n.*

reinforced, *adj., vb.*

reliable, *adj.*

remarkable, *adj.*

repay, *vb.*

reputable, *adj.*

resourceful, *adj.*

respect, *vb.*

respected, *adj., vb.*

respectful, *adj.*

responsible, *adj.*

rest, *vb.*

restful, *adj.*

revitalize, *vb.*

revive, *vb.*

reward, *n., vb.*

rich, *n., adj.*

right, *adj.*

safe, *adj.*

safety, *n.*

salutary, *adj.*

salute, *vb.*

satisfaction, *n.*

satisfactory, *adj.*

satisfy, *vb.*

satisfying, *adj.*

scrupulous, *adj.*

seasoned, *adj.*

secure, *adj.*

security, *n.*

sensational, *adj.*

sensitive, *adj.*

serious, *adj.*

service, *n., vb.*

shield, *n., vb.*

shine, *vb.*

significant, *adj.*

simplified, *adj., vb.*

skilled, *adj.*

smart, *adj.*

smile, *n., vb.*

smooth, *adj.*

solid, *adj.*

solution, *n.*

soothing, *adj.*

sophisticated, *adj.*

sparkling, *adj.*

special, *adj.*

spectacular, *adj.*

splendid, *adj.*

spontaneous, *adj.*

stable, *adj.*

standard, *n., adj.*

staunch, *adj.*

steady, *adj.*

strength, *n.*

stunning, *adj.*

stupendous, *adj.*

substantiate, *vb.*

subtle, *adj.*

success, *n.*

successful, *adj.*

superb, *adj.*

superior, *adj.*

superiority, *n.*

superlative, *adj.*

support, *n., vb.*

supportive, *adj.*

supreme, *adj.*

sure, *adj.*

surely, *adv.*

surmount, *vb.*

surmountable, *adj.*

surpass, *vb.*

sustain, *vb.*

sustaining, *adj.*

sweet, *adj.*

sympathetic, *adj.*

sympathy, *n.*

talented, *adj.*

tasteful, *adj.*

tempt, *vb.*

tempting, *adj.*

tenacious, *adj.*

tender, *adj.*

terrific, *adj.*

tested, *adj., vb.*

thank you, *n.*

thank, *vb.*

thanks, *n.*

therapeutic, *adj.*

therapy, *n.*

thorough, *adj.*

thrilling, *adj.*

thriving, *adj.*

timely, *adj.*

together, *adv.*

togetherness, *n.*

total, *n., adj.*

trained, *adj., vb.*

tranquil, *adj.*

tranquillity, *n.*

transform, *vb.*

tremendous, *adj.*

true, *adj.*

trust, *n., vb.*

trustworthy, *adj.*

understand, *vb.*

understandable, *adj.*

understanding, *adj.*

undoubtedly, *adv.*

unforgettable, *adj.*

unique, *adj.*

unlimited, *adj.*

unmatched, *adj.*

upbeat, *adj.*

vacation, *n.*

valuable, *adj.*

versatile, *adj.*

veteran, *n., adj.*

vibrant, *adj.*

vital, *adj.*

welcome, *adj.*

well, *adj.*

well-being, *n.*

well-educated, *adj.*

willing, *adj.*

winner, *n.*

winning, *adj.*

wonder, *n.*

wonderful, *adj.*

yes, *adv.*

you, *pron.*

25 Descriptive Words to Help You Sell Your Ideas, Products, and Services

Many of the words in lists 23 and 24 may also be useful in a message created to sell an idea, product, or service. The words in the following list, however, are especially effective in sales material and other persuasive messages. Some of them, in fact, such as *dazzling* and *sumptuous,* may be too exaggerated or flashy for a more conservative type of message, even though they're commonly used in sales and advertising material. (All of these words can be used as adjectives.)

absolute	awesome	challenging
absorbing	bargain	changed
abundant	basic	charming
accepted	beautified	cheerful
accessible	beautiful	chewy
acclaimed	beguiling	chic
accomplished	best	chief
actual	best-selling	choice
adaptable	better	choicest
adorable	bewitching	chosen
advanced	biggest	clarified
adventuresome	blockbuster	classic
advisory	bold	clean
all-purpose	bonus	clear
alluring	booming	closeout
amazing	boundless	colorful
ample	bountiful	colossal
amusing	breathless	comfortable
appealing	breathtaking	commanding
applicable	breezy	compact
appreciative	brief	comparable
approved	brilliant	compatible
aromatic	brisk	compelling
artistic	candid	competitive
assured	capable	complementary
astonishing	captivating	complete
attractive	cash	comprehensive
authoritative	casual	concise
authorized	celebrated	condensed
automatic	certified	confident

congenial
consequential
contemporary
convenient
cool
coordinated
correct
corrected
cost-efficient
countless
cozy
creative
crisp
critical
crucial
crunchy
current
customized
daring
dashing
dazzling
debugged
definitive
delectable
delicate
delicious
delightful
deluxe
dependable
designer
desirable
different
discounted
discriminating
distinctive
distinguished

documented
dominant
dramatic
dreamlike
durable
dynamic
dynamite
easy
economical
educated
educational
effective
effectual
effervescent
effortless
electric
electrifying
elegant
elemental
elite
embellished
eminent
enchanted
enchanting
encyclopedic
endless
endorsed
endowed
enduring
energetic
engaging
engineered
engrossing
enhanced
enjoyable
enlightening

enormous
enriched
entertaining
enthralling
enthusiastic
entire
essential
established
esteemed
estimated
every
evocative
exalted
excellent
exceptional
exciting
exclusive
exhaustive
exhilarating
expanded
expanding
experienced
expert
explosive
exquisite
extensive
extra
extraordinary
fabulous
faithful
famed
famous
fancy
fantastic
fascinating
fashionable

fast	glowing	hot
favorite	golden	hottest
featured	good	huge
felicitous	gorgeous	ideal
fetching	graceful	illuminating
finest	gracious	illustrious
firm	grand	imaginative
first	grandiose	immaculate
first-class	gratifying	immense
flexible	great	immortal
flourishing	greatest	impeccable
flowery	gripping	imperative
foolproof	groundbreaking	implemented
forceful	growing	important
foremost	guaranteed	impressive
fortunate	guidance	improved
fragrant	hallmark	improving
fresh	handmade	incisive
friendly	handsome	incomparable
fruitful	handy	increased
fulfilled	harmonious	increasing
full	haunting	incredible
functional	healthy	indestructible
furnished	heavyweight	inexpensive
futuristic	hefty	influential
galvanizing	helpful	ingenious
gargantuan	helping	innovative
gemlike	Herculean	insider's
generous	hidden	installed
genuine	high-ranking	instant
gifted	high-tech	instructive
gigantic	historic	insulated
gilded	homey	integrated
glamorous	honest	intelligible
glittering	honored	intense
glorious	hospitable	intimate

intoxicating	matchless	overpowering
intriguing	melodious	oversized
introductory	memorable	overwhelming
invaluable	mesmerizing	packed
invigorating	mighty	panoramic
inviting	mild	paramount
irresistible	miniature	passionate
juicy	minute	peaceful
jumbo	mobile	perfect
knockout	modern	perfected
landmark	modified	personalized
latest	modular	petite
lavish	monumental	phenomenal
leading	moving	picturesque
legendary	multiple	pioneer
legitimate	multipurpose	piquant
lifelike	muscular	pleasant
lifetime	mysterious	pleasing
lightweight	mystical	pliable
limitless	natural	plush
lively	neat	popular
lovable	necessary	portable
lovely	new	portentous
luminous	nostalgic	posh
luscious	notable	possible
luxuriant	noted	potent
luxurious	noteworthy	potential
magical	novel	powerful
magnificent	numerous	practical
majestic	obligatory	precious
major	only	precision
mammoth	opulent	preeminent
manageable	organic	preferred
maneuverable	original	premier
marvelous	ornate	premium
massive	outstanding	prestigious

preventive	relaxed	secure
primary	relaxing	select
principal	remarkable	selected
priority	remodeled	selective
pristine	removable	sensational
private	renewed	sensuous
prizewinning	renowned	serene
prodigious	reorganized	serviceable
productive	reproducible	sexy
professional	reputable	shapely
profitable	resonating	sheer
profuse	respected	shoestring
projected	restful	significant
Promethean	restored	simple
prominent	restructured	simplified
proposed	revealing	sizable
protected	revered	sizzling
proven	revised	skilled
pure	revitalized	sleek
quaint	revived	slim
quality	revolutionary	smart
quick	rich	smooth
radiant	rigorous	soft
rare	ripe	soothing
ravishing	riveting	sophisticated
realistic	romantic	sound
recommended	roomy	space-age
redesigned	rousing	spacious
reduced	rugged	sparkling
refined	safe	special
reformed	satisfying	spectacular
refreshing	savory	spellbinding
refundable	scented	spicy
refurbished	scheduled	splendid
reinforced	seasoned	sporty
rejuvenating	secluded	stable

staggering	thrilling	unlimited
state-of-the-art	thriving	unmatched
stirring	timeless	unparalleled
straightforward	tiny	unprecedented
striking	today's	unrelenting
strong	top	unrivaled
stunning	tough	unsurpassed
stupendous	towering	unswerving
suave	traditional	untainted
sublime	trailblazing	unyielding
substantial	trained	up-to-date
subtle	tranquil	upscale
succulent	treasured	urgent
suitable	tremendous	usable
sumptuous	trendy	user-friendly
super	triumphant	valid
superb	tropical	valuable
superior	true	vanguard
superlative	trusted	varied
supportive	ultimate	vast
supreme	ultramodern	velvety
surefire	unabridged	versatile
sweeping	unassuming	vibrant
sweet	unbeatable	vigorous
tailored	unbelievable	vintage
talented	uncommon	virtuoso
tangy	uncomplicated	vital
tantalizing	uncompromising	vivid
tasteful	unconditional	voluminous
tasty	unconventional	warm
tempting	uncut	warranted
tenacious	understandable	wealthy
tender	undisputed	wholesome
terrific	unforgettable	whopping
tested	unhurried	winning
textured	unique	winsome

wise	wondrous	worthy
wonderful	worthwhile	zesty

26
Transition Words and Phrases to Make Your Writing Flow Smoothly

Writing that sounds abrupt and choppy can often be improved by adding transition words and phrases, such as *however* and *in contrast,* between sentences and paragraphs: "Management needs to find more ways to serve the shareholders; *however,* it has other duties that are also important." Although too many transition words in a paragraph or on a page can be distracting and may add unnecessary wordiness (see examples in list 37), judicious use of words from the following list will help readers move more easily from one sentence and paragraph to another.

accordingly	at the same time
after all	because
afterward	because of
again	besides
also	best of all
although	better yet
altogether	but
an even greater	but then
and then	by all means
and yet	by reason
anyhow	clearly
as a result	consequently
assuming that	consider
at any rate	despite
at last	doubtless
at length	equally important

even more important	inasmuch as
eventually	last
evidently	later
finally	likewise
first, second, etc.	meanwhile
following	moreover
for	most important
for example	namely
for instance	naturally
for this purpose	nevertheless
for this reason	next
fortunately	no doubt
further	no wonder
furthermore	notwithstanding
hence	now
here again	obviously
here's why	on account of
however	on the contrary
if you prefer	on the other hand
immediately	on the whole
in addition	other than that
in any case	otherwise
in any event	perhaps
in brief	possibly
in comparison	rather
in conclusion	remember
in contrast	similarly
in fact	simply
in like manner	simultaneously
in other words	since
in particular	soon
in short	still
in spite of	surprisingly
in sum	that is
in summary	that's why
in the meantime	the truth is

then	to this end
therefore	toward this end
thereupon	unless
think of it	what's more
though	whence
thus	wherefore
to be sure	worse
to illustrate	yet

27

Popular Portmanteau Expressions That Blend Two Words into One

Americans have a passion for coining new words, and one of the most popular ways of doing this is by blending parts of two existing words or by combining two complete words. This process has resulted in numerous brand names, such as *Campusport* (sportswear by the Campus Sportsware Co.), and even more general blend words, such as *travelogue* (travel + monologue). Some of these terms, such as *advertorial,* also qualify as business jargon (see list 29). Although the following blend words have found their way into business writing, they should be used cautiously. Many are not as well known as *travelogue* and may not be understood by general readers.

absolete, *adj.* (absolute + obsolete) Being finished or complete.

acutangular, *adj.* (acute + angular) Having acute angles.

adaptitude, *n.* (adapt + aptitude) A special aptitude or ability.

advertorial, *n.* (advertisement + editorial) A newspaper feature that looks like an editorial but is actually paid advertising.

airdraulic, *adj.* (air + hydraulic) Referring to a process that combines pneumatic (air and other gases) and hydraulic operations.

alphanumeric, *adj.* (alphabetic + numeric) Also *alphameric;* consisting of both letters and numbers.

ambiloquence, *n.* (ambiguous + eloquence) The quality of, and skill in using, deliberately evasive, ambiguous language.

Amerasian, *n.* (American + Asian) A person having mixed American and Asian ancestry.

Amerenglish, *n.* (American + English) The form of English spoken in the United States.

Amerindian, *n.* (American + Indian) A Native American; any of the aboriginal peoples of the Western Hemisphere.

Anglistics, *n.* (Anglo + linguistics) The study of the structure and development of the English language.

anticipointment, *n.* (anticipation + disappointment) A feeling of strong expectation followed by a sense of disappointment, often used to describe a venture that fails.

applaudit, *n.* (applaud + plaudit) An especially energetic expression of approval.

automobility, *n.* (automobile + mobility) The use of cars for transportation.

badvertising, *n.* (bad + advertising) Offensive or inadequate advertising.

beautility, *n.* (beauty + utility) A combination of practical qualities and beautiful features.

bit, *n.* (binary + digit) A single character in a language having only two characters, as in the binary digits 0 and 1; the smallest unit of information recognized by a computer.

blandiloquence, *n.* (bland + grandiloquence) Calm or flattering remarks aimed at soothing emotions.

blandscape, *n.* (bland + landscape) An expanse of scenery that lacks interesting or noteworthy features.

bodacious, *adj.* (bold + audacious) Also *boldacious;* being especially daring, forward, or brazen.

brash, *adj.* (bold + rash) Being especially forward, brazen, and impulsive.

breviloquence, *adj.* (brevity + eloquence) Characterized by brevity in speaking.

bromidiom, *n.* (bromide + idiom) A commonplace expression, such as *behind the scenes,* peculiar to a particular language.

brunch, *n.* (breakfast + lunch) A combination meal served between the usual times for breakfast and lunch.

bruncheon, *n.* (breakfast + luncheon) A more recent variation of *brunch,* believed by some to be more socially correct.

brunner, *n.* (breakfast + lunch + dinner) A combination of the three main meals, often served between the usual times for lunch and dinner.

bungersome, *adj.* (bungle + cumbersome) Being awkward or clumsy.

cafetorium, *n.* (cafeteria + auditorium) A large room that can be used both as a place for food service and as an auditorium.

calligram, *n.* (calligraphy + anagram) A visual pun; a design in which letters of a word are rearranged to form a decorative pattern.

caplet, *n.* (capsule + tablet) A medicinal pill, such as a pain reliever, made in the cakelike substance of a tablet but in the elongated shape of a gelatinous capsule.

carcinomenclature, *n.* (carcinogen + nomenclature) A label for muddled government expressions that spread like a cancer.

censcissor, *vb.* (censor + scissor) To remove objectionable material from books, films, and other works.

chemagination, *n.* (chemistry + imagination) The imaginative use of chemicals in new-product development.

circannual, *adj.* (circa + annual) Referring to annual cycles or periods.

Commart, *n.* (Common + mart) The European Common Market.

compunications, *n.* (computer + communications) Communications that are handled by computers.

computeracy, *n.* (computer + literacy) The knowledge, understanding, and experience required to work with computers.

condotel, *n.* (condo + hotel) A hotel that sells suites or units under a condominium type of arrangement, with common elements shared among all owners.

corpocracy, *n.* (corporate + bureaucracy) A bureaucratic style of operation in a corporation.

correctitude, *n.* (correct + rectitude) Correct behavior and adherence to accepted rules of etiquette.

cybot, *n.* (cybernetic + robot) A type of robot capable of imitating the process of human reasoning and decision making.

datamation, *n.* (data + automation) Automatic data processing.

digerati, *n.* (digital + literati) A label for people who are highly skilled (literate) in working with digital information.

docutainment, *n.* (documentary + entertainment) A television program that dramatizes factual information.

dumbfound, *vb.* (dumb + confound) To astonish or perplex.

dunch, *n.* (dinner + lunch) A complete dinner eaten at lunchtime; a combination lunch and dinner meal eaten in the afternoon.

duologue, *n.* (duo + monologue) A long conversation between two people.

econometric, *adj.* (economic + metric) Referring to the use of mathematical and statistical methods in dealing with economic theories and problems.

enduct, *n.* (end + product) The result of a project or operation.

euphemantics, *n.* (euphemistic + semantics) The use of indirect promotional messages to advertise and sell products and services.

Eurasian, *n.* (European + Asian) A person having mixed European and Asian ancestry.

expunctuation, *n.* (expunction + punctuation) The marking of material for removal while editing a manuscript.

fuzzword, *n.* (fuzzy + buzzword) A deliberately confusing or imprecise form of jargon, such as *strategic misrepresentation* (lies), often used to impress others.

gasohol, *n.* (gasoline + alcohol) Fuel made from a blend of ethanol alcohol and gasoline.

glitterati, *n.* (glitter + literati) A label for the wealthy, fashionable, and famous.

grandificent, *adj.* (grand + magnificent) Characterized by greatness, splendor, grandeur, or lavishness.

gridlock, *n.* (grid + deadlock) An impasse or stalemate, causing complete stagnation.

guestimate, *n.* (guess + estimate) An estimate based on conjecture rather than known facts.

habitude, *n.* (habit + attitude) A certain, habitual way of thinking or acting.

humanation, *n.* (human + automation) The process of adapting human resources to the requirements of automation.

imagineering, *n.* (imagine + engineering) The implementation of creative ideas into practical form.

infopreneur, *n.* (information + entrepreneur) A person who undertakes ventures in the field of information technology.

infomercial, *n.* (information + commercial) An educational or instructional commercial television program or segment about the sponsor's product or service.

infotainment, *n.* (information + entertainment) A television program that has a mixture of news and entertainment or that dramatizes the educational content.

innoventure, *n.* (innovative + venture) A venture that begins or introduces something new.

loxygen, *n.* (liquid + oxygen) A shortened name for liquid oxygen.

megalopolitan, *adj.* (megalopolis + metropolitan) Referring to a very large metropolitan area.

mobot, *n.* (motor + robot) A motorized, mobile robot.

motorail, *n.* (motor + rail) A railway service for transporting automobiles and the occupants by rail.

opinionnaire, *n.* (opinion + questionnaire) A questionnaire designed to solicit opinions.

portmantologism, *n.* (portmanteau + neologism) A newly coined blend word.

prequel, *n.* (precede + sequel) A literary work, film, or play set in a time *before* that of an existing work, unlike a *sequel,* which follows or continues an existing work.

slang, *n.* (slovenly + language) Specially coined, often crude language usually intended to be shocking or irreverent.

specialogue, *n.* (special + catalog) A catalog slanted to a particular market.

transceiver, *n.* (transmitter + receiver) A device, such as a fax machine, that can both send and receive messages.

transonic, *adj.* (transitional + sonic) Referring to flight or flow at speeds close to the speed of sound.

workfare, *n.* (work + welfare) A form of welfare in which recipients of assistance are required to perform public service work.

28

Evasive Euphemisms for a Kinder, Gentler Message

Euphemisms are less precise and often milder substitutes for more direct, harsh, or unpleasant expressions. Although they tend to be evasive, the reasoning behind their use is the need on occasion to avoid saying something that might disturb a reader or listener. Most writing experts strongly object to their use only when the substitute sounds too misleading or silly, as in the case of *unpleasant arousal* instead of the simple, clear word *depression*. Like portmanteau words (see list 27), some euphemisms, such as *economic adjustment* (price hike), also qualify as jargon (see list 29); others, such as *close the doors* (go out of business), have been overused to the point of becoming cliches (see list 39). Writers should consider their audience and use common sense in deciding whether to adopt any of the following euphemisms.

Euphemism	Direct Reference
activist	zealot
adjustment	increase in prices

advanced in years	elderly; old
affirmative action	preferential treatment of certain groups
America first	isolationism
appearance money	bribe to participate
appropriate	steal
archivist	library clerk, museum clerk
assistance	payments to the poor
at liberty	involuntarily unemployed
awaiting employment	unemployed
away	in prison
below the salt	socially inferior
bend the rules	act illegally
biographic leverage	extortion
black economy	untaxed income from unreported sales
black market	illegal trading
black money	illegal profit
blackmail	extortion
boiler house	unscrupulous sales operation
borrow	steal
brand X	competitor's product
bump	sudden displacement or dismissal
businesslike and friendly	unproductive
challenging	unprofitable
Chinese copy	stolen copy
classic	pretentious and costly
close the doors	fail; go out of business
commission	bribe
committed	dogmatic
concessional	free; subsidized
concoct	falsify
condition	illness
conference	excuse to avoid callers
confrontation	fight; heated argument

consultancy	work given to an unwanted senior employee
contribution	bribe
controversial	disreputable; untrustworthy
convenient size	small
cordial	cool; unfriendly
corner	establish a monopoly
corporate entertainment	bribery
corporate recovery	management of insolvent companies
correction in stock market	serious decline in stock market
cozy quarters	small quarters
creative	dishonest; false
credibility gap	extent to which one is perceived to be lying
custodial engineer	janitor
cut	illegal commission or payment
debrief	question aggressively
decadent	not conforming to previous standards
deceased	dead; person who died
demanning	dismissal of employees
demise	death
deprived	poor
deselect	dismiss
devolution	decentralization; delegation of powers to lower levels
disadvantaged	poor
disciple of	supporter of someone or something taboo
dispute	strike
distinguished	over age forty
distressed	mentally ill
distribution	payment of a bribe
divert	steal

domestic engineer	someone who does or is in charge of housework
downsize	dismiss employees
downsizing	layoff, firing
early retirement	dismissal from employment
economic adjustment	price hike
economic storm	slump
economically abused	poor
economically inactive	unemployed
economy class	inexpensive class
effluent	noxious discharge
enhance	alter surreptitiously
entanglement	ill-advised association
equity retreat	fall in the stock market
ethnic	not exclusively white
exchange of views	disagreement
experienced tires	recaps; retreads
extended	dull
fact-finding mission	paid holiday
fail to win	lose
false market	conditions from improper rigging of prices
fatigue	mental illness
field merchandiser	door-to-door salesperson
financial engineering	false accounting
financial services	money lending
fishing expedition	attempt to obtain information
fix	make an illegal arrangement
flexibility	willingness to abandon principles
fly-by-night operation	shady operation that soon closes and disappears with funds
food-preparation center	kitchen
forget oneself	be guilty of a breach, as a breach of etiquette
frank	unfriendly
front	operation that hides its real activity

furlough	layoff
gender norming	accepting different standards from women
get the shorts	be insolvent
glass ceiling	level above which certain employees will not be promoted
glove money	bribe
go under	fail; go bankrupt; become insolvent
golden	excessive
golden years	old age
gracious	old; expensive
graft	bribery
grease	bribe
guest workers	foreign laborers
handout	government payment to the poor; bribe
handshake	payment upon being dismissed
high-profile	being highly visible to the public
home equity loan	second mortgage
housecleaning	destruction of incriminating records; reorganization leading to dismissals
human resources	employees; personnel
human resources manager	personnel manager
hustle	sell inexpensive goods at high prices
income protection	tax avoidance
indigent	poor
indisposed	ill; sick
industrial logic	greed
informal	without permission; illegal
inner city	slum
insider	someone using confidential information improperly

inventory adjustment	loss from overvaluation of goods or stocks
inventory leakage	stealing
involuntary severance	layoff
irregularity	dishonesty; fraud
job turning	reducing responsibility and pay
kickback	bribe; illegal payment
kite	issue a check before funds to cover it are available
knocking on doors	asking favors
lay off	dismiss from employment
learning difficulty	low intelligence; mental disability
let go	dismiss from employment
limited	stupid; incompetent
liquidity crisis	severe shortage of liquid assets or expendable funds
lived-in	untidy
loss prevention specialist	security guard
low-profile	avoiding public notice
managed news	information that is deliberately slanted
marginalized	different from the majority
marketing representative	salesperson
mature	old
misspeak	lie
mortality rate	death rate
needy and dependent persons	welfare recipients
negative contribution	sale at a loss
negative growth	decline
negative stock holding	orders that cannot be delivered
negatively privileged	poor
no longer with us	dead

nonprofit	tax-free
operator	swindler
orderly marketing	price fixing
outstanding property	expensive property
overgeared	insolvent
participate in	work for
passed away	died
patron	customer
paying guest	boarder
payoff	bribe; illicit reward
period structure	old and dilapidated structure
personal assistant	secretary
personnel ceiling reductions	employment cutbacks
physically challenged	disabled
poetic truth	lie
premium	higher-priced
preowned	used
preowned car	used car; secondhand car
prestigious	expensive
prevaricate	lie
prime	saleable
public assistance employee	civil service employee
question	persistent problem
questionable	illegal; immoral
reconditioned car	used car; secondhand car
red tape	excessively complex procedures
release	dismiss from employment
relieve	dismiss from employment
resting	unemployed
retire	dismiss from employment
revenue enhancement	taxes
reverse engineering	unauthorized copying
said out of context	said inadvisably
sanitary engineer	garbage collector

scenario	potentially dangerous scheme or plot
secluded	inconveniently isolated
security coordinator	bodyguard
senior citizen	elderly person; old person
sensible	ugly; unfashionable
slowdown	intentional refusal to do one's assigned work
sought-after	expensive
splendid oscillation	indecisiveness; disregard of a problem
sponsor	advertiser
step down	retire unwillingly
stonewall	obstruct justice; cover up; conceal
streamlining	dismissal of a number of employees
stretch the truth	lie
succumb to injuries	die
take under advisement	defer action; shelve
technical adjustment	sudden fall in stock prices
tenure	a job for life
under-the-counter	illegal
underemployed person	someone with a job below his or her level of education and ability
underprivileged	destitute; poor
undocumented	illegal
unwaged	involuntarily unemployed
verbally deficient	illiterate
visible minority	black
vulnerable	poor; inadequate
wage restraint	limit on wage increases
white elephant	unwanted possession

Business Jargon That Should Be Used Cautiously

As specialized or technical language, jargon is widespread. Law offices, real estate firms, computer operations, and many other professions and activities have their own special vocabulary. Often, the language of a certain profession or activity facilitates communication among others who share the same interests. Problems may arise, however, when someone who understands specialized terminology uses it outside the workplace with others who don't understand it. As the title indicates, therefore, the following examples of business jargon should be used cautiously, depending on the audience.

aftermarket A market for parts and accessories, such as a CD player for automobiles, created by the desire of customers to enhance their basic equipment.

angel A financial backer, contributor, or investor.

artificial reality Computer technology that simulates a real-life situation in which users can interact by attaching and using various hand and head devices.

automated attendant A computer voice-message system using prerecorded greetings and a number of voice-recorded options from which callers may select any that fits their needs.

bait and switch pricing An illegal sales tactic advertising a product at a low price to attract customers who are then urged to buy a more expensive or lower-quality substitute.

balloon payment A lump sum that is payable at the end of a loan.

bells and whistles Frills or nonessential features that are added to a product to make it more appealing.

boilerplate Standard clauses or covenants that are common in contracts, deeds, and various other documents.

bucket shop An investment brokerage that doesn't promptly process customer's buy and sell orders, in violation of the requirements of the Securities and Exchange Commission.

candy-store problem A problem for which there are many equally effective or ineffective solutions.

cohousing A community-participation concept whereby prospective residents participate in designing and building the community to meet their requirements.

contingent workforce The workforce consisting of those who do part-time, temporary, and freelance work to supplement their regular income.

cool and whizzy Usually referring to computer hardware or software with many appealing and impressively displayed features.

copreneurship The practice of two people, such as a husband and wife, running a business together as copreneurs, or entrepreneurial couples.

crossover Success or activity occurring in more than one area.

crosstalk The unwanted breakthrough or overlap that sometimes occurs between communication channels, such as the background voices you may hear on a telephone line.

cyberspace The intangible sphere in which computer users work while communicating on line; a computer-generated landscape.

demarketing Marketing that aims to discourage interest in items or activity considered harmful, such as smoking.

download To copy computer files, using a modem and the telephone lines, from a remote location to your own computer.

downtick A small or incremental decrease, such as a downtick in the stock market.

downtime An idle period when activity stops because an error has occurred or because the equipment needs repair or servicing.

dumping Selling large numbers of stock and thereby causing the price per share to drop or selling goods below cost to drive away competition.

emoticons Symbols used in E-mail messages to show emotion, such as <s>, meaning "sigh" (see examples in list 64 of Part IV).

end user The customer or client who uses a product or service.

English creep The increasing use of English as an international language and the principal business language in other countries.

enterprise zone An area that encourages investment and employment by offering tax incentives to businesses that locate there.

facadism The technique of retaining the fronts of old buildings while creating new structures behind them.

fast track The fastest and most direct route taken to reach a goal.

fifth-generation computer A robotic computer designed and programmed to simulate human thinking and activity in problem solving.

first generation The earliest or initial technology or equipment.

flanker A spin-off product that is given a name similar to that of the original product so that it can capitalize on the success of the original product.

gentrification The practice of buying and improving deteriorated urban property and selling it to higher-income people, displacing the former residents and businesspeople.

golden handcuffs A contract that pressures executives to keep their current positions for fear that a move will lead to a loss in salary or benefits.

golden parachute The guarantee of high payments to executives whose companies have lost in a takeover.

green Ecologically and environmentally concerned.

greenmail The practice of buying enough of a company's stock to threaten a hostile takeover, forcing the management to buy it back at an inflated price to prevent the takeover.

green marketing Marketing aimed at persuading the public that a company's products and methods of production are environmentally sound.

hacker An electronically skilled intruder who uses a computer to break into other people's computers and files to disrupt or destroy their data.

haircut A reduction in expenses that trims excesses without jeopardizing the main objective.

home page An information or advertising page set up at a World Wide Web site providing the starting address for multiple pages of information.

horizontal market A broad market that has a wide range of customers, such as the market for tennis shoes.

host A main computer system that provides the computing power for peripherals and remote terminals connected to it.

housekeeping routine Initial computer instructions that are generally executed only once, such as setup operations.

hype To promote something or someone through repeated and exaggerated claims.

hypertext A computer-based system that enables users to move from one place to another in any direction in a nonlinear fashion.

information superhighway A proposed worldwide network integrating computers, telephones, and cable television in all homes and businesses.

insider trading The illegal practice of using inside knowledge of a company's stock to make money.

killer technology Advanced technology that is so radical that it makes everything preceding it obsolete.

log on Also *log in;* to identify oneself on an electronic network before beginning work, giving one's name and the password to gain access and keep track of usage time.

loss leader An article sold at a loss to lure customers into a store or market.

micromanagement The planning and direction of local operations by central management.

mommy track The movement of a professional woman from professional employment to domestic life.

morphing A computer animation technique that makes it appear as though an object is changing from one shape to another; doing two or more jobs.

mouse milking Devoting considerable effort to achieve only a small or minor result.

netiquette Internet etiquette or the rules of accepted standards of behavior in using the Internet for communication and other purposes.

networking Exchanging information and communicating with others who have common interests.

niche market A new market that develops between or in addition to existing markets.

off line Not connected electronically or not under the control of a central processing unit.

on line Connected electronically or under the control of a central processing unit.

operative A determining, decisive, or important point or condition.

OPM financing Financing that is arranged by using other people's money.

outsourcing The cost-cutting practice of going to sources outside a company for labor, services, and parts, rather than using in-house resources.

peewee tech Small-company technologies.

poison pill A company's defensive strategy in a threatened takeover designed to make the takeover so expensive that the predator decides not to pursue it.

prosumer An older person who continues to work but without financial compensation.

protocol The regulation of data that enables programs on different machines to communicate with each other.

raider Also *corporate raider;* an investor that attempts to take over a company by purchasing a majority of its stock.

recareer A second career, often undertaken to avoid retirement.

rollback: A return to lower prices.

rollover Reinvestment.

rug ranking The practice of linking a secretary's career path and pay to the success of the secretary's boss.

scorched earth A self-destructive type of strategy used by a company in an attempt to discourage an unwanted corporate takeover.

screamer A customer who complains persistently.

scripting Giving a computer instructions for performing certain tasks ahead of time so that the user need not be present when the work is done.

shark repellent Efforts designed to discourage an unwanted corporate takeover by making it very expensive and difficult for the aggressor to purchase the company.

smart card A small plastic card containing a microprocessor and memory designed for holders to use in making financial transactions by machine.

surfing The process of searching for information on the Internet and exploring available sites electronically.

teflon The quality of being immune to, or being able to shed, undesirable external influences.

throughput The rate of data processing or transfer; the amount of work processed in a given period; the computer's performance in sending data through all system components.

transaction services Telephone services that enable users to complete a transaction, such as shopping by computer, over the telephone or on a computer screen.

Trojan horse Something that appears to represent normal activity but actually involves something illegal or secret.

turnaround time The time it takes to perform a task, fill an order, or receive, complete, and return something.

upload To copy computer files from a local computer and send them to a remote system on the network.

uptick A small or incremental increase, such as an uptick in the stock market.

uptime The time when equipment is operating or is available for use.

vertical market A market with a limited range of customers, such as the market for unicycles.

virus An uninvited computer program or entry in a program that disrupts or destroys data.

Web Short for the World Wide Web, an electronic system designed to enable Internet users to locate information.

white knight A corporation that takes steps to help another company being theatened by an unwanted takeover.

English Idioms That Could Cause Problems in Other Countries

Idiomatic expressions mean something different from their literal translations and therefore should be avoided with any audience that reads or translates material literally. Imagine someone in Malaysia trying to translate the sentence "We hope you have a *field day* with your new unit," meaning *enjoy* or *have great success with*. The following list has examples of idioms that may confuse certain readers. Also, any idiomatic expression that has been overused, such as *Achilles' heel,* is considered a cliche as well (see list 39) and should be avoided. In addition, some idioms are unnecessarily wordy (see list 37).

A to Z	after hours
aboveboard	against the clock
Achilles' heel	aim to prove
across the board	air one's views
act of God	airtight reason
act up	all in a day's work
after a fashion	all in all

all in good time
all the same
an off day
as a matter of fact
as far as
as good as
as regards
at close quarters
at cross purposes
at face value
at first hand
at hand
at liberty
back down
back out of something
back someone up
backlash
bad name
bank on
bare bones
be a credit to
be a headache
be at odds
be beside oneself
be big of
be driving at
be going strong
be in for something
be in good form
be in on something
be in the red
be out of practice
be rough on
be set on something
be sold on
be the end of

be tied up
be under the
  impression that
be up against
bear in mind
bears and bulls (stock
  market)
before long
beg the question
behind the scenes
behind the times
better off
beyond compare
beyond recall
bide one's time
black market
blackball
bottleneck
brace yourself
break the news
breathing space
bring someone to
  account
bring something into
  line
bring to light
bring to mind
broaden one's mind
brush-off
build on sand
buy someone off
by and by
by and large
by the way
by virtue of
by word of mouth

call into question

call it a day

call it quits

call to mind

can't help feeling

captive market

carry on

carry one's weight

carry the day

case in point

cash in on something

catch one's breath

catch sight of

change hands

change of heart

change one's mind

clean slate

clear the air

climb down

close at hand

close ranks

closed mind

come clean

come full circle

come in handy

come into play

come to grief

come to grips with

come to light

come to nothing

come to rest

corner the market

crack down on

crop up

cross one's mind

cut above

cut and dried

cut both ways

cut corners

cutthroat competition

day in and day out

dead loss

dead-end

die-hard

dig in

dip into

do away with

double back

doubt whether

down-to-earth

draw the line

drive something home

drop by

drop in

drop off

drop out

edge someone out

evenhanded

explore every avenue

face value

fall flat

fall into place

fall short

fall through

falling market

false start

false step

far and away

far cry from

fed up

feel free

field day

fifty-fifty
fighting chance
finishing touches
firm footing
first thing
firsthand
flesh out
flood the market
follow suit
foot-dragging
for good measure
for that matter
for the most part
free from
free hand
gain ground
get around to
get carried away
get something off the
    ground
get something straight
get to the bottom of
give ground
give pause
give the benefit of doubt
go a long way toward
go back on something
go easy on
go in for something
go one better
go to any lengths
golden opportunity
gray area
grow out of something
guardian angel
hand down

handout
hard-nosed
have a go at it
have a look at
have a nerve
have a way with
have had it
have half a mind to
have in mind
have it both ways
have no time for
have the edge on
head for
head start
heavy-handed
high and mighty
high places
high time
hinge on
hold back
hold forth
hold off
hold one's breath
hold sway
identical with
in a big way
in a nutshell
in a sense
in all conscience
in all good faith
in all probability
in character
in good taste
in league with
in one's element
in place of

in point of fact	lay waste
in search of	leading question
in season	lean over backward
in short order	leave a lot to be desired
in so many words	leave cold
in the balance	let something ride
in the block	let something slide
in the clear	let's face it
in the eyes of the law	lie low
in the face of it	light touch
in the long run	listen to reason
in the main	live up to
in the red	look after
in the same vein	loom large
in the wake of	loophole in the law
it stands to reason	lose face
just the same	lose ground
keep an eye on	lose heart
keep in mind	lose sight of
keep it up	lose sleep over
keep one's distance	lose touch
keep one's own counsel	lose track of
keep one's word	make a fuss
keep pace with	make a go of something
keep sight of	make a stand
keep tabs on	make capital out of
keep track of	make do
keep up appearances	make good time
kill time	make good use of
kind of	make headway
know better	make one's mark
know what's what	make something of it
know where one stands	make the grade
lame excuse	make the most of
lay down the law	make time
lay it on the line	make up for

make up for lost time

make up one's mind

make way

mark time

matter of time

mean business

meet halfway

mental block

moral support

mouthful

near miss

no earthly reason

no end to

no time at all

no way

none the wiser

none the worse for

nose for

nosedive

not cut out for

not to know someone
from Adam

of the essence

offhand

old hand

on its way out

on the face of it

on the house

on the level

on the part of

on the shelf

on top

one of these days

open mind

order of the day

out of character

out of commission

out of date

out of line

out of one's element

out of order

out of place

out of pocket

out of season

out of the question

out of thin air

out of touch

out of turn

over one's head

peace of mind

pet name

plan to stay

play fast and loose

play havoc with

play it safe

play the game

play the market

presence of mind

pressed for time

price oneself out of the
market

put a new face on it

put heads together

put on an act

put someone off

put someone wise

put something into
practice

put something off

question of the hour

race against time

rash of

ray of hope
rising market
rough time
rule of thumb
rule out something
run across
run out of
run through
saving grace
second nature
second rate
second thought
secondhand
see daylight
see eye to eye
see fit
see in black and white
see it through
see someone off
seize on
sense of proportion
serve a purpose
set an example
set great store by
set one's sights on
set the record straight
sharp tongue
shelve something
shop around
show one's hand
show one's true colors
side with someone
sit in on
size up
skin-deep
slip of the tongue

slip one's mind
small wonder
snowed under
sore point
split hairs
split the difference
stand on one's dignity
stands to reason
start from scratch
stay the course
step down
strike a chord
strike an agreement
strike it lucky
suit oneself
take a dim view of
take a hard line
take exception
take heart
take offense
take one's time
take part in
take place
take shape
take sides
take someone to task
take something amiss
take the risk
take time off
the long and the short
the small hours
there's no knowing
think something over
tie in with something
time is of the essence
time is running out

to all intents and
purposes
to good purpose
to mean business
to plague
to prune something
to table something
to the point
troubleshooter
turn a blind eye
turn a deaf ear
unmindful of
up in the air
up to date

uphill fight
water down
well-heeled
white elephant
with a free hand
with an eye toward
within the letter of the
law
without rhyme or
reason
work around the clock
work something off
year in, year out
zero in on something

31

Negative Words to Avoid in Bad-News Messages

One of the tips for composing a bad-news message, in list 15 of
Part I, is to use positive words (see the examples in list 24). Although negative words can have an adverse impact in any type of
message, they're especially risky in a bad-news message. Some
words tend to suggest something unflattering or pessimistic and
may create feelings of apprehension, dissatisfaction, anger, or
even rebellion (see also the examples of fighting words in list 32).
The words *fault* and *dispute*, for example, tend to create a sense
of apprehension, and sometimes defensiveness, in readers.
Therefore, writers need to beware of potentially negative words in
this list when they're delivering bad news to someone. (Commonly used parts of speech follow each term; for other possibilities, consult a current dictionary.)

abandon, *vb.*

abandoned, *adj., vb.*

abhor, *vb.*

abhorred, *vb.*

abolish, *vb.*

abolished, *adj., vb.*

abominable, *adj.*

abrasive, *adj.*

abscond, *vb.*

absconded, *vb.*

absurd, *adj.*

abuse, *vb.*

abused, *adj., vb.*

accident, *n.*

admonish, *vb.*

admonished, *vb.*

adversity, *n.*

affected, *adj.*

afraid, *adj.*

alarm, *n., vb.*

alarmed, *adj., vb.*

alibi, *n.*

allege, *vb.*

alleged, *adj., vb.*

altercation, *n.*

ambiguous, *adj.*

anger, *n., vb.*

angered, *vb.*

anguish, *n.*

anguished, *adj.*

annoy, *vb.*

annoyed, *adj., vb.*

antagonize, *vb.*

antagonized, *vb.*

anxiety, *n.*

apathy, *n.*

apology, *n.*

apparently, *adv.*

appease, *vb.*

appeased, *vb.*

argue, *vb.*

argued, *vb.*

argument, *n.*

assume, *vb.*

assumed, *vb.*

aversion, *n.*

bad, *adj.*

banal, *adj.*

bankrupt, *adj., vb.*

beware, *vb.*

bias, *n.*

biased, *adj.*

blame, *n., vb.*

blamed, *vb.*

bleak, *adj.*

calamity, *n.*

callous, *adj.*

cancel, *vb.*

canceled, *adj., vb.*

careless, *adj.*

carelessness, *n.*

censure, *vb.*

censured, *adj., vb.*

chaos, *n.*

cheap, *adj.*

claim, *n., vb.*

claimed, *vb.*

clash, *n., vb.*

clashed, *vb.*

collapse, *n., vb.*

collapsed, *adj., vb.*

collusion, *n.*

commonplace, *adj.*

complain, *vb.*

complained, *vb.*

complaint, *n.*

complicate, *vb.*

complicated, *adj., vb.*

contaminate, *vb.*

contaminated, *adj., vb.*

contempt, *n.*

contend, *vb.*

contended, *vb.*

contentious, *adj.*

contrived, *adj., vb.*

control, *n., vb.*

controlled, *adj., vb.*

corrupt, *adj., vb.*

crisis, *n.*

criticism, *n.*

crooked, *adj.*

crude, *adj.*

cruel, *adj.*

damage, *n., vb.*

damaged, *adj., vb.*

deadlock, *n., vb.*

deadlocked, *adj., vb.*

deceive, *vb.*

deceived, *adj., vb.*

deception, *n.*

decline, *vb.*

declined, *vb.*

defeat, *n., vb.*

defeated, *adj., vb.*

defied, *vb.*

defy, *vb.*

demagogue, *n.*

demand, *n., vb.*

demanded, *vb.*

denied, *adj., vb.*

dense, *adj.*

deny, *vb.*

deplore, *vb.*

deplored, *vb.*

deprive, *vb.*

deprived, *adj., vb.*

derelict, *n., adj.*

desert, *vb.*

deserted, *adj., vb.*

despise, *vb.*

despised, *adj., vb.*

destroy, *vb.*

destroyed, *adj., vb.*

devastate, *vb.*

devious, *adj.*

dictator, *n.*

difficult, *adj.*

disadvantage, *n.*

disadvantaged, *n., adj.*

disagree, *vb.*

disagreement, *n.*

disaster, *n.*

discredit, *vb.*

discredited, *adj., vb.*

dismal, *adj.*

dispute, *n., vb.*

disputed, *adj., vb.*

dissatisfied, *adj.*

dominate, *vb.*

dominated, *adj., vb.*

dread, *n., vb.*

dreaded, *adj., vb.*

drunk, *n., adj.*

dumb, *adj.*

emergency, *n.*

error, *n.*

evict, *vb.*

evicted, *adj., vb.*

eviction, *n.*

exaggerate, *vb.*

exaggerated, *adj., vb.*

extravagant, *adj.*

extreme, *adj.*

fail, *vb.*

failed, *adj., vb.*

failure, *n.*

fall, *n., vb.*

false, *adj.*

falsely, *adv.*

fatal, *adj.*

fault, *n.*

fear, *n., vb.*

feared, *vb.*

fiasco, *n.*

flagrant, *adj.*

flat, *adj.*

flimsy, *adj.*

force, *vb.*

forced, *vb.*

forgot, *vb.*

forsake, *vb.*

foul, *adj.*

gloss, *vb.*

gratuitous, *adj.*

grave, *adj.*

grief, *n.*

hamper, *vb.*

hampered, *vb.*

hapless, *adj.*

harass, *vb.*

harassed, *adj., vb.*

hardship, *n.*

hate, *n., vb.*

hated, *adj., vb.*

hazy, *adj.*

hinder, *vb.*

hindered, *vb.*

hogwash, *n.*

hurt, *vb.*

hurtful, *adj.*

idiot, *n.*

ignoble, *adj.*

ignorant, *adj.*

ignore, *vb.*

illiterate, *adj.*

illogical, *adj.*

imitation, *n., adj.*

immature, *adj.*

impasse, *n.*

impede, *vb.*

impeded, *vb.*

implicate, *vb.*

implicated, *vb.*

impossible, *adj.*

impractical, *adj.*

improvident, *adj.*

inadequate, *adj.*

incompetent, *adj.*

incorrect, *adj.*

indulge, *vb.*

inefficient, *adj.*

inept, *adj.*

inferior, *adj.*

inflame, *vb.*

insidious, *adj.*

insinuate, *vb.*

insist, *vb.*

insisted, *vb.*

insolvent, *adj.*

insult, *n., vb.*

intimidate, *vb.*

invalid, *adj.*

invalidate, *vb.*

irritate, *vb.*

irritated, *adj., vb.*

late, *adj.*

liable, *adj.*

liar, *n.*

lie, *n., vb.*

lied, *vb.*

liquidate, *vb.*

long-winded, *adj.*

lose, *vb.*

loss, *n.*

ludicrous, *adj.*

lying, *adj., vb.*

manipulate, *vb.*

meager, *adj.*

meddle, *vb.*

meddled, *vb.*

meddlesome, *adj.*

mediocre, *n.*

menial, *adj.*

misfortune, *n.*

misinform, *vb.*

misinformed, *adj., vb.*

misrepresent, *vb.*

misrepresented, *vb.*

monopolize, *vb.*

muddle, *n., vb.*

muddled, *adj., vb.*

mundane, *adj.*

must, *vb.*

naive, *adj.*

negate, *vb.*

negated, *vb.*

neglect, *n., vb.*

neglected, *adj., vb.*

negligence, *n.*

never, *adv.*

no, *adv.*

nonnegotiable, *adj.*

not, *adv.*

nullify, *vb.*

obligate, *vb.*

obligated, *adj., vb.*

oblique, *adj.*

obscure, *vb.*

obscured, *adj., vb.*

obstinate, *adj.*

obstruction, *n.*

obstructionist, *n.*

opinionated, *adj.*

oppose, *vb.*

oppress, *vb.*

overbearing, *adj.*

overdue, *adj.*

oversight, *n.*

partisan, *adj.*

perhaps, *adv.*

pernicious, *adj.*

pessimist, *n.*

pessimistic, *adj.*

precipitate, *vb.*

precipitated, *vb.*

predatory, *adj.*

prejudice, *n.*, *vb.*

prejudiced, *adj.*, *vb.*

premature, *adj.*

pressure, *n.*, *vb.*

pretentious, *adj.*

problem, *n.*

quibble, *vb.*

quibbled, *vb.*

radical, *adj.*

rebuke, *n.*, *vb.*

recalcitrant, *adj.*

regret, *n.*, *vb.*

repulsive, *adj.*

rude, *adj.*

ruin, *vb.*

ruined, *adj.*, *vb.*

ruthless, *adj.*

sad, *adj.*

sadly, *adv.*

sarcastic, *adj.*

senseless, *adj.*

shameful, *adj.*

shirk, *vb.*

shirked, *vb.*

shortsighted, *adj.*

shrink, *vb.*

sketchy, *adj.*

slack, *adj.*

slow, *adj.*

sorry, *adj.*

squander, *vb.*

squandered, *adj.*, *vb.*

stagnant, *adj.*

standstill, *n.*

stereotype, *n.*, *vb.*

stereotyped, *adj.*, *vb.*

straggling, *adj.*

stubborn, *adj.*

stunt, *vb.*

stunted, *vb.*

stupid, *adj.*

superficial, *adj.*

superfluous, *adj.*

taint, *vb.*

tainted, *adj.*, *vb.*

tamper, *vb.*

tampered, *vb.*

tardy, *adj.*

terrible, *adj.*

timid, *adj.*

tolerable, *adj.*

troublesome, *adj.*

ugly, *adj.*

unable, *adj.*

unacceptable, *adj.*

unfair, *adj.*

unfortunate, *adj.*

unfortunately, *adv.*

unimportant, *adj.*

unnerve, *vb.*

unnerved, *adj.*, *vb.*

unreasonable, *adj.*

unsatisfactory, *adj.*

unsuccessful, *adj.*

untimely, *adj.*

unwilling, *adj.*

unwise, *adj.*

useless, *adj.*

usurp, *vb.*

usurped, *vb.*

victim, *n.*

wanton, *adj.*

waste, *vb.*	worrisome, *adj.*
wasted, *vb.*	worry, *n., vb.*
wasteful, *adj.*	wreck, *n., vb.*
weak, *adj.*	wrong, *adj.*
weakness, *n.*	wrongful, *adj.*

32

Fighting Words and Phrases That Put Readers on the Defensive

Some words and phrases are so provocative that they shouldn't be used in business writing. Comments such as "We don't believe that" or "You should know that" are too antagonistic and strike readers as a declaration of war or a distasteful attitude of superiority. Even relatively milder comments, such as "We do not agree that," have a confrontational tone compared to the more neutral tone of "We discovered that" or "We believe that." Regardless of any sense of impatience or irritation with a reader, the use of fighting words and phrases, such as the following examples, is always ill-advised (see also examples of negative words in list 31 and loaded words in list 34).

Apparently you are not aware that . . .

Because of your mistake . . .

Because of your questionable . . .

Because you ignored proper procedure . . .

Contrary to your inference . . .

Don't tell me that . . .

Don't you realize that . . .

Even though we've told you repeatedly . . .

How can you expect others to . . .

How many times must I remind you that . . .

How many times must I tell you that . . .

I can't believe that you actually . . .

I can't believe that you seriously . . .

I don't agree with you . . .

I fail to understand why you . . .

I hope you didn't . . .

I question what you say . . .

I'm sure you must realize that . . .

If you care at all about . . .

Is there some reason why you always . . .

It is simply nonsense to say that . . .

Let me make one thing perfectly clear . . .

Let's get one thing straight . . .

Surely you don't expect us to . . .

The utter foolishness of your . . .

We are amazed that you can't . . .

We are amazed that you haven't . . .

We are amazed that you won't . . .

We are not inclined to . . .

We can't do anything until you . . .

We can't understand your . . .

We differ from you . . .

We don't believe that . . .

We expect you to . . .

We find it difficult to believe that . . .

We must insist that you . . .

We question your . . .

We take issue with . . .

What in the world makes you think that . . .

What is your problem with . . .

What makes you think that . . .

When you question our decision . . .

Who gave you permission to . . .

Whose dumb idea was it to . . .

Why can't you . . .

Why have you ignored . . .

Why is it so difficult for you to understand that . . .

Why on earth would you . . .

You apparently overlooked . . .

You did not include . . .

You do not understand . . .

You are delinquent . . .

You are out of line . . .

You are probably ignorant of the fact that . . .

You are probably unaware that . . .

You are wrong . . .

You claim that . . .

You didn't tell us that . . .

You failed to . . .

You forced me to . . .

You forgot to . . .

You have to . . .

You leave us no choice but . . .

You misrepresented . . .

You must think we're all idiots to . . .

You neglected to . . .

You obviously overlooked . . .

You overlooked . . .

You say that . . .

You should know better . . .

You should know that . . .

You surely don't expect . . .

Your action is inexcusable . . .

Your action is irresponsible . . .

Your apparent disregard for . . .

Your attitude makes no sense . . .

Your behavior makes no sense . . .

Your carelessness forced me to . . .

Your carelessness is . . .

Your complaint about . . .

Your constant inattention . . .

Your deliberate tardiness . . .

Your delinquency . . .

Your demand that . . .

Your disregard of . . .

Your dissatisfaction . . .

Your failure to . . .

Your ill-conceived suggestion to . . .

Your inability to . . .

Your insinuation about . . .

Your neglect of . . .

Your obnoxious attitude . . .

Your poor performance . . .

Your repeated violations . . .

Your shoddy work . . .

Your stubborn silence about . . .

Your thoughtlessness . . .

Your unacceptable attitude . . .

Your unacceptable work . . .

Pretentious Language That Will Make You Sound Foolish

A broad and varied vocabulary is a valuable asset and will make your writing more interesting and informative. But excessive or exclusive use of long, complex, polysyllabic words tends to sound pretentious to the general reader. Most of them prefer clear, simple words, such as *confuse*, which are easier to read and absorb than more complex words, such as *obfuscate*. Writers who overuse complex language to impress others, therefore, may be doing more harm than good to their image, especially if the readers think they sound pretentious and foolish rather than intelligent and sophisticated. Except when you need greater variety, then, select the simpler alternative for material directed to the average reader.

Pretentious Expression	Alternative
aggregation	total
anticipate	expect
approximately	about
ascertain	find out
assessed valuation	property value
assistance	aid; help
attempt	try
behest	request
bona fide	genuine
chef d'oeuvre	masterpiece
chemotherapeutic agent	drug
circa	about
cognizant	aware
commence	begin; start
commendation	praise
commercialization	commerce

concept	idea
concerning	about
conflagration	fire
construct	make
consummate	complete
customary channels	usual way
deem	think; believe
deficit	shortage
delineate	describe; draw
demonstrate	show
depressed socioeconomic area	slum
dialogue	conversation
disclosure	show; uncover
disseminate	circulate; send out
domicile	home; house
duplicate	copy
edifice	building
effected	made; did
effectuated	made; did
encourage	urge
endeavor	try
enlighten	tell
equivalent	equal
eventuality	event
facilitate	ease; help
feedback	comments
forward	send
functionalization	use
germane	relevant
hiatus	gap; interval
impair	damage; hurt; weaken
in toto	altogether; in all
inadvertency	error
inaugurate	begin; start
indebtedness	debt

individuals	people
ingress and egress	in and out
initial	first
initiate	begin; start
input	advice
inquire	ask
instantaneously	now; quickly
instrumentalities	means; ways
interface with	meet with
interrogate	ask
involving	about
ipso facto	by the very nature of the case
lethal	deadly; fatal
marketing representative	salesperson
materialize	happen
methodology	method
milieu	surroundings; environment
modus operandi	method; method of operating
multiplicity	many
multitudinous	many
nadir	low point
necessitate	require
obfuscate	confuse
obviate	prevent; do away with
optimum	best
palpable	clear; obvious; visible
parameter	limit
per annum	a year; each year
per diem	a day; each day
per se	as such
peruse	read
procure	get
promulgate	announce; declare
raison d'être	reason for
remuneration	payment

render	offer
sine qua non	essential
subsequent	after
succumb	die
terminate	end
transmit	send
utilization	use
utilize	use
vicissitude	change
wherewithal	means

34

Loaded Language
That May Reveal a Bias Toward Someone

It's hard to hide a bias. Eventually, a writer's choice of words will reveal it to the world. Unless you have a reason to express a biased view openly, select clear, basic, accurate terms. For example, if *self-confident* accurately describes someone, avoid any temptation to substitute a less accurate, slanted term, such as *arrogant*, that may reveal a hidden bias toward the person. In the following list, assume that the terms in column 1 clearly, objectively, and accurately describe someone. It's obvious then that the terms in column 2 not only will create an entirely different impression of the person, but they also will make the associated bias very obvious to a reader (see also the examples of sexist language in list 36).

Unbiased	Biased
ambitious	ruthless
assertive	pushy
blond	bleached-blond
businesslike	unfriendly
careful	nit-picky

colorful	tasteless
compassionate	bleeding-heart
complaining	whining
concerned	worried
courageous	brash
curious	nosy
delighting in	wallowing in
determined	stubborn
disagreeing	bickering
discerning	faultfinding
discussing	arguing
economical	cheap
emotional	irrational
feminist	radical
firm	stubborn
flexible	changeable
generous	wasteful
handsome	pretty-boy
harsh	catty
humanitarian	do-gooder
inexperienced	greenhorn
loud	shrill
nonviolent	weak
particular	finicky
persistent	obstinate
persuasive	nagging
private	unsociable
professional	unladylike
protective	smothering
quiet	dull
realistic	negative
requesting	demanding
self-confident	arrogant
shy	unfriendly
sophisticated	snobbish
spontaneous	impulsive

strong	macho
suspicious	paranoid
tough	difficult
unimportant	petty
unpredictable	temperamental

35

Defamatory Words That Could Get You in Trouble

Words are defamatory when they falsely and maliciously tend to damage someone's reputation, character, or good name. Defamation is so serious that it can, and often does, lead to a lawsuit. Even when something that drastic doesn't occur, the use of derogatory, disparaging, or defamatory language can cause considerable unpleasantness. Problems arise when defamatory language about someone is conveyed to a third party in speech (slander) or in writing (libel), such as in a letter or in an article. To prevent potential difficulties, legal or otherwise, avoid words such as the following when describing someone or someone's activities to a third party.

abnormal	black market	collusive
adulterer	blackmail	con artist
adultery	blackmailer	contraband
alcoholic	bogus	convict
altered records	boozer	corrupt
bad conduct	broke	corruptible
bad moral	bungling	corruption
character	buy off	counterfeiter
bankrupt	cheat	criminal
bankruptcy	cheater	criminality
bilk	cheating	crook
bilker	chiseler	crooked

deadbeat	filch	kept woman
debased	financially	kickback
deceitful	ruined	larceny
defalcation	financially	lascivious
defraud	unsound	lawbreaker
defrauder	fleece	lawless
degenerate	forged records	lewd
delinquency	forger	libelous
demented	fraud	licentious
depraved	fraudulent	loan shark
deranged	gangster	lying
dereliction	gay	malfeasance
dirty tricks	graft	malpractice
dishonest	grafted	malversation
dishonorable	heavy drinker	mental illness
disreputable	homosexual	mentally ill
distortion	hood	meritless
double-dealing	hooker	milking
drug abuser	hush money	misappropriate
drug addict	hypocrite	misappropriation
drug user	illegal	misconduct
drunk	illegality	misdeed
drunkard	illegitimate	mishandle
embezzlement	illicit	mismanagement
embezzler	immoral	misrepresentation
extort	immorality	misuse
extortion	imposter	mobster
fabrication	incompetent	nefarious
fake	inebriated	negligence
faker	inferior	neurotic
falsification	informer	on the dole
falsified	insane	on the take
falsified records	insolvent	outlawed
falsify	intolerance	pay off
felon	intoxicated	payoff
felonious	junkie	perjurer

perjury	robbery	unchaste
perversion	rumormonger	under the counter
perverted	rummy	under the table
phony	scam	underhanded
pilferer	scandalmonger	unethical
pimp	second-rate	unfaithful
piracy	shady	unfit
plagiarist	shakedown	unlawful
plagiarize	shoddy	unmarried
prevarication	shyster	mother
price fixer	slacker	unprincipled
price fixing	slanderous	unprofessional
problem drinker	smuggler	unsavory
profiteer	sneak	unscrupulous
prostitute	stealing	untrustworthy
psychopath	swindler	untruthfulness
psychotic	tax evasion	unwed mother
quack	tax fraud	unworthy of
racist	theft	villain
racketeer	thief	villainous
retarded	thievery	worthless
rob	treachery	wrongdoing
robber	two-timer	wrongful

36

Sexist Language That Readers May Not Forgive

Stereotyped, sexist language in business writing diminished noticeably in the 1990s. However, since bias is still a part of human nature, it has not disappeared completely. As readers have become more aware of discriminatory taboos, they have also become more insistent that writers use nonstereotypical, nonsexist language. Such bias-free language does not refer to a person's sex unless it's relevant to the discussion, and even then, it refers to men and women with equivalence. The following are examples of sexist words that readers may not forgive, along with suggested nonsexist alternatives (for other examples of biased language, see list 34).

Sexist	Nonsexist
according to Hoyle	according to/by the book
adman/woman; advertising man/woman	account executive; ad(vertising) agent/executive/writer/representative
advance man	advance agent; agent; representative
alderman/woman	alderperson; council member; member of the town board; town board member
all men are created equal	all people are created equal
alumna(e)/alumnus/alumni	alum; former student; graduate
anchorman/woman	anchor; anchorperson; newscaster
ancient man	ancient people/civilization/humanity
assemblyman/woman	assembly member
average man	average citizen/person
bachelor/bachelorette; old maid; spinster	single/unmarried person
bad guy	villain
bellboy/man	attendant; bellhop
Big Brother	eye of government; government spy
black worker/scientist/teacher/etc.	worker; scientist; teacher; etc.
bondsman/woman	bail bond agent; bonder; bondsperson; guarantor; surety provider
boys will be boys	children/kids will be children/kids

brotherhood	association; organization; union
brotherhood of man	human family; humanity; humankind
brotherly/sisterly love	human love; kindness
brothers/sisters	associates; brothers and sisters/ sisters and brothers; friends
businessman/woman	businessperson/executive/manager/ professional
cameraman/woman	camera operator; photographer; videographer
career girl/woman	business executive; careerist; professional
chairman/woman	chair; chairperson; moderator; presiding officer
city father	city founder/official
cleaning lady/man	cleaner; custodian; domestic worker; janitor; maintenance worker
clergyman/woman	clergy member; cleric; pastor; priest
clothes make the man	clothes make the person
comedienne	comedian; comic; humorist
common man	average citizen/person; ordinary citizen/person; common citizen/ person
company man	faithful/loyal employee
congressman/woman	member of Congress; representative; senator
councilman/woman	council member; councilor
countryman/woman	citizen; compatriot; native
craftsman/woman	artisan; crafter; craftsperson/ worker; handcrafter
craftsmanship	artisanship; artistry; quality; skilled craft work
crewman	crew member
delivery boy/girl/man/ woman	delivery person

divorcé/divorcée	divorced person; single; single person
divorced father/mother	divorced parent
doorman	doorkeeper/attendant
doubting Thomas	pessimist; skeptic
draftsman	drafter
elder statesman	elder statesperson; senior diplomat
every Tom, Dick, and Harry	every stranger off the street
everyman	average/ordinary/typical/person
fairhaired boy/girl	favorite/privileged person
family man	family-oriented person; homebody
Father Time	progress; time
father/motherland	home/native land
fellow (country)man	citizen; compatriot; friends and neighbors
fellow worker	associate; colleague; coworker
fellowship (school)	assistantship; scholarship; stipend
fellowship (social)	community; companionship; friendship
fireman	firefighter
forefather	ancestor; founder; forerunner
foreman	head juror; manager; supervisor
founding father	colonist; founder; pioneer
garbageman	garbage/trash collector; sanitation worker
gentleman's agreement	handshake; informal/unwritten agreement; your word
gentleman/woman	aristocrat; courteous/cultivated/gentleperson
Girl/Man Friday	aide; assistant; secretary
handyman	caretaker; handyperson; maintenance worker; repairer
he/him/his	he or she/she or he; him or her/her or him; his or hers/hers or his (or rewrite to use they)

headmaster/mistress	administrator; director; head; principal
heiress	heir
heroine	hero
himself	himself or herself/herself or himself
hired man	helper; hired hand/helper
Hobson's choice	no choice
hostess	host
househusband/wife	homemaker
husband/wife	spouse
idea man	creative thinker; intellectual; thinker; visionary
innocent women and children	innocent civilians/people
insurance man/woman	insurance agent/representative
jack of all trades	good at all trades; handyperson; many-talented; person of all trades
Jekyll and Hyde	alter egos; split personality
John Hancock	name; signature
journeyman	apprentice; assistant
junior executive	executive trainee
key man	key executive/individual/person
ladies and gentlemen	friends; gentlewomen and gentlemen; members of
lady	aristocrat; courteous person; gentleperson/woman
Lady Luck	luck
ladylike	courteous; proper; well bred
landlady/lord	landowner; manager; property owner; superintendent
lawman	law officer
layman	layperson
low man on the totem pole	beginner, lowest ranking individual
maid	domestic; servant

maiden name	birth name; original name
maiden voyage	first trip/voyage; initial voyage
mailman	mail carrier; postal carrier/worker
maintenance man	custodian; janitor; maintenance engineer/person/worker
mama's boy	immature/irresponsible/spoiled person
man about town	sophisticated/worldly person
man and wife	husband and wife; man and woman/woman and man; spouses
man for all seasons	all-around expert; person of many parts
man of means	powerful/rich/wealthy person
man to man	one to one; person to person
man's best friend	devoted dog; faithful friend; human's best friend
man's inhumanity to man	our inhumanity toward each other
man's/woman's work	work
man-hour	hour; labor/person/work-hour
man-sized	big; large; oversized; voracious
man/womanhood	adulthood
manhandle	abuse; batter; push around; thrash
mankind	civilization; humankind; people; society
man-made	artificial; constructed; handmade; machine made; synthetic
manpower	human resources; personnel; workforce
manservant	servant
master	accomplished; expert; gifted; proficient; skilled
master bedroom	principal/main bedroom
master key	common key
master list	complete/main/original list

master plan	model plan; overview; prototype
master/mistress	head; leader; owner; ruler; superior; teacher
master/mistress of ceremonies	announcer; emcee; host; moderator
masterful	authoritative; excellent; expert; skillful
mastermind *(n.)*	creator; originator; innovator
mastermind *(vb.)*	to direct/plan
masterpiece	great creation/piece/work
matronly	dignified; heavyset; mature
men and girls	men and women/women and men
middleman	agent; distributor; go-between; intermediary; liaison; middleperson; wholesaler
Miss/Mrs.	Ms.
modern man	modern age/civilization/peoples
Mother Earth	Earth
Mother Nature	nature
mother tongue	native language/tongue
motherland	homeland
newsman/woman	editor; newscaster/writer; reporter
night watchman	custodian; night patrol; night/ security guard
no-man's-land	hostile country; wasteland
office boy/girl	assistant; gofer; office employee/ helper/worker
ombudsman/woman	intermediary; ombudsperson; troubleshooter
parts man	parts clerk/worker; stock clerk
patrolman/woman	patrol/police officer; police; trooper
policeman/woman	officer; police officer
postmaster/mistress	head of the post office; postal chief/ director
repairman	repairperson; repairer; service representative; technician

rewrite man	rewriter
right-hand man	aide; assistant; deputy; lieutenant
salesgirl/lady/man/ woman	sales clerk/person/representative
salesmanship	sales ability/expertise/skill/ technique
serviceman/woman	repairer; service representative; technician
she/her/hers	she or he/he or she; her or him/ him or her; hers or his/his or hers (or rewrite to use they)
showmanship	production/staging genius/skill
sound man	sound controller/specialist/ technician
spokesman/woman	publicist; representative; spokesperson
sportsmanship	fair play; fairness; sporting
statesman/woman	diplomat; statesperson
statesmanship	diplomacy; political savvy; statecraft; world leadership
stationmaster	station manager
steward/stewardess	attendant; flight attendant; crew member
superman/woman	superhero/person
toastmaster/mistress	announcer; emcee; host; toastperson; presider
unmanned	uninhabited; unstaffed; lacking a crew; remote controlled
unworkmanlike	inexperienced; sloppy; unprofessional
waitress	server; waiter; waitperson
weak sister	unreliable person; weak link
welfare mother	welfare client/recipient
widow/widower	surviving spouse
wives/husbands	spouses
working man/woman	working person

workman	worker
workmen's compensation	workers' compensation
yes man	yes person

37

Wordy Phrases That Detract from Readability

Writers sometimes have trouble finding the right balance between using too many words and being so concise that they sound brusque. Both extremes detract from readability. Although some phrases, such as *as a result* (therefore) and *in many cases* (often), may legitimately be used on occasion to add variety and to avoid an overly terse tone, the phrases in column 1 seem needlessly wordy in most situations and therefore should be shortened as illustrated in column 2. (For examples of unnecessary words in a phrase that express the same idea, see list 38.)

Wordy Phrase	Preferred Short Form
a great deal of	much
a large number of	many; several
a limited number of	one, *etc.*
a majority of	most
a number of	several
a significant proportion of	some
a sizable percentage of	many
accounted for by	due to; caused by
accounted for by the fact that	because
acknowledge receipt of	have received
add the point that	add that

after very careful consideration	after considering
all of the	all
along the line of	like; about; in
an example of this is the fact that	for example
an overwhelming majority	most
another aspect of the situation to be considered is	as for; concerning; regarding
are engaged in	are; are in
are in a position to	can
are in receipt of	received
are in the process of	are
are not in a position to	cannot
arrange to send	send
as a matter of fact	in fact
as a result	therefore
as a result of	because
as of this date	now
as regards	for; about
as related to	for; about
as to	about
at a later date	later
at all times	always
at an early date	soon; at once; today; immediately; tomorrow
at that time	then
at which time	when; during
at your convenience	soon; today; tomorrow
be cognizant of	know
be in possession of	have
be in receipt of	get
be of the opinion that	believe
because of the fact that	because

by means of	by
by means of this	by this
by return mail	soon; today; tomorrow
by virtue of the fact that	because
certain person	person
come in contact with	meet
come to a decision as to	decide
concerning the nature of	about; concerning
conditions that exist in	conditions in
date of the policy	policy date
despite the fact that	despite the; although
due to the fact that	because
except in a small number of cases	usually
exhibit a tendency to	tend to
first of all	first
from the point of view of	for; to
give consideration to	consider
goes to show	proves
had occasion to be	was
have an input into	contribute to
have the ability to	be able to
have the need for	need
i.e.	*(avoid)*
if at all possible	if possible
if it is at all possible	if possible
in a satisfactory manner	satisfactorily
in a timely fashion	promptly
in accordance with your request	as you requested
in advance of	before
in any case	anyway
in case	if
in case of	if
in compliance with your request	as you requested

in due course	soon; today; tomorrow
in due time	soon; today; tomorrow
in favor of	for; to
in light of the fact that	because
in many cases	often; frequently
in many instances	often
in most cases	usually
in order that	so that
in order to	to
in rare cases	rarely
in reference to	about
in regard to	regarding; about
in relation to	about
in some cases	sometimes
in spite of the fact that	although; though
in terms of	in; for
in the case of	regarding
in the case that	if; when
in the course of	during
in the early part of	early
in the event that	if
in the field of	in
in the final analysis	finally
in the first place	first
in the majority of instances	usually
in the matter of	about
in the nature of	like
in the near future	soon; today; tomorrow
in the neighborhood of	about
in the normal course of events	normally
in the not-too-distant future	soon
in the opinion of this writer	in my opinion; I believe

in the vicinity of	near
in view of the fact that	therefore; because
inasmuch as	because
inquire as to	ask about
inside of	inside
involves the necessity of	requires
is at this time	is
is at variance with	differs from
is defined as	is
is dependent on	depends on
is indicative of	indicates
is of the opinion that	believes; thinks that
it is clear that	therefore; clearly
it is imperative that you	please
it is observed that	*(omit)*
it is often the case that	often; frequently
it is our conclusion in light of investigation	we conclude that; in conclusion
it should be noted that the	the
it stands to reason	*(omit)*
it was noted that if	if
it would not be unreasonable to assume	I assume
leaving out of consideration	disregarding
made the announcement that	announced that
make an examination of	examine
make inquiry regarding	ask about; inquire about
make mention of	mention
make use of	use
may possibly	may
needless to say	*(omit)*

not of a high order of accuracy	inaccurate
notwithstanding the fact that	although
of considerable magnitude	big; large; great
of minor importance	unimportant
on a few occasions	occasionally
on account of the conditions described	because of the conditions
on account of the fact that	because
on more than one occasion	ten, *etc.* times
on the average	on average
on the grounds that	because
on the occasion of	when; during
on the order of	about
out of	of
outside of	outside
over the long term	ultimately
owing to the fact that	because; since
perform an analysis	analyze
perhaps it may be that you	perhaps; it may be that; you may
please don't hesitate to	please
previous to	before
prior to	before
proceed to investigate	investigate
pursuant to our agreement	as we agreed
put in an appearance	appear; appeared; came; went
reach a conclusion as to	decide
reach the conclusion	conclude
refer to as	call
relative to this	about this

seldom ever	seldom
subsequent to	after
take into consideration	consider
taking this factor into consideration, it is apparent that	therefore; therefore it seems
that is	*(avoid)*
that kind of thing	that
the bulk of	most
the data show that we can	we can
the existence of	*(avoid)*
the fact that he had arrived	his arrival
the foregoing	the; this; that; these; those
the fullest possible	most; completely; fully
the information that we have in our files	our information
the only difference being that	except
the question as to whether	whether
the undersigned	I
the writer	I
there are not very many	few
this is a subject that	this subject
this is to inform you	*(omit)*
to a certain extent	in part
to a large degree	largely
to be sure	*(avoid)*
to summarize the above	in sum; in summary
under date of	dated; on
under separate cover	separately
under the circumstances	because

we are not in a position to	we cannot
we regret to say	we are sorry
we wish to acknowledge	thank you for
we would like to ask	please; would you
whether or not	whether
will you be kind enough	please
window of opportunity	opportunity
wish to bring to your attention	notice that; note that; please note
with reference to	about
with respect to	about
with the exception of	except
with the result that	so that
with this in mind, it is clear that	therefore; clearly
within the realm of possibility	possible; possibly

38

Common Redundancies That Add Deadweight to Your Writing

What's wrong with this phrase: *depreciate or decline in value?* Both *depreciate* and *decline in value* refer to the same thing; therefore, one is sufficient, and the other is redundant. A similar type of repetition can be seen in an expression such as *final result.* Since both words express "the end," *result* alone is sufficient. Although writers may intentionally use repetition for emphasis, the accidental repetition of words that express a similar idea does nothing to enhance a message; rather, it adds dead weight that detracts from clarity and professionalism. This list has examples of such common redundancies and the preferred short forms (for examples of general wordiness, see list 37).

Common Redundancy	Preferred Short Form
absolutely complete	complete
absolutely essential	essential
advance warning	warning
advise and inform	advise; inform
after the time of	after
aid and abet	aid; abet
amount of $10	$10
any and all	any; all
appraise and determine	appraise; determine
appreciate in value	appreciate
at a time when	when
attached please find	attached is
both of them	both
brief minute	minute; moment
bright and shiny	bright; shiny
city of Boston	Boston
close proximity	proximity; near
collect together	collect
color of red	red
combine into one	combine
compare and contrast	compare; contrast
complete monopoly	monopoly
completely unanimous	unanimous
consensus of opinion	consensus
cooperate and work together	cooperate; work together
cooperate together	cooperate
deeds and actions	deeds; actions
demand and insist	demand; insist
different kinds of	different
distance of three yards	three yards

during the course of	during; while; when
during the time that	during; while; when
each and every	each; every
eliminate completely	eliminate
enclosed herewith is	enclosed is; here is
enclosed please find	enclosed is; here is
end result	result; conclusion
fair and equitable	fair; equitable
fear and trembling	fear; apprehension
few and far between	seldom
few in number	few
final conclusion	conclusion; end
first and foremost	first; foremost
first began	began
for the purpose of	for; to
for the reason that	since; because
future plans	plans
future prospect	prospect
great many	many
he is a man who	he
help and assist	help; assist
hopes and aspirations	hopes; aspirations
hour of 5 P.M.	5 P.M.
immediately and at once	immediately; at once
individual person	individual; person
intents and purposes	intent(ion); purpose
large in number	many
large in size	large
make a statement saying	say
many in number	many
meeting held in	meeting in
mental attitude	attitude
month of January	January
mutual compromise	compromise

my own	my
my personal opinion	my opinion
new and innovative	new; innovative
null and void	null; void
obligation and responsibility	obligation; responsibility
one and only	one; only
one or another reason	some reason
peace and quiet	peace; quiet
period of three weeks	three weeks
period of time	period; time
pick and choose	pick; choose
plain and simple	plain; simple
point in time	then; point; time
positive growth	growth
present time	present; now
price of $10	$10
prompt and speedy	prompt; quick; speedy
question as to whether	whether
refuse and decline	refuse; decline
renovate like new	renovate
repeat again	repeat
result and effect	result; effect
resultant effect	result; effect
right and proper	right; proper
round in shape	round
rules and regulations	rules; regulations
she is a woman who	she
sick and tired	sick; tired
sign your name	sign
sincere good wishes	sincere wishes; good wishes
small in number	few
small in size	small
solid facts	facts
some reason or another	some reason

someone or other	someone
spell out in detail	spell out; detail
successful triumph	success; triumph
sum of $10	$10
temporary reprieve	reprieve
this day and age	now; today
tire and fatigue	tire; fatigue
true facts	facts
two days' time	two days
uniform and invariable	uniform; invariable
unjust and unfair	unjust; unfair
until such time as	until; when
various and sundry	various; sundry
variously different	different
visible to the eye	visible
way, shape, or form	way
wet precipitation	precipitation
widow woman	widow
year of 19XX	19XX

39

Stale Cliches That Will Make Your Writing Sound Tired and Dull

Ideas lose their originality and force through overuse. Although many cliches originated centuries ago as respected practical precepts or basic truths, the wisdom frequently lost its edge from constant use. It's the *overuse* that has made once-respected sayings seem stale, trite, and unimaginative. Writers that use such expressions, therefore, risk making their work sound tired and dull. With an international audience that translates everything literally, they also risk confusing readers. Although certain cliches, such as the *grim reaper* (death), are occasionally useful to create a picturesque image, overworked expressions in general will tend to weaken most business material.

A-1 The best quality (sometimes used legitimately in official rating systems).

ace in the hole, an A hidden advantage reserved for later use.

acid test, the A severe, conclusive test to determine truth or worth.

Actions speak louder than words What you do is more important than what you say.

all in a day's work A normal or routine matter.

all in the same boat All sharing the same risk or similar experience.

all things to all people, to be To adapt so as to please everyone.

axe to grind, an A selfish motive; something to achieve.

back to the drawing board The need to redo, redesign, or recreate something.

back to the wall, with one's Being in a desperate position, hard-pressed, or under attack.

bark up the wrong tree, to To waste time pursuing the wrong thing.

bide one's time, to To wait for the right moment or for a good opportunity.

bird's-eye view, a An overall or broad view.

blessing in disguise, a Good luck coming out of misfortune.

bone of contention, a The main point or topic of a dispute.

burn the candle at both ends, to To use one's resources and energies to excess; to overwork mentally or physically.

burn the midnight oil, to To stay up late for work or study.

bury the hatchet, to To make peace; to settle a disagreement or dispute.

business as usual Doing the same thing in the same way in spite of circumstances that call for something else; continuing to do something in the face of difficulty.

by the book Strictly by the rules; very correctly.

captain of industry, a An influential owner, manager, or leader of big business.

catbird seat, in the Being in a position of advantage or superiority.

conventional wisdom, the Generally accepted ideas.

cream of the crop, the The very best of all; the choicest members in a group.

cross that bridge when one comes to it, to To wait to decide until it is necessary to do so; to deal with a problem later.

cut and dried Commonplace, routine, or established.

dead to rights Certain; without possibility of error.

deep-six, to To discard.

die is cast, the The decision has been made.

dot the i's and cross the t's, to To be thorough; to pay attention to the details.

eleventh hour At the last minute; at the latest possible time.

Every man has his price Everyone's principles have a limit; everyone's support can be bought.

fat cat, a A wealthy person.

first magnitude, of the Prominent; outstanding.

fly in the face of, to To challenge or defy the odds.

force to be reckoned with, a Something of strength or influence that must be taken into account.

foregone conclusion, a A result already known or something already decided and therefore taken for granted.

full speed/steam ahead Proceed with all available speed and power.

get a handle on, to To succeed in coping with something difficult.

give short shrift, to To spend little time on something.

give the benefit of the doubt, to To treat as innocent when evidence isn't available to support that decision.

go for broke, to To risk everything.

good old boy, a A regular fellow; an accepted member of a cohesive or traditional group, especially one that excludes or discriminates against others.

grist for the mill Something that can be used or taken advantage of.

handwriting on the wall, the A forewarning or prediction of something bad.

hang in the balance, to To be undecided or in doubt about the outcome of something.

have a bone to pick, to To have something unpleasant to discuss, question, or argue about.

hive of industry A busy place, particularly one that is commercial.

in a nutshell Briefly; concisely.

in the long run Over a long period.

ins and outs Ramifications of or changes in a situation.

jaundiced eye, a A prejudiced view.

John Hancock One's signature.

keep at arm's length, to To keep someone at a distance; to distance oneself from something or someone.

keep one's head above water, to To stay solvent.

lay one's cards on the table, to To be candid; to reveal what you have or want.

Let the chips fall where they may Don't worry about the consequences; say what you think and do what must be done, regardless.

letter-perfect Perfect; just right.

lock, stock, and barrel Everything.

maintain the status quo, to To keep things as they are.

make or break, to To undertake something knowing that one will either succeed or fail.

Midas touch, the The ability to make money at almost anything.

moment of truth, the A time of crisis when one is put to a severe test.

more than one bargained for More than one expected or wanted from a particular situation.

movers and shakers Those with power and influence to effect change.

net result, the The outcome; the basic meaning or reason.

no-win situation, a A situation in which no one will benefit.

off the beaten track An isolated, inaccessible, or seldom-used place or route.

old-boy network, the An unofficial association of men who help each other advance, usually to the exclusion of others.

open question, an An undecided issue.

order of the day, the The agenda; the most important item or issue.

over a barrel In a weak position; at a disadvantage.

pack it in, to To quit; to give up.

paper over, to To conceal, repair, or hide the "cracks" in a situation.

paper tiger Something less formidable or menacing than it appears to be.

pay through the nose, to To be charged an exorbitant price.

pick someone's brain, to To seek information or ideas from someone who is better informed about something.

play one's cards right, to To make good decisions or moves; to use opportunities to best advantage.

point of no return, the A critical point where it is too late to reverse direction or a decision.

put a good face on it, to To make the best of things; to make a bad situation seem better.

put all one's eggs in one basket, to To risk everything on one venture.

put it on the back burner, to To postpone or delay something; to hold something in reserve.

put one's money on the line, to To back up one's opinions with an investment.

put the cart before the horse, to To take steps in an unnatural or illogical order.

read between the lines, to To determine what is really meant rather than what is actually said or written; to surmise.

read something into it, to To attach undue importance to something; to assume something more than what was actually said or done.

red herring A misleading trail or diversionary tactic.

red-letter day A memorable, special, or important day.

roll with the punches, to To adapt to adversity.

rule of thumb A rough or general guide.

run of the mill Ordinary; usual; uneventful.

short end of the stick, to get the To lose out; to get less than one is entitled to receive.

shot in the dark, a A wild guess; a conjecture.

sixth sense, a An intuitive ability; an ability to understand things that other people ordinarily miss.

sour grapes The pretense that something unattainable isn't desirable anyway.

split hairs, to To argue over petty, fine points or trifling matters.

square deal, a A fair, honest, and honorable arrangement.

stem the tide, to To stop, divert, or change the course of something, such as public opinion.

stickler for the rules Someone who strictly adheres to, or is overly fussy about, established procedure.

talk it up, to To promote, boost, or advance something.

thorn in one's side, a A source of ongoing irritation; a constantly annoying or bothersome person or thing.

throw/shed light on, to To clarify; to explain; to amplify something.

tighten one's belt, to To economize; to prepare for economic adversity.

tip of the iceberg, only the Only a small part of, or manifestation of, something much larger and, possibly, worse.

track record The history of one's accomplishments or performance.

turn of the tide A change in or reversal of fortune.

turn the tables, to To reverse something, particularly to gain an advantage.

twenty-twenty hindsight, with With a clear understanding after the fact.

wave of the future, the A strong or significant trend.

whole new ball game, a A completely changed or different situation.

with flying colors With success.

BUSINESS ENGLISH

More Than Seventy Important Grammatical Terms That Every Writer Should Know

Many of the mistakes in written material are grammatical errors. For example, writers may use the wrong case of a *pronoun* or the wrong *tense* of a *verb* (see definitions in list). But before one can watch for and correct such errors, one has to know what these terms mean. The following list introduces key grammatical terms that every writer should know, including the eight basic parts of speech: *adjective, adverb, conjunction, interjection, noun, preposition, pronoun,* and *verb*. Other lists in this part of the book, such as the six tenses of verbs in list 49, provide additional information about some of the important terms. (Terms printed in **bold face** refer to other entries in this list.)

active voice A **verb** that indicates the **subject** of a sentence is providing the action: *"He* [subject] *wrote* [verb] the letter." Compare with **passive voice.**

adjective A word that modifies (describes, explains, or limits) a **noun** or a **pronoun.** "The *business* [adjective] *writer* [noun] has arrived." *"He* [pronoun] is *unemployed* [adjective]."

adjective pronoun A **pronoun** that modifies a **noun:** *"Many* [pronoun] *writers* [noun] do freelance work."

adverb A word that modifies a **verb,** an **adjective,** another **adverb,** or a clause or sentence: *quickly* agreed [verb]; a *very* happy [adjective] manager; all *too* well [adverb]; *"Unfortunately,* the project failed [sentence]."

agreement The correspondence between words or elements, such as the singular or plural agreement between a **subject** and a **verb.** *"He* [singular subject] *is* [singular verb] late." See also **case, gender, number,** and **person.**

antecedent The **noun** or **pronoun** to which another pronoun refers: *"Ms. Schuller* [antecedent noun] understands *her* [pronoun referring to antecedent] responsibility."

appositive A word or words that identify or explain another word or words: "Mr. Lockhart, the *president* [appositive identifying Mr. Lockhart], is the keynote speaker."

article The **adjectives** *a* and *an* (indefinite articles) and *the* (definite article): *"The* technician ordered a new part."

auxiliary verb A helping, or linking, **verb,** such as *have* or *could,* that is combined with a principal verb to form a verb phrase: "They *would* [auxiliary verb] *like* [principal verb] to go."

case The property of a **noun** or **pronoun** that indicates its relation to other words in a sentence. For examples, see **nominative case, objective case,** and **possessive case.**

collective noun A **noun,** such as *family* or *members,* that denotes a group or collection of objects: "The *committee* will meet in Detroit next month."

common noun A **noun,** such as *house* or *book,* that denotes a general category or class of persons, places, things, concepts, actions, or qualities (and is not capitalized): "The *car* has a V-6 engine."

comparative degree The form of an **adjective** or **adverb** that compares two persons or things, often used with an *-er* ending or with *more* or *less:* "His report is *longer* and *more complex* [adjectives] than mine." "He worked *harder* and *more eagerly* [adverbs] than I did." Compare with **superlative degree.**

comparison The form of an **adjective** or **adverb** that indicates the degree of comparison. For examples, see **comparative degree** and **superlative degree.**

complement A word or words that complete the meaning of the thought expressed by a **verb:** "The team *studied* [verb] the *videotape* [complement: direct object]." A **direct object, pred-**

icate adjective, and **predicate nominative** are examples of complements.

compound predicate That part of a sentence consisting of two or more connected verbs or **verb** phrases: "He *proofread* [verb] and *edited* [verb] the paper."

compound sentence A sentence consisting of two or more **independent clauses** that could stand alone but are connected: *"They filed the complaint,* and *a hearing was scheduled for August 9."*

compound subject A **subject** in a sentence that consists of two or more words joined by *and, or,* or *nor:* "The *manager* and his *staff* worked well together."

compound term Two or more words expressing a single idea that are written together as one word *(businesspeople),* are joined by a hyphen *(editor-in-chief),* or are written as separate words *(post office).*

conjunction A word, such as *and* or *so,* that connects or shows the relationship between other words, phrases, clauses, or sentences: "Writers *and* books are inseparable." See also **coordinate conjunction, correlative conjunction,** and **subordinate conjunction.**

coordinate conjunction A **conjunction,** such as *but* or *nor,* that connects words, phrases, or clauses of equal value or rank, such as two **independent clauses:** "The policy may be new, *but* it is already effective."

correlative conjunction A **coordinate conjunction,** such as *either . . . or,* used in pairs or in a series: "He *not only* is a skilled writer *but also* is a polished speaker."

dangling modifier A word or words that do not logically refer to or modify another word: *"After organizing* his notes, drafting the paper was easy." (Better: "After organizing his notes, he found that drafting the paper was easy.") Compare with **misplaced modifier.**

demonstrative pronoun A **pronoun,** such as *this* or *those,* that replaces a **noun:** *"This* is our research."

dependent, or subordinate, clause A group of words in a sentence consisting of a **subject** and a **verb** that alone does not express a complete thought: "We believe *that the price is too high."* Compare with **independent clause.**

direct object A **noun** or noun equivalent that receives a verb's action and sometimes answers the question *what* or *whom* after the **verb:** "The crew installed [what?] the *podium."* Compare with **indirect object.**

expletive An introductory word, such as *it* or *there,* that occupies the position of another word, phrase, or clause: *"There* are several places we should visit in Houston." (Better: "Houston has several places we should visit.")

gender A designation of sex indicated by certain **nouns** and **pronouns,** such as *he* or *him: "She* should understand *her* rights."

gerund A **verb** form ending in *-ing* that is used as a **noun:** *"Reading* is his favorite pastime."

imperative mood An expression in the form of a command, wish, or something similar as indicted by a **verb:** *"Keep* [verb] this copy for your files." Compare with **indicative mood** and **subjunctive mood.**

indefinite pronoun A **pronoun,** such as *any* or *few,* that does not name or specify anyone or anything in particular but, rather, stands for an object generally or indefinitely: *"Both* were to blame."

independent clause A group of words in a sentence consisting of a **subject** and a **predicate** that forms a complete thought by itself: *"They* [subject] *completed the project* [predicate] though four members had the flu." Compare with **dependent, or subordinate, clause.**

indicative mood An expression indicated by a **verb** that states or questions a fact. "You *were* [verb—fact] involved." "*Were* [verb—question] you involved?" Compare with **imperative mood** and **subjunctive mood.**

indirect object A **noun** or noun equivalent that always occurs before the **direct object** and indicates to whom or for whom something is done: "The editor gave the *reporter* [indirect object] a new assignment [direct object]."

infinitive A **verb** form used as a **noun,** an **adjective,** or an **adverb** and often preceded by *to:* "To *write* [noun] was her desire." "Her desire to *write* [adjective] is obvious." "She stopped to *write* [adverb]."

interjection A word or phrase expressing sudden or strong feeling: *Hey! Oh! Great!*

interrogative pronoun A **pronoun,** such as *who* or *which,* that asks a question: "*What* did the article say about our program?"

intransitive verb A **verb** that does not need an object to complete its meaning: "She *works* steadily." Compare with **transitive verb.**

irregular verb A **verb** that forms the past **tense** and the past **participle** by internal changes: *ring* [present tense]; *rang* [past tense]; *rung* [past participle]. Compare with **regular verb.**

misplaced modifier A **modifier** positioned so that it seems to modify the wrong word or phrase: "She *only* typed the report [didn't do anything else]." (Better: "She typed *only* the report [didn't type anything else].") Compare with **dangling modifier.**

modifier A word or group of words, such as **adjectives** or **adverbs,** that restrict, qualify, or expand the meaning of another word: "The *computer* [adjective] equipment processed material *rapidly* [adverb]."

mood The form of a **verb** that shows the manner in which an action or state of being should be regarded. For examples, see **imperative mood, indicative mood,** and **subjunctive mood.**

nominative case The **case** of a **predicate** noun or of a **noun** or **pronoun** in a **subject** that denotes the person or thing taking action: "She is a skilled *manager* [predicate noun]." *"He* [subject pronoun] wrote to the agency." Compare with **objective case** and **possessive case.**

nonrestrictive clause A **dependent,** or **subordinate, clause,** usually set off with commas, that is not essential to the meaning of a sentence: "The old equipment, *which is hard to operate,* will soon be replaced." Compare with **restrictive clause.**

noun A word or words that name a person *(Mike),* place *(San Diego),* thing *(computer),* concept or idea *(automation),* action *(operation),* or quality *(perfection).*

number The property of a **noun, pronoun,** or **verb** that indicates how many things are being referred to: *"Many* [plural pronoun] *writers* [plural noun] *prefer* [plural verb] to work alone."

objective case The **case** of a **noun** or **pronoun** used as a **direct object** of a **verb** or **preposition** "She *complimented* [verb] *me* [object of verb]." "They drove *to* [preposition] the *station* [object of preposition]." Compare with **nominative case** and **possessive case.**

participle A **verb** form that is used as an **adjective:** "The *revised* [from verb *revise*] figures revealed a decline in sales."

passive voice A **verb** that indicates the **subject** of a sentence is receiving the action: "The *report* [subject] *was written* [verb] by Bob Pruitt." Compare with **active voice.**

person The form of a **personal pronoun** that identifies the person speaking or spoken to or the person or thing spoken of: *I* [first person] am; *you* [second person] are; *he* [third person] is.

personal pronoun A **pronoun,** such as *me* or *they,* that indicates whether reference is to the person speaking or spoken to or the person or thing spoken of: *"It* is a beautifully designed magazine."

phrasal preposition Two or more words, such as *along with,* regarded as a single **preposition:** *"According to* the program, the international speaker is from Japan." Compare with **prepositional phrase.**

possessive case The **case** of a **noun** or **pronoun** that denotes possession or a relationship: *man's* [possession] car; *her* [relationship] accountant. Compare with **nominative case** and **objective case.**

predicate That part of a sentence containing a **verb** and other words that makes a statement about the **subject:** "The secretary [subject] *transcribed* [verb] *her notes right after the meeting."*

predicate adjective An **adjective** that follows an **auxiliary verb** and describes the **subject:** "The *company* [subject] *is* [auxiliary verb] *well known* [predicate adjective] in Europe."

predicate nominative A **noun** or **pronoun** in the **predicate** of a sentence that is in the **nominative case:** "Mrs. Shaw is a friendly *receptionist* [predicate noun]."

preposition A word that indicates the relation between its object (**noun** or **pronoun**) and some other word, such as a **verb:** "She *flew* [verb] *to* [preposition] *Toronto* [object]."

prepositional phrase A **preposition,** its object, and any **modifiers** of the object: "The exhibits were set *up in the auditorium."* Compare with **phrasal preposition.**

pronoun A word that takes the place of a **noun** (its **antecedent**): *"It* [the X Company] was founded on July 14, 1992."

proper noun A **noun** that names a particular person, place, thing, concept, action, or quality (and is always capitalized): "On *Tuesday,* the tour group will visit the *Great Wall of China."*

reflexive, or intensive, pronoun A **pronoun,** such as *himself* or *themselves,* formed by adding *-self* or *-selves* to a **personal pronoun** or **indefinite pronoun:** "I trained *myself* to operate the press."

regular verb A **verb** that forms the past tense by adding *-d* or *-ed* to the present tense: *call* [present tense]; *called* [past tense]; *have/has/had called* [past participle]. Compare with **irregular verb.**

relative adjective A **pronoun,** such as *whose* or *what,* used as an *adjective* and linking an adjective clause to an **antecedent:** "She is the *woman* [antecedent] *whose* [pronoun] *story won an award* [adjective clause]."

relative adverb An **adverb,** such as *where* or *why,* that refers to an **antecedent** in the main clause but modifies a word in the **dependent, or subordinate, clause:** "They found the *box* [antecedent], *where* [modifies *were stored*] the supplies were stored."

relative pronoun A **pronoun,** such as *whom* or *which,* that replaces a **noun** and relates a **dependent,** or **subordinate, clause** to a main clause: "The proposal went to the *director* [antecedent] *who* [relative pronoun] *made a decision* [dependent clause]."

restrictive clause A **dependent,** or **subordinate, clause** that is essential to a sentence's meaning (and therefore should not be set off with commas): "The employee *with the most points* wins a free vacation." Compare with **nonrestrictive clause.**

subject That part of a sentence about which a statement is made in the **predicate:** *"The twin towers* [subject] *were actually built ten years apart* [predicate]."

subjunctive mood An expression of an action or state of being indicated by a **verb** as conditional, hypothetical, doubtful, possible, contrary to fact, or desired: "If I *were* you, I'd put that in writing." Compare with **imperative mood** and **indicative mood.**

subordinate conjunction A **conjunction,** such as *since* or *unless,* that connects a **dependent,** or **subordinate, clause** to the main clause: *"Because* [subordinate conjunction] *he was overworked* [dependent clause], they hired more people."

superlative degree The form of an **adjective** or **adverb** that compares more than two persons or things, often used with an *-est* ending or with *most* or *least:* "Of the three reports, his report is the *longest* and *most complex* [adjectives]." "Of the three people, he worked the *hardest* and *most eagerly* [adverbs]." Compare with **comparative degree.**

tense The form of a **verb** that indicates the time of an action or state of being: *wrote* [past], *had written* [past perfect], *write* [present], *have written* [present perfect], *will write* [future], *will have written* [future perfect].

transitive verb A **verb** that needs a **direct object:** "Bill *saved* [verb] *the photograph* [object]." Compare with **intransitive verb.**

verb A word or words that express an action, such as *run,* or a state of being, such as *am:* "The play *lasted* three hours."

verbal A **verb** form used as another part of speech. For examples, see **gerund, infinitive,** and **participle.**

voice The form of a **verb** that indicates whether a **subject** is the doer or receiver of an action. For examples, see **active voice** and **passive voice.**

41

Nouns Ending in -s That May Be Singular or Plural

Some nouns appear to be plural but may refer to something as a single category or unit and are therefore treated as singular and used with a singular verb: "The human *species is* known as *Homo sapiens.*" When the noun refers to the various items or people in a category or unit, it should be treated as plural and used with a plural verb: "Fourteen endangered *species are* on display at the museum." The following are examples of other nouns that may be either singular or plural, depending on the intended meaning. However, dictionaries sometimes differ about whether a noun may be treated as singular, plural, or both. (For examples of nouns that are commonly singular, see list 42; for those that are commonly plural, see list 43.)

acoustics	metaphysics
aerobics	obstetrics
aesthetics	physics
analytics	poetics
apologetics	politics
athletics	scissors
dynamics	semantics
economics	statics
electronics	statistics
ethics	tactics
genetics	tweezers
means *(wealth or way)*	wages
mechanics	whereabouts

Nouns Ending in -s That Are Commonly Singular

The following list has examples of nouns that look like plural nouns but are usually treated as singular and are therefore used with a singular verb: "*Metrics* is the use or study of metrical study in verse." However, dictionaries sometimes differ about whether a noun may be treated as singular, plural, or both. (For examples of nouns that are commonly plural, see list 43; for those that may be singular or plural, see list 41.)

aeronautics	news
billiards	optics
civics	phonetics
hydraulics	phonics
hydromechanics	physics
linguistics	pneumatics
magnetics	spherics
mathematics	tectonics

Nouns Ending in -s That Are Commonly Plural

This list has examples of nouns that are spelled as plural nouns and are usually treated as plural, therefore requiring a plural verb: "The human *vitals are* clearly marked on the company's new medical poster." However, dictionaries sometimes differ about whether a noun may be treated as singular, plural, or both. (For examples of nouns that are commonly singular, see list 42; for those that may be singular or plural, see list 41.)

analects	lyrics	spoils
annals	monies	suds
ashes	nuptials	thanks
clothes	pants	thongs
eaves	proceeds	tongs
goods	remains	trousers
lees	riches	
links	shears	

Nouns and Adjectives That Designate Nationality Worldwide

Writers who prepare international communications need to take extra precautions to avoid mistakes that might offend or annoy a reader in another country. Just as many people dislike having their names misspelled or mispronounced, many also are annoyed by the incorrect use of a nationality designation. Many such designations are logical: For example, most writers know that a native of South Korea is correctly called a *Korean*. But other designations are less obvious: Not everyone knows that a native of Madagascar is a *Malagasy*. This list includes government-approved nationality designations for countries worldwide.

Country	Noun	Adjective
Afghanistan	Afghan(s)	Afghan
Albania	Albanian(s)	Albanian
Algeria	Algerian(s)	Algerian
Andorra	Andorran(s)	Andorran
Angola	Angolan(s)	Angolan
Antigua and Barbuda	Antiguan(s), Barbudan(s)	Antiguan, Barbudan

Argentina	Argentine(s)	Argentine
Armenia	Armenian(s)	Armenian
Australia	Australian(s)	Australian
Austria	Austrian(s)	Austrian
Azerbaijan	Azerbaijani(s)	Azerbaijani
Bahamas	Bahamian(s)	Bahamian
Bahrain	Bahraini(s)	Bahraini
Bangladesh	Bangladeshi(s)	Bangladesh
Barbados	Barbadian(s)	Barbadian
Belarus	Belarusian(s)	Belarusian
Belgium	Belgian(s)	Belgian
Belize	Belizean(s)	Belizean
Benin	Beninese	Beninese
Bhutan	Bhutanese	Bhutanese
Bolivia	Bolivian(s)	Bolivian
Bosnia and Herzegovina	Bosnian(s), Herzegovinian(s)	Bosnian, Herzegovinian
Botswana	Motswana *(sing.)*, Batswana *(pl.)*	Motswana *(sing.)*, Batswana *(pl.)*
Brazil	Brazilian(s)	Brazilian
Brunei	Bruneian(s)	Bruneian
Bulgaria	Bulgarian(s)	Bulgarian
Burkina Faso	Burkinabe	Burkinabe
Burma (Myanma)	Burmese	Burmese
Burundi	Burundian(s)	Burundi
Cambodia	Cambodian(s)	Cambodian
Cameroon	Cameroonian(s)	Cameroonian
Canada	Canadian(s)	Canadian
Cape Verde	Cape Verdean(s)	Cape Verdean
Central African Republic	Central African(s)	Central African
Chad	Chadian(s)	Chadian
Chile	Chilean(s)	Chilean
China	Chinese	Chinese
Colombia	Colombian(s)	Colombian

Comoros	Comoran(s)	Comoran
Congo	Congolese	Congolese *or* Congo
Costa Rica	Costa Rican(s)	Costa Rican
Croatia	Croat(s)	Croatian
Cuba	Cuban(s)	Cuban
Cyprus	Cypriot(s)	Cypriot
Czech Republic	Czech(s)	Czech
Denmark	Dane(s)	Danish
Djibouti	Djiboutian(s)	Djiboutian
Dominica	Dominican(s)	Dominican
Dominican Republic	Dominican(s)	Dominican
Ecuador	Ecuadorian(s)	Ecuadorian
Egypt	Egyptian(s)	Egyptian
El Salvador	Salvadoran(s)	Salvadoran
Equatorial Guinea	Equatorial Guinean(s) *or* Equatoguinean(s)	Equatorial Guinean *or* Equatoguinean
Eritrea	Eritrean(s)	Eritrean
Estonia	Estonian(s)	Estonian
Ethiopia	Ethiopian(s)	Ethiopian
Fiji	Fijian(s)	Fijian
Finland	Finn(s)	Finnish
France	Frenchman(men), Frenchwoman (women)	French
Gabon	Gabonese	Gabonese
Gambia, The	Gambian(s)	Gambian
Georgia	Georgian(s)	Georgian
Germany	German(s)	German
Ghana	Ghanaian(s)	Ghanaian
Greece	Greek(s)	Greek
Grenada	Grenadian(s)	Grenadian
Guatemala	Guatemalan(s)	Guatemalan
Guinea	Guinean(s)	Guinean
Guinea-Bissau	Guinea-Bissauan(s)	Guinea-Bissauan

Guyana	Guyanese	Guyanese
Haiti	Haitian(s)	Haitian
Honduras	Honduran(s)	Honduran
Hungary	Hungarian(s)	Hungarian
Iceland	Icelander(s)	Icelandic
India	Indian(s)	Indian
Indonesia	Indonesian(s)	Indonesian
Iran	Iranian(s)	Iranian
Iraq	Iraqi(s)	Iraqi
Ireland	Irishman(men), Irishwoman (women) *(sing.)*, Irish *(pl.)*	Irish
Israel	Israeli(s)	Israeli
Italy	Italian(s)	Italian
Ivory Coast	Ivorian(s)	Ivorian
Jamaica	Jamaican(s)	Jamaican
Japan	Japanese	Japanese
Jordan	Jordanian(s)	Jordanian
Kazakhstan	Kazakhstani(s)	Kazakhstani
Kenya	Kenyan(s)	Kenyan
Kiribati	I-Kiribati(s)	I-Kiribati
Korea, North	Korean(s)	Korean
Korea, South	Korean(s)	Korean
Kuwait	Kuwaiti(s)	Kuwaiti
Kyrgyzstan	Kyrgyz(s)	Kyrgyz
Laos	Lao(s) *or* Laotian(s)	Lao *or* Laotian
Latvia	Latvian(s)	Latvian
Lebanon	Lebanese	Lebanese
Lesotho	Mosotho *(sing.)*, Basotho *(pl.)*	Basotho
Liberia	Liberian(s)	Liberian
Libya	Libyan(s)	Libyan
Liechtenstein	Liechtensteiner(s)	Liechtenstein
Lithuania	Lithuanian(s)	Lithuanian
Luxembourg	Luxembourger(s)	Luxembourg

Macedonia, The Former Yugoslav Republic of	Macedonian(s)	Macedonian
Madagascar	Malagasy	Malagasy
Malawi	Malawian(s)	Malawian
Malaysia	Malaysian(s)	Malaysian
Maldives	Maldivian(s)	Maldivian
Mali	Malian(s)	Malian
Malta	Maltese	Maltese
Marshall Islands	Marshallese	Marshallese
Mauritania	Mauritanian(s)	Mauritanian
Mauritius	Mauritian(s)	Mauritian
Mexico	Mexican(s)	Mexican
Micronesia	Micronesian(s)	Micronesian
Moldova	Moldovan(s)	Moldovan
Monaco	Monacan(s) *or* Monegasque(s)	Monacan *or* Monegasque
Mongolia	Mongolian(s)	Mongolian
Morocco	Moroccan(s)	Moroccan
Mozambique	Mozambican(s)	Mozambican
Namibia	Namibian(s)	Namibian
Nauru	Nauruan(s)	Nauruan
Nepal	Nepalese	Nepalese
Netherlands	Dutchman(men), Dutchwoman (women)	Dutch
New Zealand	New Zealander(s)	New Zealand
Nicaragua	Nicaraguan(s)	Nicaraguan
Niger	Nigerien(s)	Nigerien
Nigeria	Nigerian(s)	Nigerian
Norway	Norwegian(s)	Norwegian
Oman	Omani(s)	Omani
Pakistan	Pakistani(s)	Pakistani
Palau	Palauan(s)	Palauan
Panama	Panamanian(s)	Panamanian

Papua New Guinea	Papua New Guinean(s)	Papua New Guinean
Paraguay	Paraguayan(s)	Paraguayan
Peru	Peruvian(s)	Peruvian
Philippines	Filipino(s)	Philippine
Poland	Pole(s)	Polish
Portugal	Portuguese	Portuguese
Qatar	Qatari(s)	Qatari
Romania	Romanian(s)	Romanian
Russia	Russian(s)	Russian
Rwanda	Rwandan(s)	Rwandan
Saint Kitts and Nevis	Kittsian(s), Nevisian(s)	Kittsian, Nevisian
Saint Lucia	Saint Lucian(s)	Saint Lucian
Saint Vincent and the Grenadines	Saint Vincentian(s) *or* Vincentian(s)	Saint Vincentian *or* Vincentian
San Marino	Sammarinese	Sammarinese
Sao Tome and Principe	Sao Tomean(s)	Sao Tomean
Saudi Arabia	Saudi(s)	Saudi *or* Saudi Arabian
Senegal	Senegalese	Senegalese
Serbia and Montenegro	Serb(s), Montenegrin(s)	Serbian, Montenegrin
Seychelles	Seychellois	Seychelles
Sierra Leone	Sierra Leonean(s)	Sierra Leonean
Singapore	Singaporean(s)	Singapore
Slovakia	Slovak(s)	Slovak
Slovenia	Slovene(s)	Slovene
Solomon Islands	Solomon Islander(s)	Solomon Islander
Somalia	Somali(s)	Somali
South Africa	South African(s)	South African
Spain	Spaniard(s)	Spanish
Sri Lanka	Sri Lankan(s)	Sri Lankan
Sudan	Sudanese	Sudanese

Suriname	Surinamer(s)	Surinamese
Swaziland	Swazi(s)	Swazi
Sweden	Swede(s)	Swedish
Switzerland	Swiss	Swiss
Syria	Syrian(s)	Syrian
Taiwan	Chinese	Chinese
Tajikistan	Tajik(s)	Tajik
Tanzania	Tanzanian(s)	Tanzanian
Thailand	Thai	Thai
Togo	Togolese	Togolese
Tonga	Tongan(s)	Tongan
Trinidad and Tobago	Trinidadian(s), Tobagonian(s)	Trinidadian, Tobagonian
Tunisia	Tunisian(s)	Tunisian
Turkey	Turk(s)	Turkish
Turkmenistan	Turkmen(s)	Turkmen
Tuvalu	Tuvaluan(s)	Tuvaluan
Uganda	Ugandan(s)	Ugandan
Ukraine	Ukrainian(s)	Ukrainian
United Arab Emirates	Emirian(s)	Emirian
United Kingdom	Briton(s), British *(collective pl.)*	British
Uruguay	Uruguayan(s)	Uruguayan
Uzbekistan	Uzbek(s)	Uzbek
Vanuatu	Ni-Vanuatu	Ni-Vanuatu
Venezuela	Venezuelan(s)	Venezuelan
Vietnam	Vietnamese	Vietnamese
Western Samoa	Western Samoan(s)	Western Samoan
Yemen	Yemini(s)	Yemeni
Zaire	Zairian(s)	Zairian
Zambia	Zambian(s)	Zambian
Zimbabwe	Zimbabwean(s)	Zimbabwean

45

Basic Forms of Common Pronouns

Pronouns are one of the most used—and sometimes misused—parts of speech in the English language. To avoid mistakes, writers should know the basic forms of common *personal, demonstrative, interrogative, relative, reflexive,* and *indefinite pronouns.* See the definitions of these terms in list 40. To learn more about this familiar part of speech, see also list 46 in which common pronouns are classified by case.

Class of Pronoun	Basic Forms
Personal	
First person	I, me, my, mine, we, us, our, ours
Second person	you, yours
Third person	he, him, his, she, her, hers, it, its, they, them, their, theirs
Demonstrative	this, that, these, those
Interrogative	who, whom, whose, which, what
Relative	who, whom, whose, that, which, what
Reflexive, or intensive	myself, yourself, himself, herself, itself, oneself, ourselves, yourselves, themselves
Indefinite	all, another, any, anybody, anyone, anything, both, each, each one, each other, either, everybody, everyone, everything, few, many, most, neither, nobody,

none, no one, nothing, one, ones,
one another, other, others,
several, some, somebody,
someone, something, such

46
Pronouns Classified by Case

Like nouns, pronouns are characterized by one of three cases: nominative, objective, or possessive. The *case* indicates a pronoun's relationship to other words in a sentence. For example, if a pronoun is the subject of a sentence, or could be substituted for the subject, it's in the *nominative case:* "*It* [subject] is *he* [could be substituted for subject] who placed that call." If a pronoun is the object of a preposition or verb, it's in the *objective case:* "She *stopped* [verb] *him* [object of verb] from triggering the alarm." If the pronoun indicates possession, ownership, or a similar relationship, it's in the *possessive case:* "Is that *your* [indicates possession] computer?"

Nominative Case	Objective Case	Possessive Case
I	me	my
you	you	your
he	him	his
she	her	her
it	it	its
we	us	our
they	them	their
who	whom	whose

47

The Most Widely Used English Prepositions

Many of the more than 150 prepositions in the English language are used by writers every day. Prepositions such as *to* show the relation between a word called its *object* and another word called its *antecedent*: "He *went* [antecedent: verb] *to* [preposition] the *office* [object: noun]." Some prepositions also function as other parts of speech. For example, the word *through* can be used as a preposition (drove *through* the city) but also can be used as an adverb (break *through* the barrier) or an adjective (*through* traffic). The following widely used prepositions are presented in two groups: basic one-word prepositions and phrasal (compound) prepositions of two to three words.

Basic Prepositions

aboard	beside(s)	mid
about	between	midst
above	beyond	near
across	but	notwithstanding
after	by	of
against	concerning	off
along	considering	on
alongside	despite	on to
amid(st)	down	onto
among(st)	during	opposite
around	except(ing)	out
at	for	outside
barring	from	over
before	in	past
behind	inside	pending
below	into	per
beneath	like	regarding

respecting	till	unto
round	to	up
save	touching	upon
saving	toward(s)	via
since	under	with
through	underneath	within
throughout	until (*or* till)	without

Phrasal Prepositions

according to	from among
ahead of	from behind
along with	from beneath
alongside of	from between
apart from	from over
as against	from under
as between	in accordance with
as compared with	in addition to
as far as	in apposition with
as for	in back of
as near as	in behalf of
as to	in case of
as well as	in comparison to
aside from	in comparison with
away from	in compliance with
because of	in consequence of
by means of	in consideration of
by reason of	in default of
by virtue of	in front of
by way of	in lieu of
contrary to	in opposition to
due to	in place of
except for	in preference to
exclusive of	in reference to
for the sake of	in regard to
from above	in respect to

in spite of	regardless of
in view of	relating to
inclusive of	relative to
independently of	round about
inside of	up to
instead of	with a view to
on account of	with reference to
on behalf of	with regard to
opposite to	with respect to
out of	with the intention of
outside of	with the view of
owing to	without regard to

48

Common Connecting and Correlative Conjunctions

Conjunctions, like the prepositions in list 47, also show the relation between words and may indicate the relation between phrases, clauses, or entire sentences. The most familiar form is the connecting conjunction: When a conjunction joins words or sentences, it's called a *coordinate* (or *coordinating*) *conjunction:* "She wrote the editorial, *and* the company published it." When it connects a subordinate element, such as a dependent clause, to another part of the sentence, it's called a *subordinate* (or *subordinating*) *conjunction:* "Although we're running late, we expect to attend the meeting." Another form of conjunction, called a *correlative conjunction,* is always used in a pair: "*Either* Tim will handle the assignment, *or* Jill will do it."

Coordinate and Subordinate Conjunctions

after	and
also	as
although	as if

as long as	so
as often as	so that
as soon as	still
as though	than
because	that
before	then
both	therefore
but	though
but that	till
either	unless
even if	until
except	what
except for	whatever
for	when
for the purpose of	whence
how	whenever
however	where
if	whereas
in case	whereat
in order that	whereby
in spite of	wherefore
in that	wherein
inasmuch as	whereof
lest	whereupon
neither	wherever
nevertheless	whether
nor	which
notwithstanding	whichever
now that	while
only	whither
or	who
provided	whoever
provided that	why
save	with a view to
seeing	without
since	yet

Correlative Conjunctions

although . . . yet	now . . . now
as . . . as	now . . . then
as . . . so	so . . . as
both . . . and	so . . . as (that)
either . . . or	such . . . as (that)
if . . . then	though . . . yet
neither . . . nor	whereas . . . therefore
not only . . . but also	whether . . . or

49

The Six Basic Verb Tenses

For a writer to express accurately the time when an action occurs, verbs must be used in the proper *tense*. The three main divisions of time that verbs express are the *present, past,* and *future.* These three times, or verb tenses, can be further broken down to show time even more specifically. The three additional tenses that indicate this more precise action are the *present perfect, past perfect,* and *future perfect tenses.* This list gives an example of the use of each tense.

Present tense: Denoting something occurring in the present: "I *write.*"

Past tense: Denoting something occurring in the past: "I *wrote.*"

Future tense: Denoting something occurring in the future: "I *will write.*"

Present perfect tense: Denoting something occurring in the past but having an effect on the present: "I *have finished* my writing."

Past perfect tense: Denoting something occurring before a specific moment in the past: "When you called, I already *had finished* my writing."

Future perfect tense: Denoting something that will have occurred before some future time: "I *will have finished* my writing by the time you return from the post office."

The Three Principal Parts of More Than One Hundred Irregular Verbs

Forming the past tense and the past participle of irregular verbs can be difficult. (To learn more about tenses, refer to the examples in list 49.) With regular verbs, such as *bill* (send an invoice), all you have to do is add *-d* or *-ed* to the present form of the verb: *bill* (present), *billed* (past), *have/has/had billed* (past participle). But with irregular verbs, such as *sing*, you often have to use entirely different words for the past and past participle forms: *sing* (present), *sang* (past), *have/has/had sung* (past participle). To form the past participle in the following list, remember to add *have*, *has*, or *had* before the words in the third column.

Present	Past	Past Participle
abide	abode/abided	abode/abided
arise	arose	arisen
awake	awoke/awaked	awoke/awaked
be (am)	was	been
bear	bore	borne
beat	beat	beaten/beat
become	became	become
begin	began	begun
behold	beheld	beheld
bid *(command)*	bade	bidden

bid *(offer to buy)*	bid	bid
bind	bound	bound
bite	bit	bit
bleed	bled	bled
blow	blew	blown
break	broke	broken
breed	bred	bred
bring	brought	brought
broadcast	broadcast/ broadcasted	broadcast/ broadcasted
build	built	built
burst	burst	burst
buy	bought	bought
cast	cast	cast
catch	caught	caught
choose	chose	chosen
cleave	cleaved/cleft/clove	cleaved/cleft/ clove/cloven
cling	clung	clung
come	came	come
cost	cost	cost
creep	crept	crept
cut	cut	cut
deal	dealt	dealt
do	did	done
draw	drew	drawn
drink	drank	drunk
drive	drove	driven
eat	ate	eaten
fall	fell	fallen
feed	fed	fed
feel	felt	felt
fight	fought	fought
find	found	found
flee	fled	fled
fling	flung	flung

fly	flew	flown
forbid	forbade	forbidden
forget	forgot	forgotten/forgot
forsake	forsook	forsaken
freeze	froze	frozen
get	got	got
give	gave	given
go	went	gone
grind	ground	ground
grow	grew	grown
hang *(suspend)*	hung	hung
have	had	had
hide	hid	hidden
hit	hit	hit
hold	held	held
hurt	hurt	hurt
keep	kept	kept
know	knew	known
lay *(place)*	laid	laid
lead	led	led
leave	left	left
lend	lent	lent
let	let	let
lie *(recline)*	lay	lain
lose	lost	lost
make	made	made
mean	meant	meant
meet	met	met
mistake	mistook	mistaken
pay	paid	paid
put	put	put
read	read	read
rid	rid	rid
ride	rode	ridden
ring	rang	rung
rise	rose	risen

run	ran	run
say	said	said
see	saw	seen
seek	sought	sought
sell	sold	sold
send	sent	sent
set	set	set
shake	shook	shaken
shed	shed	shed
shine *(give light)*	shone	shone
shoot	shot	shot
show	showed	shown/showed
shrink	shrank	shrunk/shrunken
shut	shut	shut
sing	sang	sung
sink	sank	sunk
sit	sat	sat
sleep	slept	slept
slide	slid	slid
sling	slung	slung
speak	spoke	spoken
speed	sped	sped
spend	spent	spent
spill	spilt/spilled	spilled
spin	spun	spun
split	split	split
spread	spread	spread
spring	sprang	sprung
stand	stood	stood
steal	stole	stolen
stick	stuck	stuck
sting	stung	stung
stink	stank	stunk
strike	struck	struck/stricken
string	strung	strung
strive	strove	striven

swear	swore	sworn
sweep	swept	swept
swim	swam	swum
swing	swung	swung
take	took	taken
teach	taught	taught
tear	tore	torn
tell	told	told
think	thought	thought
thrive	throve/thrived	thriven/thrived
throw	threw	thrown
thrust	thrust	thrust
tread	trod	trodden
understand	understood	understood
wake	woke/waked	woken/waked
wear	wore	worn
weave	wove	woven
win	won	won
wind	wound	wound
wring	wrung	wrung
write	wrote	written

51

Adjectives That Can't Be Compared

Writers use many adjectives (words that describe other words), including those that express some quality: a *perfect* letter. When such words are used literally, in their strictest sense, they don't allow for comparison. For example, something that is truly perfect can't be *more* or *less* perfect than something else that is also truly perfect. They're both the most that they can be. However, something can be *less than*, or *not*, perfect. The following list has examples of adjectives that logically can't be compared when they're used in a literal, strict sense. In general, then, such words should not be used with *more, most, less,* or *least* or with the endings *-er* or *-est* (for example, not *more final*).

absolute	irreversible
best	irrevocable
complete	limitless
devoid	meaningless
empty	mortal
endless	omnipotent
enduring	perfect
entire	perpetual
eternal	primary
everlasting	replete
exact	round
extinct	simultaneous
fatal	square
final	terminal
full	ultimate
illimitable	unanimous
inadmissible	unendurable
incessant	unique
indestructible	universal
inestimable	untouchable
inevitable	whole
infinite	worst
infinitesimal	worthless

One Hundred Common Prefixes and What They Mean

Writers need a large and varied vocabulary to express many different ideas and to suitably vary their remarks. Adding a *prefix* (letters such as *un-*) to the front of a word or the main part of a word is one way to create an entirely new word and thereby enlarge one's vocabulary. In contemporary writing, most prefixes are attached without a hyphen (*un + important = unimportant*), unless a prefix precedes a proper noun (*un-American*). This list has one hundred prefixes, common definitions, and an example of use (for the other common type of affix, see list 53).

a- On; toward: *across*

ab- Away from: *absent*

ad- Toward; near; at: *adjoin*

ambi- Around; both: *ambivalence*

ante- Before: *antedate*

anti- Opposite; opposed to: *antisocial*

aqua- Water; liquid: *aquaduct*

audio- Sound; hearing: *audiographic*

auto- Self; automatic: *automobile*

baro- Weight; pressure: barometer

be- Completely; on all sides: *behalf*

bi- Involving two: *bimonthly*

bio- Life; living organism: *biosphere*

by- Out of the way; secondary: *bypass*

centi- One hundredth: *centimeter*

chrono- Time: *chronometer*

circum- Around: *circumnavigate*

co- With; together; jointly: *coexist*

com- With; jointly; together: *commix*

con- With; jointly; together: *concurrent*

contra- Against: *contradistinction*

counter- Contrary: *counterproposal*

de- Reverse; remove: *defame*

deci- One-tenth: *deciliter*

deka- Ten: *dekagram*

di- Having two: *diode*

dia- Across; through; apart: *diametrical*

dis- Negation; reversal; absence of; opposite of: *disagreement*

duo- Two: *duopoly*

epi- Above; upon; over: *epicenter*

equi- Equal: *equilibrium*

ex- Outside of; former: *ex–police officer*

extra- Outside; beyond: *extralegal*

extro- Outward: *extrovert*

for- Completely; excessively: *forspent*

fore- Before in time: *foresight*

geo- Earth: *geomagnetic*

hecto- One hundred: *hectometer*

hemi- Half; partial: *hemisphere*

homo- Same: *homograph*

hydro- Water; liquid; hydrogen: *hydroelectric*

hyper- Over; above; beyond: *hyperspace*

hypo- Beneath; under; deficient: *hyponormal*

il- Not: *illogical*

im- Not: *imperfect*

in- In; not: *inconsistent*

infra- Within; below: *infrared*

inter- Between; among: *interstate*

intra- Within: *intrastate*

intro- Inside; in; into: *introjection*

ir- In; not: *irreversible*

iso- Equal: *isobaric*

kilo- One thousand: *kilobyte*

macro- Large; inclusive: *macromanagement*

mal- Bad; abnormal: *maladjusted*

meso- Intermediate: *mesomorph*

micro- Small: *micromanagement*

mid- Middle: *midway*

milli- One-thousandth: *millimeter*

mini- Miniature; small: *minibus*

mis- Bad; wrong: *misspell*

mono- One; single: *monograph*

multi- Many: *multinational*

neo- New; recent: *neoconservative*

non- Not: *nonabrasive*

ob- Inverse; against: *objectionable*

octo- Eight: *octogenarian*

olig- Few: *oligopoly*

out- Exceeding: *outgrow*

pan- All: *panchromatic*

para- Beside; near: *paraprofessional*

per- Through; proportion: *percentile*

peri- About; around: *peripheral*

phono- Speech; sound: *phonograph*

photo- Light: *photocomposition*

poly- Many; much: *polysyllable*

post- After: *postrecession*

pre- Before: *preschool*

pro- Substituting; supporting: *pro-American*

pseudo- False: *pseudointellectual*

psycho- Mental: *psychodynamics*

quadri- Four: *quadrilateral*

re- Back; again: *response*

retro- Backward; behind: *retroactive*

self- Oneself; automatic: *self-sealing*

semi- Half: *semiautomatic*

sub- Inferior; under: *subhead*

super- Superior; over: *supersized*

supra- Above; transcending: *supranational*

sym- With; similar: *symbolic*

syn- With; similar; at the same time: *synchronous*

tele- Distance: *telecommunications*

trans- Across; transfer: *transmit*

ultra- Beyond: *ultrascientific*

un- Release; reverse; not: *uninterested*

under- Below; inferior: *understaffed*

up- Up: *upstairs*

vari- Variety; difference: *variation*

vice- Deputy: *vice president*

xero- Dry: *xerography*

53
One Hundred Common Suffixes and What They Mean

Like prefixes, described in list 52, suffixes also consist of letters attached to words or the main parts of words. However, suffixes, such as *-ment*, are attached at the end: *manage + ment = management*. Also like prefixes, suffixes provide a way to enlarge one's vocabulary by creating another word, such as *management*, from a basic word, such as *manage*. This list has one hundred suffixes, common definitions, and an example of use.

-ability Ability; inclination: *transportability*

-able Capable of; inclined to: *predictable*

-acity Quality or state of: *veracity*

-age Collection; result: *damage*

-al Relating to: *instructional*

-an One belonging to: *European*

-ance State of; action: *continuance*

-ancy Condition; quality; *redundancy*

-ant Causing; being: *hesitant*

-archy Rule; government: *oligarchy*

-arium Place; housing: *planetarium*

-art Habitually performing or characterized by: *braggart*

-ate Characterized by; act on: *demonstrate*

-cade Procession: *motorcade*

-centric Kind or number of centers: *concentric*

-chrome Color: *monochrome*

-cide Killer: *insecticide*

-cline Slope: *incline*

-cracy Government; rule: *democracy*

-cy State; condition: *solvency*

-dom Condition: *officialdom*

-ed Having; characterized by: *bigoted*

-eer Engaged in: *profiteer*

-en Consisting of; become: *strengthen*

-ence State of: *independence*

-ent State of: *complacent*

-er Performer of action: *writer*

-ery Practice: *fishery*

-escent Becoming: *coalescent*

-ese Relating to: *Chinese*

-et Small: *snippet*

-fic Causing: *prolific*

-fold Divided into parts: *fourfold*

-form Having the form of: *plexiform*

-ful Full of; able to: *helpful*

-fy Form; make: *amplify*

-genic Suitable for production: *telegenic*

-gon Having angles: *decagon*

-gram Written material: *monogram*

-graph Written material: *hectograph*

-hood Condition; quality: *statehood*

-ia Belonging to: *memorabilia*

-ial Pertaining to: *managerial*

-ian Of; resembling: *Floridian*

-ible Capable of: *deducible*

-ic Characterized by: *graphic*

-ician Specialist: *technician*

-ics Pertaining to: *athletics*

-ide Chemical properties: *sulfide*

-ile Division: *decile*

-ine Of; resembling; substance: *chlorine*

-ing Action; process: *computing*

-ion Act; process: *regulation*

-ish Of; like; preoccupation: *selfish*

-ism System; process: *liberalism*

-ist Agent; doer; adherent: *specialist*

-ite Native of; follower: *urbanite*

-ity Condition; degree: *alkalinity*

-ive Tending toward: *active*

-ization Action; process: *decentralization*

-ize Cause to be; render: *capitalize*

-less Without: *jobless*

-like Resembling: *businesslike*

-ling Characterized by: *underling*

-log(ue) Discourse: *monolog(ue)*

-logy Expression; study of: *psychology*

-ly Like; characterized by: *quarterly*

-ment Act; process: *government*

-meter Measuring device: *thermometer*

-metry Science of measuring: *trigonometry*

-morphous Shape; form: *polymorphous*

-most Most; nearest: *innermost*

-ness State; quality: *darkness*

-oid Resembling: *celluloid*

-ome Mass: *phyllome*

-on Unit: *magneton*

-onym Word; name: *pseudonym*

-or Performer of action: *actor*

-ory Place for; characterized by: *depository*

-osis Abnormal condition: *symbiosis*

-ous Characterized by: *poisonous*

-phone Sound: *telephone*

-plastic Forming; growing: *neoplastic*

-scope Instrument for viewing: *telescope*

-sect Cut; divide: *dissect*

-ship State; condition; body: *readership*

-some Characterized by; group: *threesome*

-stat Regulating device: *thermostat*

-th State; quality: *dearth*

-tude State; quality: *plenitude*

-ty Condition; quality: *priority*

-ule Small: *minuscule*

-ure Body; act; process: *tenure*

-urgy Technique or process for working with: *metallurgy*

-ward In a certain direction: *downward*

-ways In a certain manner; position: *sideways*

-wide Extending throughout: *citywide*

-wise In a certain direction: *counterclockwise*

-work Product; production: *teamwork*

-worthy Suitability; of sufficient worth: *creditworthy*

54

More Than Two Hundred Compound Terms and Their Proper Spelling

Whereas prefixes and suffixes, described in lists 52 and 53, consist of letters attached to other words or the main parts of words, *compound terms* are combinations of two or more complete words, such as *tax + payer = taxpayer*. Although some authorities also loosely refer to new words formed with prefixes and suffixes as compounds, this list has only new terms formed by combining complete words. Some compounds are usually written closed (*businessperson*), others are hyphenated (*self-confident*), and a few are written open (*first aid*). A common part of speech is given after each term; for examples of other parts of speech, refer to a current dictionary).

aforementioned, *adj.*

aforesaid, *adj.*

after-hours, *adj.*

aftertaste, *n.*

afterthought, *n.*

air conditioner, *n.*

air-condition, *vb.*

airspace, *n.*

airtight, *adj.*

all right, *adv.*

all-around, *adj.*

all-important, *adj.*

all-time, *adj.*

anyhow, *adv.*

anyplace, *adv.*

anything, *pron.*

attorney general, *n.*

audiofrequency, *n.*

audiovisual, *adj.*

backup, *adj.*

ball bearing, *n.*

ballpark, *n.*

ballplayer, *n.*

ballpoint, *adj.*

bankbook, *n.*

beforehand, *adv.*

billboard, *n.*

birthplace, *n.*

blue book, *n.*

blue ribbon, *n.*

blueprint, *n.*

boardinghouse, *n.*

bondholder, *n.*

bookcase, *n.*

bookend, *n.*

bookkeeper, *n.*

bookkeeping, *n.*

bookmaker, *n.*

bookseller, *n.*

bookstore, *n.*

bottom line, *n.*

boxcar, *n.*

brain trust, *n.*

brainpower, *n.*

brainstorm, *n.*

brainwash, *vb.*

break-in, *n.*

breakout, *n.*

breakthrough, *n.*

breakup, *n.*

briefcase, *n.*

broadcast, *n.*

buildup, *n.*

burnout, *n.*

businessperson, *n.*

by-election, *n.*

by-product, *n.*

bylaw, *n.*

byline, *n.*

bypass, *n.*

car pool, *n.*

cardboard, *n.*

carryall, *n.*

carryover, *n.*

case study, *n.*

caseload, *n.*

casework, *n.*

cashbook, *n.*

catchword, *n.*

catlike, *adj.*

check mark, *n.*

check-in, *adj.*

checkbook, *n.*

checklist, *n.*

checkout, *adj.*

checkpoint, *n.*

checkup, *n.*

city-state, *n.*

classmate, *n.*

classroom, *n.*

clean-cut, *adj.*

cleanup, *n.*

clear-cut, *adj.*

clearing house *or*
   clearinghouse, *n.*

clipboard, *n.*

close-up, *n.*

closeout, *adj.*

comeback, *n.*

common law, *n.*

common sense, *n.*

copyedit, *vb.*

copywriter, *n.*

cost-effective, *adj.*

countdown, *n.*	filmstrip, *n.*
court-martial, *n.*	fingertip, *n.*
courtroom, *n.*	fireproof, *adj.*
courtyard, *n.*	first aid, *n.*
crackdown, *n.*	foolproof, *adj.*
cross section, *n.*	foothold, *n.*
cross talk, *n.*	free trade, *n.*
cross-examine, *vb.*	free will, *n.*
cross-index, *n.*	freelance, *adj.*
cross-reference, *n.*	freeliving, *adj.*
crossover, *n.*	ghostwriter, *n.*
crossroads, *n.*	good-bye, *n.*
day care, *n.*	goodwill, *n.*
day labor, *n.*	groundwork, *n.*
daytime, *n.*	half hour, *n.*
deadline, *n.*	halftime, *n.*
die-hard, *adj.*	halfway, *adj.*
double entry, *n.*	handbook, *n.*
double-check, *vb.*	handmade, *adj.*
double-cross, *vb.*	headline, *n.*
double-space, *vb.*	holdover, *n.*
downplay, *vb.*	holdup, *n.*
downtime, *n.*	horsepower, *n.*
downtown, *n.*	jet lag, *n.*
dry cleaner, *n.*	job lot, *n.*
dry goods, *n.*	keystroke, *n.*
dry-clean, *vb.*	laborsaving, *adj.*
everybody, *pron.*	landholder, *n.*
everyplace, *adv.*	landowner, *n.*
everything, *pron.*	lawmaker, *n.*
everywhere, *adv.*	layoff, *n.*
extracurricular, *adj.*	layout, *n.*
eyewitness, *n.*	lead time, *n.*
fairway, *n.*	letterhead, *n.*
farfetched, *adj.*	life-style, *n.*
filmmaker, *n.*	lifeline, *n.*

lightweight, *adj.*

lineup, *n.*

looseleaf, *adj.*

loudspeaker, *n.*

lowdown, *n.*

markdown, *n.*

marketplace, *n.*

moneylender, *n.*

moneymaker, *n.*

moreover, *adv.*

nation-state, *n.*

nationwide, *adj.*

nearby, *adv.*

network, *n.*

nevertheless, *adv.*

newfound, *adj.*

newscast, *n.*

newsstand, *n.*

newsworthy, *adj.*

nightlife, *n.*

nonetheless, *adv.*

nonprofit, *adj.*

noontime, *n.*

notebook, *n.*

noteworthy, *adj.*

notwithstanding, *adv.*

nowadays, *adv.*

odd lot, *n.*

off-line, *adj.*

offhand, *adv.*

officeholder, *n.*

offset, *adj.*

on-line, *adj.*

once-over, *n.*

overall, *adv.*

overrate, *vb.*

paperwork, *n.*

passbook, *n.*

passerby, *n.*

payroll, *n.*

percent, *n.*

pipeline, *n.*

postmark, *n.*

postwar, *adj.*

president-elect, *n.*

proofread, *vb.*

pushbutton, *adj.*

put-down, *n.*

put-on, *n.*

readout, *n.*

rollback, *n.*

rundown, *n.*

salesclerk, *n.*

salesperson, *n.*

schoolteacher, *n.*

scratchpad, *n.*

self-concern, *n.*

send-up, *n.*

sendoff, *n.*

setback, *n.*

setup, *n.*

shortcut, *n.*

showdown, *n.*

sideline, *n.*

stand-in, *n.*

standby, *n.*

statewide, *adj.*

stock market, *n.*

stockbroker, *n.*

stockpile, *n.*

stopgap, *adj.*

takeoff, *n.*

takeout, *n.*	turnover, *n.*
takeover, *n.*	twofold, *adj.*
taxpayer, *n.*	underrate, *vb.*
textbook, *n.*	underway, *adj.*
thereafter, *adv.*	vice president, *n.*
throwback, *n.*	viewfinder, *n.*
tie-in, *n.*	viewpoint, *n.*
tie-up, *n.*	waterpower, *n.*
timecard, *n.*	wavelength, *n.*
timesaving, *adj.*	wildlife, *n.*
timetable, *n.*	windup, *n.*
titleholder, *n.*	workforce, *n.*
trade-in, *n.*	work load, *n.*
trade-off, *n.*	workday, *n.*
trademark, *n.*	wristwatch, *n.*
transcontinental, *adj.*	yearbook, *n.*

55

The Fourteen Principal Marks of Punctuation

Finding an acceptable balance between too little and too much punctuation can be a challenge. Readers in other countries, for example, benefit from slightly more punctuation, because it adds clarity and guides them through each sentence. U.S. readers, however, have become accustomed to less punctuation, such as no comma after a short introductory word: "Thus we will postpone the vote." When used properly, though, the following are all legitimate marks of punctuation that will help readers avoid misreading a complex sentence.

Apostrophe ('): *"It's* [contraction for *It is*] true that the machine has had *its* [adjective] share of problems."

Brackets [ ]: "We easily reached an agreement in the past (in 1996 [or 1997?]) and hope to do so in the future."

Colon (:): The source of the quote is John Hill, "Communication Pitfalls," *Business Writing Weekly* 14, no. 6 (1994): 21.

Comma (,): "Although I like the Model A210, I would rather use my old A110."

Dash (—): "The tests—called 'verbal exercises' in the manual—were more difficult than we expected."

Ellipsis points (. . .): According to Dr. Learner, "The real computer revolution . . . [designates missing words] is yet to come."

Exclamation point (!): "Clearance Sale! Bargain Prices!"

Hyphen (-): "Although she is a well-known speaker at many technical conferences, she is not well known outside the conference circuit."

Parentheses ( ): "The redesigned ink refill provides low-friction, smooth writing for all Magic Pearl pens (not for use in Style-Writer pens)."

Period (.): "The new employee, T. R. McGinley, reminds me of JFK when he was in his early thirties."

Question mark (?): "Ms. Jenkins asked who is in charge of maintenance; do you have the person's name and number?"

Quotation marks (' "): The company bulletin clearly stated that "the new insurance plan will cover 'all' employees"; however, according to my boss, "Senior employees will not be covered under part B of the plan."

Semicolon (;): "The workshop will be held simultaneously in three locations: Tampa, Florida; Madison, Wisconsin; and Salt Lake City, Utah."

Virgule, solidus, or slash (/): "The product summary states that the M/V1000 operates at 160 rev./min."

56

Essential Diacritical Marks
to Use with Foreign Words

To indicate a particular phonetic value, one of the diacritical marks, or *diacritics,* in this list may be added to the associated letter(s) in a word. Most U.S. writers use these marks with foreign words, as with the French expression *à compte* (on account). But accents may also be used to distinguish any words—domestic or foreign—that might be confused because they're spelled the same but have different meanings, as in *résumé* (curriculum vitae) and *resume* (to begin again). List 57 has naturalized foreign words that need no accents, but less familiar foreign words should always be written in an italic face and include the accenting requirements of the language of origin.

acute accent: é	tilde: ñ	haček: č
grave accent: è	macron: ō	diaeresis: ö
circumflex: ô	breve: ŭ	cedilla: ç

57

Anglicized Foreign Words
That Do Not Need Italics or Accents

The English language has borrowed numerous words from other languages. For example, both Latin and French terms are widely used in certain professions, such as law, medicine, retail fashions, and meal service. Unfamiliar words should be written in an italic face and accented as required in the language of origin (see the diacritical marks in list 56). However, some of the words have been completely adapted to English use *(anglicized)*. When that has happened, it's no longer necessary to italicize or accent the word. Although accents and italics may be omitted in the following words, follow the preferred style of your employer or that of the publisher or publication for which you are writing.

a la carte	cortege
a la king	coulee
a la mode	coup d'etat
a priori	coup de grace
aide memoire	coupe
aide-de-camp	creme
alias	crepe
angstrom	crepe de chine
aperitif	critique
applique	debacle
apropos	debonair
auto(s)-da-fe	debut
blase	debutante
bona fide	decollete
boutonniere	dejeuner
brassiere	denouement
buffet	depot
cabana	eclair
cafe	eclat
cafeteria	ecru
camouflage	elan
canape	elite
cause celebre	ennui
chaperon	entree
chateau	ersatz
chauffeur	etude
chic	ex officio
cliche	facade
cloisonne	faience
communique	fete
confrere	frappe
connoisseur	garcon
consomme	glace

gratis

grille

gruyere

habitue

hors d'oeuvres

ingenue

jardiniere

litterateur

materiel

matinee

melange

melee

menage

mesalliance

metier

moire

naive

naivete

nee

nom de plume

opera bouffe

opera comique

papier mache

piece de resistance

pleiade

porte cochere

porte lumiere

portiere

pousse cafe

premiere

protege

puree

rale

recherche

regime

rendezvous

repertoire

risque

role

rotisserie

roue

saute

seance

smorgasbord

soiree

souffle

status quo

suede

table d'hote

tableau

tete-a-tete

verbatim

vicuna

vis-a-vis

58

Words That Are Commonly Written in Italics

When preparing a document, writers should follow the preferred style of their employers or that of the publishers or publications for which they write. Although the treatment of names and terms may differ among organizations, certain words are generally written in an italic face in all cases. This list gives examples of such words. (Refer to list 59 for examples of words that should be enclosed in quotation marks.)

Foreign terms (if unfamiliar): *cahier* (French: notebook).

Words or letters referred to as such: "The word *profile* was substituted for the term *biographical summary*."

Words or terms being defined: "The *phoenix* is a legendary bird that rises from the ashes to live again."

Words or terms being emphasized: "No, he wasn't fired; he was merely *transferred* to another location."

Legal cases: The case of *Jones* v. *California;* the *Jones* case.

Species or subspecies and genus names: *Homo* (genus) *sapiens* (species).

Book, pamphlet, and similar titles and subtitles: *The Modern Business Writer* [title]: *A Guide to Composition* [subtitle].

Magazine and newspaper titles: *U.S. News and World Report; New York Times Book Review*.

Motion picture titles: *Liar, Liar*.

Television series titles: *Chicago Hope*.

Play titles: *Phantom of the Opera*.

Poem titles (long): *Paradise Lost.*

Musical composition titles (long): *Don Giovanni; William Tell Overture.*

Painting, drawing, sculpture, and other art titles: Picasso's *Les Demoiselles d'Avignon.*

Ship and submarine names: *Ocean Spirit;* USS *Windstar.*

Aircraft and spacecraft names: *Spirit of Saint Louis; Columbia* space shuttle.

Satellite names: *Sputnik II.*

Words That Are Commonly Enclosed in Quotation Marks

Just as it's common to write certain words in italics (see list 58), it's also common to enclose other words in quotation marks. For example, it's widely understood that when you quote someone verbatim, those words should be enclosed in quotation marks. However, it's not so obvious whether certain names and terms should be italicized or enclosed in quotation marks. This list gives examples of words that are usually set in a roman type, such as that used in this sentence, and enclosed in quotation marks.

Quoted words from speeches or published works (when not set apart or displayed as a blocked quotation): On page 3, he said that "moderate inflation, to some, has surprising merit."

Words being emphasized or used in a different way (when not italicized): I think he's trying to "reinvent" himself.

Slang expressions: The article said she was caught passing "hot paper."

Irony (if meaning may not be obvious): Yes, we heard about the lower dividends and, like many others, were "delighted" at the news.

Chapter and part titles of a book: "The Art of Selling."

Periodical and newspaper articles and features: "Computer Filing at the New Company."

Essay titles: "The Walmartization of America."

Speech titles: "Long-Range Planning at the City Council."

Manuscript, dissertation, report, and other unpublished work titles: "A Study of Economic Reforms in the 1900s."

Song titles (short): "Star-Spangled Banner."

Poem titles (short): "Winter's Delight."

Television and radio program and episode titles (nonseries): National Geographic's "Tigers of the Snow."

60

A Collection of the Most Frequently Misspelled English Words

Good writers are not necessarily good spellers. In the age of computer spell-checkers, this is less of a problem than it used to be. However, writers aren't always sitting at their computers. Even when they are, spell-checkers may be inadequate since they can't discern differences such as *whole* and *hole*. Therefore, it's still important to watch one's spelling. Problems often arise with certain words that have been troublesome to many writers throughout the ages. For example, should you write *accomodate* or *accom-*

modate? Should you write *accidently* or *accidentally*? The following list has many more words that are among the most frequently misspelled in the English language.

abdicate	across
aberration	adapt
abhorrence	address
absence	adducible
absurd	adept
accede	adequate
accelerator	adjustment
accept	admirable
acceptance	admissible
access	advantageous
accessible	advertisement
accessory	advertising
accidentally	advisable
accommodate	advise
accommodation	adviser *or* advisor
accompanied	advisory
accompanying	aerogram *or*
accordance	aerogramme
accrued	aesthetic
accumulate	affect *(vb.: influence)*
accuracy	affects
accustom	affidavit
achieve	affinity
achieved	affluent
achievement	aggravate
acknowledge	agreeable
acknowledgment	aisle
acoustic	alienable
acquaintance	all right
acquiesce	allotment
acquire	allotted
acquitted	allowable

allowance

allude

almost

already

altar *(n.: structure)*

alter *(vb.: change)*

altogether

aluminum

alumnus

amateur

ambassador

amendment

among

amortize

analogous

analyses *(pl.)*

analysis *(s.)*

analyze

angel

angle

announce

announcement

annoyance

annual

antecedent

anticipate

antithetical

anxiety

anxious

apocalypse

apologize

apparatus

apparel

apparent

appearance

appliance

applicable

applicant

appointment

appraisal

appreciable

appropriate

approximate

archaeology

archetype

archipelago

architect

archive

arctic

argument

arrangement

article

ascend

ascertain

assassin

assessment

assiduous

assignment

assistance

assistant

associate

assured

attendance

attention

attorneys

audible

auditor

authorize

auxiliary

available

awkward

baccalaureate

bachelor

balloon

bankruptcy

barbarous

bargain

baroque

barren

basis

beggar

beginning

believe

believing

beneficial

beneficiary

benefited

benign

binary

biscuit

bloc *(n.: political unit)*

bologna

bookkeeper

bouillon

boundary

boutonniere

brilliant

brochure

bruised

budget

bulletin

buoy

buoyant

bureau

business

businessperson

busy

caddie *(golf)*

caddy *(tea)*

cafeteria

calculable

calendar

campaign

canceled *or* cancelled

cancellation

candelabra

candidate

cannot

capital *(n.: money; town)*

capitol *(n.: building)*

career

carriage

casualty

catalog *or* catalogue

catechism

category

Caucasian

cede

cellar

cemetery

censor *(delete)*

censure *(criticize)*

chancellor

changeable

changing

characteristic

charisma

chauffeur

chlorophyll

choice

choose

cigarette

cinnamon

circuit

circumstances
client
clientele
clique
coalesce
coarse
coconut
codicil
collapsible
collar
collateral
colloquial
colonel
column
combustible
coming
commission
commitment
committed
committee
commodity
comparable
comparative
comparatively
comparison
compatible
compel
compelled
competent
competitor
complaisant
complement *(vb.: complete)*
compliment *(vb.: flatter)*
comprehensible
compromise

concede
conceivable
conceive
concern
concession
concurred
conference
conferrable
confident
confidential
configuration
congratulate
connoisseur
conscience
conscientious
conscious
consensus
consequence
consequential
consignment
consistent
consonant
consul *(n: diplomatic official)*
consulate *(n: consul's residence)*
contemptible
continuous
controlling
controversy
convenience
convenient
cordially
corespondent *(n.: law)*
corporation
correspondence

correspondent *(n.:*
   writer)
corrigible
corroborate
corruptible
council *(governing body)*
councilor *or* councillor
   (n.: council member)
counsel *(n: lawyer; vb.:*
   to advise)
counselor *or* counsellor
   (n.: lawyer)
courteous
courtesy
coverage
credibility
credible
creditable
creditor
crescendo
criticism
criticize
cruelty
cryptic
curiosity
current
curriculum
cursor
customer
cyanide
database *or* data base
dealt
debatable
debater
debtor
deceitful

deceive
decide
decision
deducible
deductible
defendant
defense
defensible
deference
deferred
deficient
deficit
definite
definitely
definitive
delegate
delicatessen
demagogue
demonstrable
dependent
depositor
deprecate
depreciate
depreciation
derisive
derivative
descendant
describe
description
desirable
desktop publishing
desperate
destructible
deteriorate
develop
development

device *(n.: object)*
devise *(vb.: arrange)*
diagnostic
dialog *or* dialogue
diaphragm
dichotomy
dictionary
dietitian
difference
different
digestible
dilemma
dilettante
director
disappear
disappoint
disastrous
discernible
discipline
discourse
discrepancy
discriminate
disk
disparate
dissatisfaction
dissatisfied
dissipate
divisible
drought
drudgery
dyeing *(vb.: coloring)*
dying *(vb.: near death)*
eagerly
ecclesiastical
economical
ecstasy

edible
edition
effect *(n.: result)*
effects
efficiency
efficient
effluent
egregious
eighth
eligible
eliminate
eloquent
elusive
embarrass
embarrassment
emergency
eminent
emphasis
emphasize
employee
enclose
encumbrance
encyclopedia
endeavor
endorse
endorsement
enemy
enterprise
enthusiasm
envelope
environment
equaled
equipment
equipped
equivalent
especially

essence

essential

etiquette

euphoria

evince

exaggerate

exceed

excel

excellence

excellent

except

excessive

exercise

exhaust

exhaustible

exhibit

exhilarate

exhilaration

existence

expedite

expenditure

expense

experience

explanation

expressible

extensible

extension

extraordinary

extremely

facetious

facilitate

facilities

factitious

fallible

familiar

familiarize

fantasize

fantasy

fascinate

favorable

favorite

feasible

February

fictitious

fiery

finally

financial

financially

financier

flammable

flaunt

flexible

flowchart *or* flow chart

forbade

forcible

foreign

foremost

forfeit

formally

formerly

fortuitous

forty

forward

fourth

frantically

fraudulent

freight

friend

fruition

fulfill

fulfillment

fungus

furthermore
gaily
gallant
gasoline
gauge *or* gage
generally
genius
genuine
glamour *or* glamor
good-bye *or* good-by
gourmet
government
governor
graffiti
grammar
grandeur
grateful
grief
grievance
grievous
guarantee
guerilla
guidance
gullible
hallelujah
handkerchief
handled
harangue
harass
hardware
hazardous
height
heinous
hemorrhage
hesitancy
hesitant

hesitate
heterogeneous *or*
   heterogenous
hindrance
holiday
homogeneous *or*
   homogenous
hoping
horrible
humorous
hundredths
hurriedly
hygienic
hyperbole
hypocrisy
icicle
identical
idiosyncrasy
idyll *or* idyl
ignorant
illegible
imaginary
imitation
imitative
immediately
immigration
imminent
impedance
imperative
imperiled
impossible
impromptu
inasmuch as
inaugurate
incarcerate
incidentally

inconvenience

incredible

incredulous

incurred

indebtedness

indelible

independence

independent

indict

indigestible

indispensable

individual

induce

inducement

industrious

inevitable

inferable

infinite

inflammable

influential

ingenious *(clever)*

ingenuous *(naive)*

inimitable

initial

innocence

innuendo

inoculate

inquiry

insignia

insistent

installment

instance

integral

intellectual

intelligence

intelligible

intention

intentionally

intercede

interest

interface

intermittent

internment

interrupted

intervene

inventory

investor

invincible

irrelevant

irresistible

irritable

itemized

itinerary

itself

jeopardize

jeopardy

judge

judgment

juggle

justifiable

ketchup *or* catsup

khaki

knell

knoll

knowledge

knowledgeable

knuckle

kosher

laboratory

landlord

laudable

legible

legitimate

leisure

length

lenient

letterhead

liable

liaison

library

license

licorice

lightning

likable

likelihood

likely

liquefy

liquidation

literature

livelihood

loneliness

loose *(adj.: unfastened)*

lose *(vb.: mislay)*

magazine

maintain

maintenance

management

manual

manufacturer

manuscript

marital

marriage

Massachusetts

material *(n.: substance)*

materiel *(n.: equipment)*

mathematics

maximum

meager

medical

medicinal

medicine

medieval

megabyte

memorandum

menus

merchandise

messenger

microprocessor

mileage

miniature

minimum

miscellaneous

mischievous

Mississippi

misspell

modernize

momentous

monochrome

monolog *or* monologue

morale

mortgage

murmur

muscle

necessary

negligible

negotiate

neighborhood

neither

nestle

nevertheless

newsstand

niche

nickel

nil

ninetieth

ninety

ninth

no one

nobody

noticeable

notoriety

nowadays

nuclear

nucleus

oblige

oblivious

obstacle

occasion

occasionally

occupant

occur

occurred

occurrence

occurring

offense

offering

official

omission

omit

omitted

operate

opinion

opportunity

optimistic

ordinary

organization

organize

original

oscillate

ostensible

outrageous

overdue

overrun

pageant

paid

pamphlet

pantomime

paradigm

parallel

paralyze

parameter

parliament

partial

participant

particularly

pastime

patronage

peculiar

perceive

percent

perceptible

peremptory

perfectible

periphery

permanent

permissible

permitted

perquisite

persecute

perseverance

persistent

personal *(adj.: private)*

personnel *(n.: employees)*

perspicuous

persuade

persuasible

phase

phenomenon

physically

physician

picaresque

picnic

picnicking

picturesque

piece

planning

plausible

pleasant

pleasure

plebeian

plebiscite

plow

politician

portentous

possess

possession

possibly

practicable

practical

practically

practice

precede

precedence

precedent

precipitous

precision

predictable

preferable

preference

preferred

prejudice

preliminary

premium

preparation

prerequisite

presence

prestigious

prevalent

previous

price list

primitive

principal *(n.: person;*
   money; adj.: chief)

principle *(n.: rule)*

privilege

probably

procedure

proceed

prodigy

professor

programmer

prominent

promissory

promulgate

pronunciation

propeller

prophecy *(n.: prediction)*

prophesy *(vb.: predict)*

prosecute

protocol

pseudonym

psyche

psychiatrist

psychology

purchase

pursue

quantity

quay

questionnaire

queue

quiet

quite

quixotic

quiz

quizzes

realize

really

rearrange

reasonable

recede

receipt

receive

recently

recession

recipe

recognize

recognized

recommend

reconnaissance

recurrence

reducible

refer

referable

referee

reference

referendum

referred

referring

region

registrar

regrettable

reign

reimburse

relieve

religious

remember

reminisce

remittance

renege

renewal

repeat

repertoire

repetition

representative

repressible

reproducible

requirement

reservoir

residual

resistance

resistible

respectfully

respectively

response

responsibility

responsible

restaurant

reticence

retractable

retrieve

reversible

rhetoric

rheumatism

rhythm

rhythmical

ridiculous

route

saccharin

sacrifice

sacrilegious

safety

salable *or* saleable

salary

sarcasm

satisfactory

scarcely

scenario

scenery

scepter

schedule

schism

science

scythe

secede

secession

secretary

securities

seize

semantic

sensible

sensual

sentinel

separate

sequence

sequential

serendipity

sergeant

serviceable

several

severely

sheriff

shipment

shipping

shone

shown

siege

significant

similar

simile

simultaneous

sincerity

smolder

solemn

soliloquy

someone

somewhat

sophomore

specialize

specimen

specious

speech

spell-checker *or* spell
    checker

stationary *(adj.:*
    immobile)

stationery *(n.: paper)*

statistics

strenuous

strictly

studying

suave

submitted

subpoena

subscriber

substantial

succeed

successful

suddenness

sufficient

suffrage

summarize

superintendent

supersede

supervisor

suppress

surprise

survey

susceptible

sustainable

syllable

syllabus

symmetrical

symmetry

synchronize

tangible

tariff

telecommunications

temperament

temperature

temporary

tendency

terrestrial

theater

their

there

thesaurus

thorough

thousandth

throughout

tied

time-sharing

tournament

toward *or* towards

tragedy

tranquillity *or*
    tranquility

transcendent

transfer

transferable

transferred

trauma

treacherous

treasurer

tremendous

tried

trivial

truly

twelfth

tying

typeface

typical

typing

tyranny

ultimately

unanimous

underrate

undoubtedly

unequivocal

unfortunately

universally

unnecessary

until

unusual

urgent

usable

usage

usually

vacancy

vaccination

vacillate

vacuum

valuable

various

vector

vehicle	weird
vendible	whether
vendor	wholesale
vengeance	wholly
vicinity	withhold
vicious	worthwhile
victory	wreck
vigilance	wrestle
villain	writing
visible	written
vitiate	yacht
vivacious	yaw
volatile	yea
volume	yearn
voluntary	yield
volunteer	zephyr
warehouse	zero
warrant	zigzag
weather	zinc
Wednesday	zodiac

REFERENCE LIBRARY

61

Principal Languages Throughout the World

The following list gives the major languages spoken in each country, designates those that are considered official languages, and specifies those that are commonly used in business dealings. When English isn't an accepted business language, some companies prefer to have their messages to another country translated into that country's language. (The addresses of two translator associations are included in list 76 of Part V.)

Afghanistan: Pashtu (business); Tajik; Uzbek; Hazara; English (business)

Albania: Albanian (official: Tosk dialect; business); Greek

Algeria: Arabic (official; business); French (business); misc. Berber dialects

Andorra: Catalan (official); French (business); Spanish (business); Castilian

Angola: Portuguese (official; business); misc. African languages

Antigua and Barbuda: English (official; business); misc. local dialects

Argentina: Spanish (official; business); English; Italian; German; French

Armenia: Armenian (official; business); Russian

Australia: English (business); misc. native languages

Austria: German (business)

Azerbaijan: Azeri (business); Russian; Armenian

Bahamas, The: English (business); Creole

Bahrain: Arabic (business); English (business); Farsi, Urdu

Bangladesh: Bangla (official); English (business)

Barbados: English (business)

Belarus: Byelorussian (business); Russian

Belgium: Dutch (business); French (business); German

Belize: English (official; business); Spanish (business); Maya, Garifuna

Benin: French (official; business); Fon; Yoruba; misc. tribal languages

Bhutan: Dzongkha (official); Tibetan and Nepalese dialects; English (business)

Bolivia: Spanish (official; business); Quechua (official); Aymara (official); English

Bosnia and Herzegovina: Serbo-Croatian (business)

Botswana: English (official; business); Setswana

Brazil: Portuguese (official; business); Spanish; French

Brunei: Malay (official); English (business); Chinese

Bulgaria: Bulgarian (business); misc. other languages

Burkina Faso: French (official; business); misc. tribal languages

Burma: Burmese; English (business); misc. other languages

Burundi: Kirundi (official); French (official; business); Swahili

Cambodia: Khmer (official; business); French (business)

Cameroon: English (official; business); French (official; business); misc. African languages

Canada: English (official; business); French (official; business)

Cape Verde: Portuguese (business); Crioulo

Central African Republic: French (official; business); Sangho; Arabic; Hunsa; Swahili

Chad: French (official; business); Arabic (official; business); Sara; Sango; misc. other languages and dialects

Chile: Spanish (business)

China: Chinese; Mandarin (business); English (business); misc. local dialects

Colombia: Spanish (business)

Comoros: Arabic (official; business); French (official; business); Comoran

Congo: French (official; business); Lingala; Kikongo

Costa Rica: Spanish (official; business); English

Croatia: Serbo-Croatian (business)

Cuba: Spanish (business)

Cyprus: Greek; Turkish; English (business)

Czech Republic: Czech (business); Slovak (business)

Denmark: Danish (business); Faroese; Greenlandic; German

Djibouti: French (official; business); Arabic (official; business); Somali; Afar

Dominica: English (official; business); French patois

Dominican Republic: Spanish (business)

Ecuador: Spanish (official; business); Quechua and other Indian languages

Egypt: Arabic (official; business); English (business); French

El Salvador: Spanish (business); Nahua

Equatorial Guinea: Spanish (official; business); pidgin English; Fang; Bubi; Ibo

Eritrea: Tigre; Kunama; misc. Cushitic dialects; Nora Ban; Arabic; for business: use language of local area

Estonia: Estonian (official; business); Latvian; Lithuanian; Russian

Ethiopia: Amharic (official; business); Tigrinya; Orominga; Guaraginga; Somali; Arabic; English (business)

Fiji: English (official; business); Fijian; Hindustani

Finland: Finnish (official; business); Swedish (official; business); Lapp, Russian

France: French (business); misc. regional dialects

Gabon: French (official; business); Fang; Myene; Bateke, Bapounou/Eschira; Bandjabi

Gambia, The: English (official; business); Mandinka; Wolof; Fula

Georgia: Georgian (official; business); Armenian; Azeri; Russian

Germany: German (business)

Ghana: English (official; business); misc. African languages

Greece: Greek (official; business); English; French

Grenada: English (official; business); French patois

Guatemala: Spanish (business); misc. Indian dialects and languages

Guinea: French (official; business); misc. tribal languages

Guinea-Bissau: Portuguese (official; business); Criolo; misc. African languages

Guyana: English (business); misc. Amerindian dialects

Haiti: French (official; business); Creole (business)

Honduras: Spanish (business); misc. Indian dialects

Hungary: Hungarian (business)

Iceland: Icelandic (business)

India: Hindi; English (business); all official: Bengali, Telugu; Marathi; Tamil; Urdu; Gujarati; Malayalam; Kannada

Indonesia: Bahasa Indonesia (official); English (business); Dutch; Javanese

Iran: Persian and Persian dialects; Turkic and Turkic dialects; Kurdish; Luri; Baloch; Arabic; Turkish; English (business); Farsi (business)

Iraq: Arabic (business); Kurdish (official in Kurdish region); Assyrian; Armenian; English (business)

Ireland: English (business); Irish Gaelic (business)

Israel: Hebrew (official; business); English (business); Arabic

Italy: Italian (business); German; French; Slovene

Ivory Coast: French (official; business); Dioula and other dialects

Jamaica: English (business); Creole

Japan: Japanese (business); English (business)

Jordan: Arabic (official; business); English (business)

Kazakhstan: Kazakh, or Qazaqz (official; business); Russian (business)

Kenya: English (official; business); Swahili (official); misc. indigenous languages

Kiribati: English (official; business); Gilbertese

Korea, North: Korean (official; business); English (business)

Korea, South: Korean (official; business); English (business)

Kuwait: Arabic (official; business); English (business)

Kyrgyzstan: Kirghiz, or Kyrgyz (official; business); Russian

Laos: Lao (official); French (business); English; misc. ethnic languages

Latvia: Lettish (official; business); Lithuanian; Russian

Lebanon: Arabic (official; business); French (official); Armenian; English (business)

Lesotho: English (official; business); Sesotho; Zulu; Xhosa

Liberia: English (official; business); misc. Niger-Congo languages

Libya: Arabic (business); English (business); Italian

Liechtenstein: German (official, business); Alemannic dialect

Lithuania: Lithuanian (official; business); Polish; Russian

Luxembourg: Luxembourgisch; German (business); French (business); English

Macedonia: Macedonian (business); Albanian; Turkish; Serbo-Croation

Madagascar: French (official; business); Malagasy (official)

Malawi: English (official; business); Chichewa (official); misc. regional languages

Malaysia: Malay (official); English (business); misc. Chinese dialects; Tamil; misc. tribal languages

Maldives: Divehi; English (business)

Mali: French (official; business); Bambara; misc. African languages

Malta: Maltese (official; business); English (official; business)

Marshall Islands: English (official; business); two Malayo-Polynesian dialects; Japanese

Mauritania: Hasaniya Arabic (official; business); Wolof (official); French (business); Pular; Soninke

Mauritius: English (official; business); Creole; French (business); Hindi; Urdu; Hakka; Bojpoori

Mexico: Spanish (business); misc. Mayan dialects

Micronesia, Federated States of: English (official; business); Trukese; Pohnpeian; Yapese; Kosrean

Moldova: Moldovan (official; business); Russian; Gagauz

Monaco: French (official; business); English; Italian; Monegasque

Mongolia: Khalkha Mongol (business); Turkic; Russian (business); Chinese

Morocco: Arabic (official; business); French (business); Spanish (business); misc. Berber dialects

Mozambique: Portuguese (official; business); misc. indigenous dialects

Namibia: Afrikaans (business); German (business); English (business); misc. indigenous languages

Nauru: Nauruan (official); English (business)

Nepal: Nepali (official); English (business); misc. languages and dialects

Netherlands: Dutch (business); English (business)

New Zealand: English (official; business); Maori

Nicaragua: Spanish (official; business); English; misc. Indian languages

Niger: French (official; business); Hausa; Djerma

Nigeria: English (official; business); Hausa; Yoruba; Ibo; Fulani

Niue: Polynesian (business); English (business)

Norway: Norwegian (official; business)

Oman: Arabic (official; business); English (business); Baluchi; Urdu; misc. Indian dialects

Pakistan: Punjabi; Urdu (official; business); English (official; business); Sindhi; Pashtu; Balochi

Palau: English (official; business); Palauan (official in 13 of 16 states); Sonsorolese (official in Sonsoral); Anguar and Japanese (official in Anguar): Tobi (official in Tobi)

Panama: Spanish (official; business); English (business)

Papua New Guinea: English (business); Motu

Paraguay: Spanish (official; business); Guarani

Peru: Spanish (official; business): Quechua (official); Aymara

Philippines: Filipino (official); English (official; business); Spanish (business)

Poland: Polish (business)

Portugal: Portuguese (business)

Qatar: Arabic (official; business); English (business)

Romania: Romanian (business); Hungarian; German

Russia: Russian (business); misc. other languages

Rwanda: Kinyarwanda (official); French (official; business); Kiswahili

Saint Kitts and Nevis: English (business)

Saint Lucia: English (official; business); French patois

Saint Vincent and the Grenadines: English (business); French patois

San Marino: Italian (business)

Sao Tome and Principe: Portuguese (official; business)

Saudi Arabia: Arabic (business); English (business)

Senegal: French (official; business); Wolof; Pulaar; Diola; Mandingo

Serbia and Montenegro: Serbo-Croatian (business); Albanian

Seychelles: English (official; business); French (official; business); Creole

Sierra Leone: English (official; business); Mende; Temne; Krio

Singapore: Chinese (official); Malay (official); Tami (official); English (official; business)

Slovakia: Slovak (official; business); Hungarian

Slovenia: Slovenian (business); Serbo-Croatian

Solomon Islands: Melanesian pidgin; English (business)

Somalia: Somali (official); Arabic (business); Italian (business); English (business)

South Africa: all official: Afrikaans (business); English (business); Ndebele; Pedi; Sotho; Swazi; Tsonga; Tswana; Venda; Xhosa (business); Zulu

Spain: Castilian Spanish (business); Catalan; Galician; Basque

Sri Lanka: Sinhala (official); Tamil; English (business)

Sudan: Arabic (official; business); Nubian; Ta Bedawie; Nilotic; Nilo-Hamitic; misc. Sundanic languages; English (business)

Suriname: Dutch (official; business); English (business); Sranang Tongo, or Taki-Taki; Hindustani; Javanese

Swaziland: English (official; business); siSwati (official)

Sweden: Swedish (business)

Switzerland: German (business); French (business); Italian (business); Romansch

Syria: Arabic (official; business); Kurdish; Armenian; Aramaic; Circassian; French; English (business)

Taiwan: Mandarin Chinese (official; business); Taiwanese; misc. Hakka dialects; English (business)

Tajikistan: Tajik (official; business); Russian

Tanzania: Swahili (official); English (official; business)

Thailand: Thai (business); English (business)

Togo: French (official; business); Ewe; Mina; Dagomba; Kabye

Tonga: Tongan; English (business)

Trinidad and Tobago: English (official; business); Hindi; French; Spanish

Tunisia: Arabic (official; business); French (business)

Turkey: Turkish (official; business); Kurdish; Arabic

Turkmenistan: Turkmen (official; business); Russian; Uzbek

Tuvalu: Tuvaluan; English (business)

Uganda: English (official; business); Luganda; Swahili; misc. Bantu and Nilotic languages

Ukraine: Ukrainian (business); Russian; Romanian; Polish; Hungarian

United Arab Emirates: Arabic (official; business); Persian; English (business); Hindi; Urdu

United Kingdom: English (business); Welsh; Scottish form of Gaelic

Uruguay: Spanish (business); Brazilero

Uzbekistan: Uzbek (business); Russian; Tajik

Vanuatu: English (official; business); French (official); pidgin

Venezuela: Spanish (official; business); misc. native Amerindian dialects

Vietnam: Vietnamese (official; business); French (business); Chinese; English; Khmer; misc. tribal languages

Western Sahara: Hassaniya Arabic (business); Moroccan Arabic (business)

Western Samoa: Samoan (Polynesian); English (business)

Yemen: Arabic (business); English (business)

Zaire: French (business); Lingala; Swahili

Zambia: English (official; business); misc. indigenous languages

Zimbabwe: English (official; business); Shona; Sindebele

62

Major Currencies of the World

Writers preparing financial information for, or receiving such information from, international readers must know the currencies of the respective countries. The following list gives the basic currencies and subcurrencies (fractional units) used in countries throughout the world (N.A. = not available). To find out more about pending currency changes, especially in newly formed countries, contact a bank that has an international department.

Afghanistan: afghani (Af) = 100 puls

Albania: lek (L) = 100 quintars

Algeria: Algerian dinar (DA) = 100 centimes

Andorra: French franc (F) = 100 centimes; Spanish peseta (Pta) = 100 centimos

Angola: new kwanza (NKz) = 100 kwei

Antigua and Barbuda: East Caribbean dollar (EC$) = 100 cents

Argentina: new peso (N.A.) = 100 centavos

Armenia: dram (N.A.) = 100 luma

Australia: Australian dollar ($A) = 100 cents

Austria: Austrian schilling (S) = 100 groschen

Azerbaijan: manat (N.A.) = 100 gopik

Bahamas, The: Bahamian dollar (B$) = 100 cents

Bahrain: Bahraini dinar (BD) = 1,000 fils

Bangladesh: taka (Tk) = 100 poiska

Barbados: Barbadian dollar (Bds$) = 100 cents

Belarus: Belarusian rubel (BR) = N.A.

Belgium: Belgian franc (BF) = 100 centimes

Belize: Belizean dollar (Bz$) = 100 cents

Benin: CFA franc (CFAF) = 100 centimes

Bhutan: ngultrum (Nu) = 100 chetrum

Bolivia: boliviano ($B) = 100 centavos

Bosnia and Herzegovina: dinar (D) = 100 paras

Botswana: pula (P) = 100 thebe

Brazil: real (R$) = 100 centavos

Brunei: Bruneian dollar (B$) = 100 cents

Bulgaria: lev (Lv) = 100 stotinki

Burkina Faso: CFA franc (CFAF) = 100 centimes

Burma: kyat (K) = 100 pyas

Burundi: Burundi franc (BFu) = 100 centimes

Cambodia: new riel (CR) = 100 sen

Cameroon: CFA franc (CFAF) = 100 centimes

Canada: Canadian dollar (Can$) = 100 cents

Cape Verde: Cape Verdean escudo (CVEsc) = 100 centavos

Central African Republic: CFA franc (CFAF) = 100 centimes

Chad: CFA franc (CFAF) = 100 centimes

Chile: Chilean peso (Ch$) = 100 centavos

China: yuan (¥) = 10 jiao

Colombia: Colombian peso (Col$) = 100 centavos

Comoros: Comoran franc (CF) = 100 centimes

Congo: CFA franc (CFAF) = 100 centimes

Costa Rica: Costa Rican colon (C) = 100 centimos

Croatia: Croatian kuna (HRK) = 100 paras

Cuba: Cuban peso (Cu$) = 100 centavos

Cyprus: Cypriot pound (£C) = 100 cents; Turkish lira (TL) = 100 kurus

Czech Republic: koruna (Kc) = 100 haleru

Denmark: Danish krone (DKr) = 100 oere

Djibouti: Djiboutian franc (DF) = 100 centimes

Dominica: East Caribbean dollar (EC$) = 100 cents

Dominican Republic: Dominican peso (RD$) = 100 centavos

Ecuador: sucre (S/) = 100 centavos

Egypt: Egyptian pound (£E) = 100 piasters

El Salvador: Salvadoran colon (C) = 100 centavos

Equatorial Guinea: CFA franc (CFAF) = 100 centimes

Eritrea: birr (Br) = 100 cents

Estonia: Estonian kroon (EEK) = 100 cents

Ethiopia: birr (Br) = 100 cents

Fiji: Fijian dollar (F$) = 100 cents

Finland: markka (FMk) = 100 pennia

France: franc (F) = 100 centimes

Gabon: CFA franc (CFAF) = 100 centimes

Gambia, The: dalasi (D) = 100 bututs

Georgia: lari (N.A.) = N.A.

Germany: deutsche mark (DM) = 100 pfennige

Ghana: new cedi (C) = 100 pesewas

Greece: drachma (Dr) = 100 lepta

Grenada: East Caribbean dollar (EC$) = 100 cents

Guatemala: quetzal (Q) = 100 centavos

Guinea: Guinean franc (FG) = 100 centimes

Guinea-Bissau: Guinea-Bissauan peso (PG) = 100 centavos

Guyana: Guyanese dollar (G$) = 100 cents

Haiti: gourde (G) = 100 centimes

Honduras: lempira (L)= 100 centavos

Hungary: forint (Ft) = 100 filler

Iceland: Icelandic krona (Kr) = 100 aurar

India: Indian rupee (Re) = 100 paise

Indonesia: Indonesian rupiah (Rp) = 100 sen (sen discontinued)

Iran: 10 Iranian rial (IR) = 1 toman (domestic figures generally referred to by toman)

Iraq: Iraqi dinar (ID) = 1,000 fils

Ireland: Irish pound (£I) = 100 pence

Israel: new Israeli shekel (NIS) = 100 new agorot (sing. agora)

Italy: Italian lira (Lit) = 100 centesimi

Ivory Coast: CFA franc (CFAF) = 100 centimes

Jamaica: Jamaican dollar (J$) = 100 cents

Japan: yen (¥) = N.A.

Jordan: Jordanian dinar (JD) = 1,000 fils

Kazakhstan: tenge (N.A.) = N.A.

Kenya: Kenyan shilling (KSh) = 100 cents

Kiribati: Australian dollar ($A) = 100 cents

Korea, North: North Korean won (Wn) = 100 chon

Korea, South: South Korean won (W) = 10 chon (theoretical)

Kuwait: Kuwaiti dinar (KD) = 1,000 fils

Kyrgyzstan: som (N.A.) = N.A.

Laos: new kip (NK) = 100 at

Latvia: lat = 100 cents

Lebanon: Lebanese pound (£L) = 100 piasters

Lesotho: loti (L) = 100 lisente

Liberia: Liberian dollar (L$) = 100 cents

Libya: Libyan dinar (LD) = 1,000 dirhams

Liechtenstein: Swiss franc, franken, or franchi (SwF) = 100 centimes, rappen, or centesimi

Lithuania: lita (N.A.) = N.A.

Luxembourg: Luxembourg franc (LuxF) = 100 centimes

Macedonia: pataca (P) = 100 avos

Madagascar: Malagasy franc (FMG) = 100 centimes

Malawi: Malawian kwacha (MK) = 100 tambala

Malaysia: ringgit (M$) = 100 sen

Maldives: rufiyaa (Rf) = 100 laari

Mali: CFA franc (CFAF) = 100 centimes

Malta: Maltese lira (LM) = 100 cents

Marshall Islands: U.S. dollar (US$) = 100 cents

Mauritania: ouguiya (UM) = 5 khoums

Mauritius: Mauritian rupee (MauR) = 100 cents

Mexico: new Mexican peso (Mex$) = 100 centavos

Micronesia, Federated States of: U.S. dollar (US$) = 100 cents

Moldova: leu (N.A.) = N.A.

Monaco: French franc (F) = 100 centimes

Mongolia: tughrik (Tug) = 100 mongos

Morocco: Moroccan dirham (DH) = 100 centimes

Mozambique: metical (Mt) = 100 centavos

Namibia: South African rand (R) = 100 cents

Nauru: Australian dollar ($A) = 100 cents

Nepal: Nepalese rupee (NR) = 100 paisa

Netherlands: guilder, gulden, or florin (f.) = 100 cents

New Zealand: New Zealand dollar (NZ$) = 100 cents

Nicaragua: gold cordoba (C$) = 100 centavos

Niger: CFA franc (CFAF) = 100 centimes

Nigeria: naira (N) = 100 kobo

Norway: Norwegian krone (NKr) = 100 oere

Oman: Omani rial (RO) = 1,000 baiza

Pakistan: Pakistan rupee (PRe) = 100 paisa

Palau: United States dollar (US$) = 100 cents

Panama: balboa (B) = 100 centesimos

Papua New Guinea: kina (K) = 100 toea

Paraguay: guarani (G) = 100 centimos

Peru: nuevo sol (S/.) = 100 centimos

Philippines: Philippine peso (P) = 100 centavos

Poland: zloty (Zl) = 100 groszy

Portugal: Portuguese escudo (Esc) = 100 centavos

Qatar: Qatari riyal (QR) = 100 dirhams

Romania: leu (L) = 100 bani

Russia: ruble (R) = 100 kopeks

Rwanda: Rwandan franc (RF) = 100 centimes

Saint Kitts and Nevis: East Caribbean dollar (EC$) = 100 cents

Saint Lucia: East Caribbean dollar (EC$) = 100 cents

Saint Vincent and the Grenadines: East Caribbean dollar (EC$) = 100 cents

San Marino: Italian lira (Lit) = 100 centesimi (also mints its own coins)

Sao Tome and Principe: dobra (Db) = 100 centimos

Saudia Arabia: Saudi rial (SR) = 100 halalas

Senegal: CFA franc (CFAF) = 100 centimes

Serbia and Montenegro: Yugoslav new dinar (YD) = 100 paras

Seychelles: Seychelles rupee (SRe) = 100 cents

Sierra Leone: leone (Le) = 100 cents

Singapore: Singapore dollar (S$) = 100 cents

Slovakia: koruna (Sk) = 100 halierov

Slovenia: tolar (SIT) = 100 stotins

Solomon Islands: Solomon Islands dollar (SI$) = 100 cents

Somalia: Somali shilling (So. Sh.) = 100 cents

South Africa: rand (R) = 100 cents

Spain: peseta (Pta) = 100 centimos

Sri Lanka: Sri Lankan rupee (SLRe) = 100 cents

Sudan: Sudanese pound (£Sd) = 100 piastres

Suriname: Surinamese guilder, gulden, or florin (Sf.) = 100 cents

Swaziland: lilangeni (E) = 100 cents

Sweden: Swedish krona (SKr) = 100 oere

Switzerland: Swiss franc, franken, or franco (SwF) = 100 centimes, rappen, or centesimi

Syria: Syrian pound (£S) = 100 piastres

Taiwan: New Taiwan dollar (NT$) = 100 cents

Tajikistan: Rajik (N.A.) = N.A.

Tanzania: Tanzanian shilling (TSh) = 100 cents

Thailand: baht (B) = 100 satang

Togo: CFA franc (CFAF) = 100 centimes

Tonga: pa'anga (T$) = 100 seniti

Trinidad and Tobago: Trinidad and Tobago dollar (TT$) = 100 cents

Tunisia: Tunisian dinar (TD) = 1,000 millimes

Turkey: Turkish lira (TL) = 100 kurus

Turkmenistan: manat (N.A.) = N.A.

Tuvalu: Tuvaluan dollar ($T) or Australian dollar ($A) = 100 cents

Uganda: Uganda shilling (USh) = 100 cents

Ukraine: karbovanet (N.A.) = N.A.; to be replaced by hryvnya (N.A.) = N.A.

United Arab Emirates: Emirian dirham (Dh) = 100 fils

United Kingdom: British pound (£) = 100 pence

Uruguay: Uruguayan peso ($Ur) = 100 centesimos

Uzbekistan: som (N.A.) = N.A.

Vanuatu: vatu (VT) = 100 centimes

Venezuela: bolivar (Bs) = 100 centimos

Vietnam: new dong (D) = 100 xu

Western Sahara: Moroccan dirham (DH) = 100 centimes

Western Samoa: tala (WS$) = 100 sene

Yemen: Yemeni rial (N.A.) = N.A.

Zaire: zaire (Z) = 100 makuta

Zambia: Zambian kwacha (ZK) = 100 ngwee

Zimbabwe: Zimbabwean dollar (Z$) = 100 cents

63

Commonly Abbreviated Internet Phrases

Some Internet communicators use an abbreviated form of expression, such as *TTYL* (talk to you later), for informal, conversational comments and as a way of personalizing their messages. (For other types of conversational shorthand, see list 64; for nonconversational abbreviations, see list 65.) The number of these informal abbreviations are rapidly increasing. Although they are appealing as a way of shortening an electronic message and making it seem friendlier, some (ROTM—right on the money) are trite and overworked, and others (GOK—God only knows) are too casual for most business use. In general, avoid the following abbreviations in professional business communications and formal documents.

AAMOF	As a matter of fact
AFAIK	As far as I know
AFK	Away from the keyboard
BBFN	Bye-bye for now
BBL	Be back later
BTW	By the way
BYKT	But you knew that
CMIIW	Correct me if I'm wrong
DIIK	Damned if I know

EOL	End of lecture
EOT	End of thread
F2F	Face to face (meeting)
FCOL	For crying out loud
FITB	Fill in the blank
FOTCL	Falling off the chair laughing
FWIW	For what it's worth
FYA	For your amusement
FYI	For your information
GD&R	Grinning, ducking, and running
GLG	Goofy little grin
GOK	God only knows
HHOJ	Ha, ha, only joking
HHOK	Ha, ha, only kidding
HHOS	Ha, ha, only serious
IAC	In any case
IAE	In any event
IANAL	I am not a lawyer
IMCO	In my considered opinion
IMHO	In my humble opinion
IOW	In other words
IRL	In real life
IWBNI	It would be nice if
JADP	Just another data point
JASE	Just another system error
KISS	Keep it simple, stupid
LAT	Lovely and talented
LOL	Laughing out loud
MORF	Male or female?
NRN	No reply necessary
OIC	Oh, I see
OOC	Out of character
OTOH	On the other hand
PMJI	Pardon my jumping in
RL	Real life
ROFL, ROTFL	Rolling on the floor laughing

ROTM	Right on the money
RSN	Real soon now (maybe never)
RUMOF	Are you male or female?
S!MT!!OE!!!	Sets! my teeth!! on edge!!!
SITD	Still in the dark
TAFN	That's all for now
TIA	Thanks in advance
TIC	Tongue in cheek
TMOT	Trust me on this
TPTB	The powers that be
TTFN	Ta-ta for now
TTYL	Talk to you later
TTYTT	To tell you the truth
TYVM	Thank you very much
WADR	With all due respect
YMMV	Your mileage may vary
YOYOW	You own your own words

64

Widely Used E-Mail Emoticons

Like the abbreviations of Internet phrases in list 63, emoticons—also called *smileys* or *smiley-face symbols* because of the way they look—are a form of conversational shorthand. These symbols, such as '-) (winking), are used to make electronic messages more personal and, especially, to show emotion or attitude, such as irony, that might not otherwise be obvious. The list also includes *nonsmiley-face symbols*, such as <g> (grin). Both smiley and nonsmiley symbols should be used only in informal communications with people you know and should be avoided in professional business messages and formal documents. *Caution:* When using such symbols, be certain that the recipient knows and uses the same ones; some communicators may have adopted a different version.

:-)	Basic smiley
,-)	Winking and happy
:'->	Happy and crying
:-"	Whistling
,-}	Wry and winking
;-)	Winking
):-)	Impish
:-?	Licking one's lips
:-b...	Drooling
:-0	Talkative
:-d	Said with a smile
<g>	Grin
<l>	Laugh
>:D	Demonic laugh
<L> *or* :D	Laughing
:-D	Laughing at you
:/)	Not funny
:-/	Skeptical
:->	Sarcastic
<J>	Joking
<jk>	Just kidding
<i>	Irony
:-7 *or* ;^)	Smirking
%}	Eyes crossed and smirking
:-J	Tongue in cheek
:-(	Sad, unhappy
(:-(*or* :-c	Very unhappy
:(	Frowning, upset
<:/&	Stomach in knots
<s>	Sigh
:-e	Disappointed
:-o	Surprised

>:-> *or* >:-<	Angry
:-#	Lips are sealed
:-V	Shouting
:-@	Screaming
;-(*or* :'-(*or* :,(	Crying
:-(	Boo hoo
:-t	Pouting
:—\	Undecided
I-O	Yawning, snoring
I-I	Asleep
:-I	Indifferent
:-&	Tongue-tied
I-o	Bored
:-!	Foot in mouth
:-$	Biting one's tongue
:-*	Oops!
<>	No comment
[:]	Robot
<:-I	Dunce
?—(	Black eye
:P	Sticking out tongue
>;->	Lewd remark
:-P	Nyahhh!
=:o	Argh!
:-(*)	Made me sick
&-I	Made me cry
:-S	Incoherent
:-w	Speak with forked tongue
\\/	Live long and prosper
...	Back in a sec
X-(	Brain dead
(-:	Left-handed
::-)	Wears glasses
8:-)	Glasses on forehead
':-(	Very hot
)8-)	Ready to party all night

| L:-) | Just graduated |
| [:-) | Wearing a Walkman |

65

Information Technology Abbreviations

Business writers use many abbreviations, especially those involving information technology. The following abbreviations include *acronyms*—abbreviations pronounced like an actual word *(BASIC)*—and *initialisms*—abbreviations pronounced letter by letter *(LCD)*. Although many computer abbreviations, such as *PC*, are capitalized, the general trend is toward lowercase letters *(cpu)*. Punctuation is minimal, although an abbreviation in lowercase letters that is spelled the same as a word, such as *it.* (information technology), usually ends with a period to distinguish it from the actual word. Whereas the previous two lists had abbreviations and symbols that should be used only in very informal, conversational communications, the following abbreviations are widely used in *technical* business documents.

abm, ABM	Automated batch mixing
abp, ABP	Actual block processor
acc, ACC	Accumulator
ace., ACE	Automatic circuit exchange
acf	Advanced communication function
acl, ACL	Access control list
acr	Abandon call and retry
acu	Address control unit; automatic calling unit
a/d	Analog to digital
adc, ADC	Analog-to-digital converter
ade	Automatic data entry
adl, ADL	Automatic data link

adp, ADP	Automated/automatic data processing
adsl, ADSL	Asynchrononous digital subscriber loop
aex, AEX	Automatic electronic exchange
af	Audiofidelity; audiofrequency
ai	Artificial intelligence
AIX	Advanced interactive executive
alcom	Algebraic compiler; algebraic computer
ALTRAN	Algebraic translator
alu, ALU	Arithmetic logic unit
am., AM	Amplitude modulation
a/m	Auto/manual
anacom	Analog computer
ANSI	American National Standards Institute
AOL	America Online
apa	All points addressable
api, API	Application program interface
apu	Auxiliary power unit
ar	Achievement ratio; aspect ratio; auditory reception
ar, AR	Address register
ARP	Address resolution protocol
aru	Analog remote unit; audio response unit
as., AS	Autonomous system
asc	Automatic sequence control; automatic switching center; auxiliary switch closed
ASCII	American Standard Code for Information Interchange
asic, ASIC	Application-specific integrated circuit
asm	Auxiliary-storage management
asr, ASR	Answer-send-receive
atl	Analog threshold logic
AUTOVON	Automatic voice network

aux, AUX	Auxiliary device
b	Bit
ba, BA	Binary add; bus available
bac, BAC	Binary asymmetric channel
BAM	Basic access method
bar., BAR	Base address register; buffer address register
BASIC	Beginner's All-Purpose Symbolic Instruction
bau	Basic assembly unit
bbp	Building-block principle
bbs	Bulletin board system
bc	Binary code; binary counter
bcd	Binary-coded data; binary-coded decimal
bd.	Baud
ber	Basic encoding rules
bex, BEX	Broadbank exchange
bfr., BFR	Buffer
bi	Buffer index
bi., BI	Binary
bios, BIOS	Basic input-output system
bit, bit.	Binary digit
BITNET	Because It's Time Network
biu	Basic information unit
bix, BIX	Binary information exchange
bjf	Batch-job format
bm, BM	Buffer mark; buffer modules
bn, BN	Binary number (system)
bof, BOF	Beginning of file
bot, BOT	Beginning of tape
bpi	Bits per inch; bytes per inch
bps	Bits per second; bytes per second
bpu	Base production unit
bs	Binary subtraction

bsc	Basic message switching center; binary synchronous communication
bsd	Bit storage density
btl, BTL	Beginning tape level
btu	Basic transmission unit
c	Computer; cycle
cad.	Cartridge-activated device
cad., CAD	Computer-aided design
cad./cam., CAD/CAM	Computer-aided design/computer-aided manufacturing
cal, CAL	Computer-aided learning; Conversational Algebraic Language
cam.	Central-address memory; computer-addressed memory
cam., CAM	Computer-aided manufacturing
cap., CAP	Computer-aided production
car., CAR	Computer-assisted retrieval
cat., CAT	Computer-aided testing
caw	Cam-action wheel; channel address word
cbl, CBL	Computer-based learning
cbt, CBT	Computer-based training
CBX	Computer branch exchange
ccb	Command control block
ccc	Central computer complex; command control console; computer-command control
CCITT	Consultative Committee for International Telephony and Telegraphy
ccr	Command control receiver; computer character recognition; control circuit resistance
cdb	Current data bit
cdc	Call-directing code

CD-ROM	Compact disk, read-only memory
CERT	Computer Emergency Response Team
cet	Cumulative elapsed time
cff	Computer forms feeder
cfp	Computer forms printer
cga, CGA	Computer graphics adapter
cgh	Computer-generated hologram
cgi, CGI	Computer graphics interface
cic	Command input coupler
cim	Computer-input microfilm; computer-integrated manufacturing
CIS	CompuServe Information Service
ciu	Computer interface unit
CIX	Commercial Internet Exchange
cla	Communication line adaptor
cll	Circuit load logic
clp, CLP	Command language processor
clu	Central logic unit
cm, c/m	Communications multiplexor
c/m	Control and monitoring; cycles per minute
cmi, CMI	Computer-managed instruction
cml	Circuit micrologic; current mode logic
COBOL	Common Business-Oriented Language
com, COM	Computer-output microfilm
compac, COMPAC	Computer program for automatic control
cot., COT	Card or tape reader
cp	Central processor
c/p	Control panel
cpa	Critical-path analysis
cph	Characters per hour; cycles per hour
cpi	Characters per inch
cpl	Characters per line; common program language

cpm	Cards per minute; characters per minute; counts per minute; critical path method; cycles per minute
cp/m	Control program for microcomputers
cps	Central processing system; characters per second; critical path scheduling; cycles per second
cpu, CPU	Central processing unit
crf	Control relay forward
crm	Critical reaction measure; crucial reaction measure
crt, CRT	Cathode-ray tube
crtu	Combined receiving and transmitting unit
c/s	Call signal; cycles per second
csect	Control section; cross section
csl	Computer-simulation language; computer-sensitive language
cst	Channel status indicator; channel status table
csu	Central statistical unit; circuit-switching unit; constant-speed unit
ctm	Communications terminal modules
cts, CTS	Clear to send
ctu	Central terminal unit
ctx	Computer telex exchange
cub., CUB	Control unit busy
cum	Central unit memory
CWIS	Campus-Wide Information System
cwp, CWP	Communicating word processor
cx	Control transmitter
cx, CX	Central exchange
dam., DAM	Direct-access method
dasd, DASD	Direct-access storage device
dat	Digital audiotape
datacom	Data communications

dav	Data above voice
db, dB	Decibel
dbam, DBAM	Database-access method
dbase	Database
dBu	Decibel unit
d-bug	Debug(ged)(ging)
dd	Digital data; digital display
DDBMS	Distributed database management system
ddc	Direct digital control
dde	Direct data entry
ddis	Data display
ddl	Data definition language; data description language; digital data link
ddm	Data demand module
dds	Digital display scope; digital dynamics simulator
de/me	Decoding memory
des, DES	Data encryption standard
dfa	Digital fault analysis
dfd	Data function diagram
dfg	Digital function generator; diode function generator
dia	Document interchange architecture
dian	Digital analog
didad	Digital data display
di/do.	Data input/data output
dif	Data-interchange format
dig. r-o	Digital readout
div	Data in voice; digits in voice
dl, d/l	Data link
dlu	Digitizer logic unit
dma, DMA	Direct memory access
dmb	Dual-mode bus
dmc	Digital microcircuit

dms	Digital multiplex switching
DNS	Domain Name Server (Internet)
dos, DOS	Disk operating system
dov, DOV	Data over voice
dp	Data processing
dpi	Dots per inch
dr.	Destructive readout
draw./, DRAW	Direct read after write
drdw, DRDW	Direct read during write
dri	Data rate indicator; data reduction interpreter
dro	Destructive readout
drs	Data-reduction system
drt	Data-review technique
ds, DS	Data set
dscb	Data set control block
dsr, DSR	Data set ready
ds&r	Data storage and retrieval
DSS	Digital satellite system
d to a	Digital to analog
dtp, DTP	Desktop publishing
dtr	Distribution tape reel
dtr, DTR	Data terminal ready
duv, DUV	Data under voice
DVD	Digital videodisk
dvi	Digital video interactive
dvl	Direct voice line
EBCDIC	Extended binary coded decimal interchange code
ecm	Extended core memory
edac, edc	Error detection and correction
edc	Electronic digital computer
edi	Electronic data interchange
edp, EDP	Electronic data processing
ehf	Extra high frequency; extremely high frequency

EIDE	Enhanced Integrated Drive Electronics
EISA	Extended Industry Standard Architecture
elf., ELF	Extra low frequency; extremely low frequency
elv, ELV	Extra low voltage; extremely low voltage
emm	Expanded memory manager
ems	Expanded memory specification
emux	Electronic multiplexer
ENIAC	Electronic Numerical Integrator and Calculator
eo, EO	End of operation
e-o	Electro-optical
eob, EOB	End of block (character)
eof, EOF	End of file
eoj, EOJ	End of job
eol, EOL	End of line
eolb, EOLB	End-of-line block
eom, EOM	End of message
eor, EOR	End of record; end of run
eot, EOT	End of tape; end of transmission
EPROM	Erasable programmable read-only memory
etb, ETB	End-of-transmission block
etx, ETX	End of text
evt	Effective visual transmission
f, F	Feedback
FAQ	Frequently asked questions (E-mail)
fat., FAT	File allocation table
f/b	Feedback; front to back (ratio)
fca	Frequency control and analysis
fdm	Frequency division multiplexing
fe, FE	Format effective
ff, FF	Form feed
flf, FLF	Flip-flop (computer)

fm, FM	Frequency modulation
FORTRAN	Formula Translation (language)
fps	Frames per second
f&r	Feed and return
fs, FS	File separation
FTP	File transfer protocol (E-mail)
gb, GB	Gigabyte (computer storage capacity)
GDT	Graphic display terminal
GIF	Graphics interchange format
gigo, GIGO	Garbage in, garbage out
gps, GPS	Graphics positioning system
GUI	Graphical User Interface
hdlc, HDLC	High-level data link control
hdtv, HDTV	High-definition television
hf, HF	High frequency
hpfs, HPFS	High-performance file system
HSP	High-speed printer
HTML	Hypertext Markup Language
HTTP	Hypertext Transfer Protocol
ibw	Information bandwidth
ic	Input circuit; integrated circuit
icff	Intercommunication flip-flop
idac	Interim digital-analog converter
idp	Information data processing; input data processing; integrated data processing
if., IF	Information feedback
IGP	Interior Gateway Protocol
ildf	Integrated logistic data file
i/o	Input/output
i&o	Input and output
iob	Input-output buffer
i/p	Input
IP	Internet protocol
ipfm	Integral pulse frequency modulation
ir	Information retrieval

i&r	Information and retrieval
IRC	Internet relay chat
is., IS	Information services
ISA	Industry Standard Architecture
isam, ISAM	Indexed sequential access method
ISDN	Integrated Services Digital Network
ISO	International Standards Organization
ISP	Internet service provider
is&r	Information storage and retrieval
isv	Independent software vendor
it., IT	Information technology
itv, ITV	Interactive TV
ixc	Interexchange
k, K	About one thousand (computer storage capacity)
kb	Keyboard
kbe	Keyboard entry
LAN	Local-area network
LAWN	Local-area wireless network
lb	Line buffer
lc	Liquid crystal
lcd, LCD	Liquid crystal display
lcm	Large-core memory
l-d	Low density
led, LED	Light-emitting diode
lf	Line feed; low frequency
li	Line item
linac	Linear accelerator
ll, l/l	Lower limit
l/l	Line by line
lna	Low-noise amplifier
lp	Linear programming
lpcw	Long-pulse continuous wave
lpm	Lines per minute
mac, MAC	Medium-access control
MAN	Metropolitan area network

mar., MAR	Memory address register
mb, MB	Memory buffer (computer storage)
mbr	Memory buffer register
mcga, MCGA	Multicolor graphics array
mcvf	Multichannel voice frequency
m-d, modem	Modulator-demodulator
m/e	Mechanical/electrical
mf	Medium frequency
mfm	Modified frequency modulation
mh	Magnetic heading
micr, MICR	Magnetic-ink character recognition
MIME	Multipurpose Internet mail extension
mis, MIS	Management information system; manager of information services
ml	Machine language
mmx	Memory multiplexer
mpx	Multiplex
mt	Machine translation
mud., MUD	Multiuser domain/dungeon
mux	Multiplex(er)
mx	Multiplex
nc, NC	Numerical control
ndr, ndro	Nondestructive readout
netiquette	Internet etiquette
NFS	Network File System
nic	Network interface card
NII	National Information Infrastructure
NIS	Network Information Service
nop, NOP	No-operating instruction
nos, NOS	Network operating system
oc	Open circuit
ocr, OCR	Optical character reader; optical character recognition
odt	On-line debugging technique
oem	Original equipment manufacturer
olc	On-line computer

olrt	On-line real time
oop, OOP	Object-oriented programming
o/p	Output
os, OS	Operating system
osi, OSI	Open system interconnection
pa	Paper advance; power amplifier
PBX	Private branch exchange
pc	Printed circuit; program counter
p/c	Processor controller; pulse counter
pcb	Printed circuit board
pdn, PDN	Public data network
pf	Performance factor; pulse frequency
pfm	Power factor meter; pulse frequency modulation
pfr	Peak flow rate
pim, PIM	Personal information manager
pm	Primary memory; pulse modulation
pmm	Pulse mode multiplex
po	Power oscillator
POST	Power-on self-test
PPP	Point-to-point protocol
ptm	Pulse-time modulation
RAM	Random-access memory
REM	Recognition memory
rf	Radio frequency
rgb, RGB	Red-green-blue (monitor)
ri	Random interval
rip., RIP	Routing information protocol
ROM	Read-only memory
rps	Revolutions per second
rsi, RSI	Repetitive strain injury
r/w	Read/write
RXD	Receive data
sam., SAM	Sequential-access method; serial access memory
SAP	Service advertising protocol

s/c	Short circuit
scc	Serial communications controller
scsi, SCSI	Small computer system interface
shf	Superhigh frequency
SLIP	Serial line Internet protocol
SMTP	Simple mail transfer protocol
s/n	Signal to noise (ratio)
SOHO	Small office–home office
SPG	Service protocol gateway
spl, SPL	Systems programming language
SPOOL	Simultaneous peripheral operations on line
SPX	Sequenced packet exchange
SRAM	Static RAM
ssdd, SSDD	Single-side double-density (diskette)
ssp	Systems support program
SVGA	Super video graphics array
TCP/IP	Transmission control protocol/Internet protocol
TIA	The Internet Adapter
TIFF	Tagged image file format
tof, TOF	Top of file
TOPS	Transparent operating system
TTY	Teletypewriter
twx, TWX	Teletypewriter exchange
txd, TXD	Transmit data
uhf, UHF	Ultrahigh frequency
ulf, ULF	Ultralow frequency
ulsi, ULSI	Ultra large scale integration
UPS	Uninterruptible power supply
URL	Uniform Resource Locator (Internet)
USASCII	USA Standard Code for Information Interchange
UNIVAC	Universal Automatic Computer
VDT	Video display terminal
vf	Video frequency

vga, VGA	Visual graphics array
vhf, VHF	Very high frequency
vhp, VHP	Very high performance
vlsi, VLSI	Very large scale integration
vo	Voice-over
vof	Variable operating frequency
vox, VOX	Voice-operated device
vr, VR	Virtual reality
VRAM	Video RAM
VRML	Virtual reality modeling language
WAIS	Wide Area Information Servers (Internet)
WAN	Wide area network
WORM	Write-once, read-many
WWW	World Wide Web
WYSIWG (pronounced *wiz-ee-wig*)	What you see is what you get (desktop publishing)
WYSIWYP (pronounced *wiz-ee-whip*)	What you see is what you print (desktop publishing)
xcvr	Transceiver
XGA	Extended graphics array
xmt, XMT	Transmit

66

Metric Weights and Measures

Although the metric system has been in existence since the eighteenth century and has been adopted by many countries, the United States still uses its customary measures along with the metric measures. The metric system is widely used in international trade, but both metric and customary units are used in U.S. domestic business. A writer, therefore, needs to know how to convert one type of unit to another. The following lists give the common metric prefixes, their use with base units, and the multiplication factors that are used to convert a metric unit to a customary unit.

METRIC PREFIXES

Prefix	Multiplication Factor	Symbol
exa-	1,000,000,000,000,000,000 (10^{18}) (one quintillion)	E
peta-	1,000, 000, 000, 000, 000 (10^{15}) (one quadrillion)	P
tera-	1, 000, 000, 000, 000 (10^{12}) (one trillion)	T
giga-	1,000,000,000 (10^9) (one billion)	G
mega-	1,000,000 (10^6) (one million)	M
kilo-	1,000 (10^3) (one thousand)	k
hecto-	100 (10^2) (one hundred)	h
deka-	10 (ten)	da
deci-	0.1 (10^{-1}) (one-tenth)	d
centi-	0.01 (10^{-2}) (one-hundredth)	c
milli-	0.001 (10^{-3}) (one-thousandth)	m
micro-	0.000,001 (10^{-6}) (one-millionth)	μ

nano-	0.000,000,001 (10^{-9}) (one-billionth)	n
pico-	0.000,000,000,001 (10^{-12}) (one-trillionth)	p
femto-	0.000,000,000,000,001 (10^{-15}) (one-quadrillionth)	f
atto-	0.000,000,000,000,000,001 (10^{-18}) (one-quintillionth)	a

METRIC PREFIXES USED WITH BASE UNITS

Weight: 1 *kilo*gram = 1,000 grams
1 *hecto*gram = 100 grams
1 *deka*gram = 10 grams
(1 gram = 1 gram)
1 *deci*gram = 0.1 gram
1 *centi*gram = 0.01 gram
1 *milli*gram = 0.001 gram

Length: 1 *kilo*meter = 1,000 meters
1 *hecto*meter = 100 meters
1 *deka*meter = 10 meters
(1 meter = 1 meter)
1 *deci*meter = 0.1 meter
1 *centi*meter = 0.01 meter
1 *milli*meter = 0.001 meter

Volume: 1 *hecto*liter = 100 liters
1 *deka*liter = 10 liters
(1 liter = 1 liter)
1 *centi*liter = 0.01 liter
1 *milli*liter = 0.001 liter

MULTIPLICATION FACTORS FOR CONVERTING UNITS

When You Know	Multiply by	To Find
Metric Length		
millimeters	0.04	inches
centimeters	0.39	inches
meters	3.28	feet
meters	1.09	yards
kilometers	0.62	miles
Customary Length		
inches	25.40	millimeters
inches	2.54	centimeters
feet	30.48	centimeters
yards	0.91	meters
miles	1.61	kilometers
Metric Area		
square centimeters	0.16	square inches
square meters	1.20	square yards
square kilometers	0.39	square miles
hectares (10,000m²)	2.47	acres
Customary Area		
square inches	6.45	square centimeters
square feet	0.09	square meters
square yards	0.84	square meters
square miles	2.60	square kilometers
acres	0.40	hectares
Metric Mass and Weight		
grams	0.035	ounce
kilograms	2.21	pounds
metric tons (1000 kg)	1.10	short tons
Customary Mass and Weight		
ounces	28.35	grams
pounds	0.45	kilograms

short tons (2000 lb)	0.91	tons (metric)

Metric Volume

milliliters	0.20	teaspoons
milliliters	0.06	tablespoons
milliliters	0.03	fluid ounces
liters	4.23	cups
liters	2.12	pints
liters	1.06	quarts
liters	0.26	gallons
cubic meters	35.32	cubic feet
cubic meters	1.35	cubic yards

Customary Volume

teaspoons	4.93	milliliters
tablespoons	14.79	milliliters
fluid ounces	29.57	milliliters
cups	0.24	liters
pints	0.47	liters
quarts	0.95	liters
gallons	3.79	liters
cubic feet	0.03	cubic meters
cubic yards	0.76	cubic meters

Metric Speed

kilometers per hour	0.62	miles per hour

Customary Speed

miles per hour	1.61	kilometers per hour

67

Basic Math Signs and Symbols

Writers who prepare technical or statistical documents must know the basic math signs and symbols. This list has more than a hundred such signs and symbols that are used in business material.

Sign	Meaning
+	Plus
−	Minus
×	Multiplied by
÷	Divided by
=	Equal to
±	Plus or minus
∓	Minus or plus
≐	Plus or equal to
++	Double plus
≏	Difference between
−:	Difference excess
≡	Indentical with, congruent
≢	Not identical with
≠	Not equal to
≈	Nearly equal to
≅	Equals approximately
≧	Equal to or greater than
≦	Equal to or less than
<	Less than
⊐	Less than
>	Greater than
⊏	Greater than
≷	Greater than or less than
≮	Not less than

≯	Not greater than
≦	Less than or equal to
≤	Less than or equal to
≦	Less than or equal to
≲	Less than or equal to
≶	Less than or greater than
≧	Greater than or equal to
≥	Greater than or equal to
≧	Greater than or equal to
≳	Greater than or equal to
≎	Equivalent to
≠	Not equivalent to
≢	Not equivalent to
⊂	Included in
⊃	Excluded from
~	Difference
∽	Difference
⧧	Equal and parallel
≐	Approaches a limit
$\underline{m}$	Is measured by
⊥	Perpendicular to
⊥s	Perpendiculars
∥	Parallel
∥s	Parallels
∦	Not parallel
∠	Angle
⦣	Angle
⦢	Angle
∠s	Angles
∟	Right angle
⩭	Equal angles
△	Triangle
△s	Triangles
/	Rising diagonal
\	Falling diagonal
//	Parallel rising diagonal

\\	Parallel falling diagonal
///	Rising parallels
\\\	Falling parallels
|||	Triple vertical
≡	Quadruple parallels
⌒	Arc
⌣	Arc
v̂	Sector
⌀	Diameter
∴	Hence, therefore
∵	Because
·	Multiplied by
:	Ratio
::	Proportion
≑	Geometrical proportion
√	Square root
∛	Cube root
∜	Fourth root
ⁿ√	nth root
<	Horizontal radical
Σ	Summation
Π	Product sign
π	Pi
∪	Union sign
∩	Intersection sign
!	Factorial sign
∅	Empty set; null set
∈	Is an element of
∉	Is not an element of
Δ	Delta
∝	Variation
∞	Infinity
⊢	Assertion sign
∂	Partial differential
∂	Partial differential
∫	Integral

$\oint$	Contour integral
$\hookleftarrow$	Horizontal integral
/	Single bond
|	Single bond
\	Single bond
|	Single bond (punched to right)
\\\\	Double bond
||	Double bond
//	Double bond
⋮	Triple bond
↔	Reaction goes both right and left
↕	Reaction goes both up and down
⇋	Equilibrium reaction beginning at right
⇌	Equilibrium reaction beginning at left
⇌	Reversible reaction beginning at left
⇋	Reaction begins at right and is completed to left
⇉	Reaction begins at right and is completed to right
⇄	Reaction begins at left and is completed to right
⇄	Reaction begins at left and is completed to left
⇋	Reversible reaction beginning at right
↕	Reversible
⇑	Elimination
⇓	Absorption
⇅	Exchange
↗	Reversible reaction
↖	Reversible reaction

68
Greek Letter Symbols

Business writers use Greek letters in math and other technical material. When the letters are handwritten on a manuscript to be sent to a printer or desktop publishing operator, they should be clearly identified as uppercase or lowercase letters.

Name	Uppercase Letter	Lowercase Letter
alpha	A	α
beta	B	β
gamma	Γ	γ
delta	Δ	δ
epsilon	E	ε
zeta	Z	ζ
eta	H	η
theta	Θ	θ
iota	I	ι
kappa	K	κ
lambda	Λ	λ
mu	M	μ
nu	N	ν
xi	Ξ	ξ
omicron	O	o
pi	Π	π
rho	P	ρ
sigma	Σ	σ
tau	T	τ
upsilon	Υ	υ
phi	Φ	φ
chi	X	χ
psi	Ψ	ψ
omega	Ω	ω

V

RESOURCES

69

Important International Organizations

These international organizations may have information of interest to writers who communicate with international readers and those whose employers deal in international trade. (For additional sources of international information, see lists 70–72.)

African, Caribbean, and Pacific Countries, Avenue Georges Henri 451, B-1200, Brussels, Belgium.

African Development Bank, 01, BP 1387, Abidjan 01, Ivory Coast.

Agency for Cultural and Technical Cooperation, 13 quai Andre-Citroen, F-75015, Paris, France.

Arab Bank for Economic Development, Sayed Abdel Rahman El Mahdi Avenue, P.O. Box 2640, Khartoum, Sudan.

Arab Fund for Economic and Social Development, P.O. Box 21923, Safat 13080, Kuwait.

Arab League, Midan Attahrir, Tahrir Square, P.O. Box 11642, Cairo, Egypt.

Arab Monetary Fund, P.O. Box 2818, Abu Dhabi, United Arab Emirates.

Asia Pacific Economic Cooperation, Ministry of Trade and Industry, Public Relations, 8 Shenton Way No. 48-01, Treasury Building, Singapore, Singapore.

Asian Development Bank, 6 ADB Avenue, Mandaluyong, METRO Manila, Philippines.

Association of Southeast Asian Nations, Jalan Sisingamangaraja 70A, Kebayoran Baru, P.O. Box 2072, Jakarta 12110, Indonesia.

Bank for International Settlements, Centralbannplatz 2, CH-4002 Basel, Switzerland.

Benelux Economic Union, rue de la Regence 39, B-1000, Brussels, Belgium.

Caribbean Community and Common Market, CARICOM, P.O. Box 10827, Bank of Guyana Building, 3rd floor, Avenue of the Republic, Georgetown, Guyana.

Caribbean Development Bank, P.O. Box 408, Wildey, Saint Michael, Barbados.

Central African Customs and Economic Union, BP 969, Banqui, Central African Republic.

Central African States Development Bank, BDEAC, Place du Gouvernement, BP 1177, Brazzaville, Congo.

Central American Bank for Economic Integration, Apartado Postal 772, Tegucigalpa DC, Honduras.

Central American Common Market, 4A Avda 10-25, Zona 14, Apdo Postal 1237, 01901 Guatemala City, Guatemala.

Colombo Plan, Colombo Plan Bureau, P.O. Box 596, 12 Melbourne Avenue, Colombo 4, Sri Lanka.

Commission for Social Development, c/o ECOSOC/DPCSD, United Nations, New York, NY 10017.

Commission on Human Settlements, c/o HABITAT, P.O. Box 30030, Nairobi, Kenya.

Commonwealth, c/o Commonwealth Secretariat, Marlborough House, Pall Mall, London SW1Y5HX, United Kingdom.

Commonwealth of Independent States, Kirov Street 17, 220000 Minsk, Belarus.

Council of Arab Economic Unity, BP 925100, Amman, Jordan.

Council of Europe, Palais de l'Europe, F-67075, Strasbourg CEDEX, France.

Customs Cooperation Council, rue de l'Industrie 26-38, B-1040 Brussels, Belgium.

East African Development Bank, 4 Nile Avenue, P.O. Box 7128, Kampala, Uganda.

Economic and Social Commission for Asia and the Pacific, United Nations Building, Rajadamnern Avenue, Bangkok 10200, Thailand.

Economic and Social Commission for Western Asia, P.O. Box 927115, Amman, Jordan (temporary address).

Economic and Social Council, United Nations, New York, NY 10017.

Economic Commission for Africa, P.O. Box 3001-3005, Addis Ababa, Ethiopia.

Economic Commission for Europe, Palais des Nations, CH-1211 Geneva 10, Switzerland.

Economic Commission for Latin America and the Caribbean, Edificio Naciones Unidas, Avenida Dag Hammarskjold, Casilla 179 D, Santiago, Chile.

Economic Community of Central African States, CEEAC, BP 2112, Libreville, Gabon.

Economic Community of West African States, 6 King George V Road, PMB 12745, Lagos, Nigeria.

Economic Cooperation Organization, 5 Hejab Avenue, Bd Kesh-avarz, P.O. Box 14155-6176, Teheran, Iran.

European Bank for Reconstruction and Development, One Exchange Square, London EC2A 2EH, United Kingdom.

European Free Trade Association, 9-11 rue de Varembe, CH-1211 Geneva 20, Switzerland.

European Investment Bank, Bd Konrad Adenauer 100, L-2950 Luxembourg, Luxembourg.

European Union, c/o European Commission, rue de la Loi 200, B-1049 Brussels, Belgium.

Gulf Cooperation Council, P.O. Box 7431, Riyadh 11462, Saudi Arabia.

Inter-American Development Bank, 1300 New York Avenue, NW, Washington, DC 10577.

International Bank for Reconstruction and Development [World Bank], 1818 H Street, NW, Washington, DC 20433.

International Chamber of Commerce, 38 Cours Albert 1st, F-75008 Paris, France.

International Confederation of Free Trade Unions, International Trade Union House, Bd Emile Jacqmain 155, B-1210 Brussels, Belgium.

International Development Association, 1818 H Street, NW, Washington, DC 20433.

International Energy Agency, 2 rue Andre Pascal, F-75775 Paris CEDEX 16, France.

International Finance Corporation, 1818 H Street, NW, Washington, DC 20433.

International Labor Organization, International Labor Office, 4 route des Morillons, CH-1211 Geneva 22, Switzerland.

International Monetary Fund, 700 19th Street, NW, Washington, DC 20431.

International Organization for Standardization, CP56, 1 rue de Varembe, CH-1211 Geneva 20, Switzerland.

International Telecommunication Union, Place des Nations, 1211 Geneva 20, Switzerland.

International Telecommunications Satellite Organization, IN-TELSAT, 3400 International Drive, NW, Washington, DC 20008.

Islamic Development Bank, P.O. Box 5925, Jeddah 21432, Saudi Arabia.

Latin American Economic System, SELA, Avda Francisco de Miranda, Torre Europa, piso 4, Chacaito, Apartado de Correos 17035, Caracas 1010-A, Venezuela.

Nordic Council, Tyrgatan 7, Box 19506, S-104 32 Stockholm, Sweden.

Nordic Investment Bank, Fabiansgatan 34, PB 249 SF-00171 Helsinki, Finland.

North Atlantic Cooperation Council, c/o NATO, B-1110 Brussels, Belgium.

North Atlantic Treaty Organization, B-110 Brussels, Belgium.

Organization for Economic Cooperation and Development, 2 rue Andre Pascal, F-75775 Paris CEDEX 16, France.

Organization of African Unity, P.O. Box 3243 Addis Ababa, Ethiopia.

Organization of American States, corner of 17th Street and Constitution Avenue, NW, Washington, DC 20006.

Organization of Arab Petroleum Exporting Countries, P.O. Box 20501, Safat 13066, Kuwait.

Organization of Eastern Caribbean States, P.O. Box 179, The Morne, Castries, Saint Lucia.

Organization of Petroleum Exporting Countries, Obere Donaustrasse 93, A-1020 Vienna, Austria.

South Asian Association for Regional Cooperation, P.O. Box 4222, Kathmandu, Nepal.

South Pacific Commission, Anse Vata BP D5 Noumea CEDEX, New Caledonia.

Southern African Development Community, Private Bag 008, Gaborne, Botswana.

United Nations, New York, NY 10017.

United Nations Conference on Trade and Development, Palais des Nations, CH-1211 Geneva 10, Switzerland.

United Nations Development Program, One United National Plaza, New York, NY 10017.

United Nations Industrial Development Organization, Vienna International Center, P.O. Box 300, A-1400 Vienna, Austria.

Universal Postal Union, Bureau International de l'UPU, Weltpoststrasse 4, CH-3000 Berne 15, Switzerland.

West African Development Bank, BOAD, BP 1172, 68 av de la liberation, Lome, Togo.

Western European Union, rue de la Regence 4, B-1000 Brussels, Belgium.

World Health Organization, CH-1211 Geneva 27, Switzerland.

World Trade Organization [replacing **General Agreement on Tariffs and Trade**], 154 rue de Lausanne, CH-1211 Geneva 21, Switzerland.

70

Foreign Embassies in the United States

Writers who need to learn more about the people with whom they communicate in other countries or who need to describe social, economic, or other conditions in the countries may find such information in the foreign embassies located in the United States. You may, for example, want to know the correct way to state someone's title in your letter or may need to describe a region in the other country where your company would like to market a product. This list has the addresses of all important foreign embassies in the United States. (See list 71 for addresses of U.S. embassies throughout the world.) Address your letter to the Embassy of [Country Name], unless another office is indicated (see *Cuba*, for example).

Afghanistan: 2341 Wyoming Avenue, NW, Washington, DC 20008.

Albania: 1511 K Street, NW, Suite 1010, Washington, DC 20005.

Algeria: 2118 Kalorama Road, NW, Washington, DC 20008.

Angola: 1819 L Street, NW, Suite 400, Washington, DC 20036.

Antigua and Barbuda: 3216 New Mexico Avenue, NW, Washington, DC 20011.

Argentina: 1600 New Hampshire Avenue, NW, Washington, DC 20009.

Armenia: 1660 L Street, NW, Suite 210, Washington, DC 20036.

Australia: 1601 Massachusetts Avenue, NW, Washington, DC 20036.

Austria: 3524 International Court, NW, Washington, DC 20008.

Azerbaijan: 927 15th Street, NW, Washington, DC 20005 (temporary address).

Bahamas, The: 2220 Massachusetts Avenue, NW, Washington, DC 20008.

Bahrain: 3502 International Drive, NW, Washington, DC 20008.

Bangladesh: 2201 Wisconsin Avenue, NW, Washington, DC 20007.

Barbados: 2144 Wyoming Avenue, NW, Washington, DC 20008.

Belarus: 1619 New Hampshire Avenue, NW, Washington, DC 20009.

Belgium: 3330 Garfield Street, NW, Washington, DC 20008.

Belize: 2535 Massachusetts Avenue, NW, Washington, DC 20008.

Benin: 2737 Cathedral Avenue, NW, Washington, DC 20008.

Bolivia: 3014 Massachusetts Avenue, NW, Washington, DC 20008.

Bosnia and Herzegovina: 1707 L Street, NW, Suite 760, Washington, DC 20036.

Botswana: 3400 International Drive, NW, Suite 7M, Washington, DC 20008.

Brazil: 3006 Massachusetts Avenue, NW, Washington, DC 20008.

Brunei: 2600 Virginia Avenue, NW, Washington, DC 20037.

Bulgaria: 1621 22nd Street, NW, Washington, DC 20008.

Burkina Faso: 2340 Massachusetts Avenue, NW, Washington, DC 20008.

Burma: 2300 S Street, NW, Washington, DC 20008.

Burundi: 2233 Wisconsin Avenue, NW, Suite 212, Washington, DC 20007.

Cameroon: 2349 Massachusetts Avenue, NW, Washington, DC 20008.

Canada: 501 Pennsylvania Avenue, NW, Washington, DC 20001.

Cape Verde: 3415 Massachusetts Avenue, NW, Washington, DC 20007.

Central African Republic: 1618 22nd Street, NW, Washington, DC 20008.

Chad: 2002 R Street, NW, Washington, DC 20009.

Chile: 1732 Massachusetts Avenue, NW, Washington, DC 20036.

China: 2300 Connecticut Avenue, NW, Washington, DC 20008.

Colombia: 2118 Leroy Place, NW, Washington, DC 20008.

Comoros: c/o United Nations, 336 East 45 Street, 2nd Floor, New York, NY 10017 (temporary address).

Congo: 4891 Colorado Avenue, NW, Washington, DC 20011.

Costa Rica: 2114 S Street, NW, Washington, DC 20008.

Croatia: 2343 Massachusetts Avenue, NW, Washington, DC 20008.

Cuba: Cuban Interests Section, c/o Swiss Embassy, 2630 and 2639 16th Street, NW, Washington, DC 20009.

Cyprus: 2211 R Street, NW, Washington, DC 20008.

Czech Republic: 3900 Spring of Freedom Street, NW, Washington, DC 20008.

Denmark: 3200 Whitehaven Street, NW, Washington, DC 20008.

Djibouti: 1156 15th Street, NW, Suite 515, Washington, DC 20005.

Dominican Republic: 1715 22nd Street, NW, Washington, DC 20008.

Ecuador: 2535 15th Street, NW, Washington, DC 20009.

Egypt: 3521 International Court, NW, Washington, DC 20008.

El Salvador: 2308 California Street, NW, Washington, DC 20008.

Equatorial Guinea: 57 Magnolia Avenue, Mount Vernon, NY 10553 (temporary address).

Eritrea: 910 17th Street, NW, Suite 400, Washington, DC 20006.

Estonia: 1030 15th Street, NW, Suite 1000, Washington, DC 20005.

Ethiopia: 2134 Kalorama Road, NW, Washington, DC 20008.

Fiji: 2233 Wisconsin Avenue, NW, Suite 240, Washington, DC 20007.

Finland: 3301 Massachusetts Avenue, NW, Washington, DC 20008.

France: 4101 Reservoir Road, NW, Washington, DC 20007.

Gabon: 2233 Wisconsin Avenue, NW, Suite 200, Washington, DC 20007.

Gambia, The: 1155 15th Street, NW, Suite 1000, Washington, DC 20005.

Georgia: 1511 K Street, NW, Suite 424, Washington, DC 20005.

Germany: 4645 Reservoir Road, NW, Washington, DC 20007.

Ghana: 3512 International Drive, NW, Washington, DC 20008.

Greece: 2221 Massachusetts Avenue, NW, Washington, DC 20008.

Grenada: 1701 New Hampshire Avenue, NW, Washington, DC 20009.

Guatemala: 2220 R Street, NW, Washington, DC 20008.

Guinea: 2112 Leroy Place, NW, Washington, DC 20008.

Guinea-Bissau: 918 16th Street, NW, Mezzanine Suite, Washington, DC 20006.

Guyana: 2490 Tracy Place, NW, Washington, DC 20008.

Haiti: 2311 Massachusetts Avenue, NW, Washington, DC 20008.

Honduras: 3007 Tilden Street, NW, Washington, DC 20008.

Hungary: 3910 Shoemaker Street, NW, Washington, DC 20008.

Iceland: 1156 15th Street, NW, Suite 1200, Washington, DC 20005.

India: 2107 Massachusetts Avenue, NW, Washington, DC 20008.

Indonesia: 2020 Massachusetts Avenue, NW, Washington, DC 20036.

Iran: Iranian Interests Section, c/o Pakistani Embassy, 2209 Wisconsin Avenue, NW, Washington, DC 20007.

Iraq: Iraqi Interests Section, c/o Algerian Embassy, 1801 P Street, NW, Washington, DC 20036.

Ireland: 2234 Massachusetts Avenue, NW, Washington, DC 20008.

Israel: 3514 International Drive, NW, Washington, DC 20008.

Italy: 1601 Fuller Street, NW, Washington, DC 20009.

Ivory Coast: 2424 Massachusetts Avenue, NW, Washington, DC 20008.

Jamaica: 1520 New Hampshire Avenue, NW, Washington, DC 20036.

Japan: 2520 Massachusetts Avenue, NW, Washington, DC 20008.

Jordan: 3504 International Drive, NW, Washington, DC 20008.

Kazakhstan: 3421 Massachusetts Avenue, NW, Washington, DC 20008 (temporary address).

Kenya: 2249 R Street, NW, Washington, DC 20008.

Korea, South: 2540 Massachusetts Avenue, NW, Washington, DC 20008.

Kuwait: 2940 Tilden Street, NW, Washington, DC 20008.

Kyrgyzstan: 1511 K Street, NW, Suite 705, Washington, DC 20036.

Laos: 2222 S Street, NW, Washington, DC 20008.

Latvia: 4325 17th Street, NW, Washington, DC 20011.

Lebanon: 2560 28th Street, NW, Washington, DC 20008.

Lesotho: 2511 Massachusetts Avenue, NW, Washington, DC 20008.

Liberia: 5201 16th Street, NW, Washington, DC 20011.

Lithuania: 2622 16th Street, NW, Washington, DC 20009.

Luxembourg: 2200 Massachusetts Avenue, NW, Washington, DC 20008.

Madagascar: 2374 Massachusetts Avenue, NW, Washington, DC 20008.

Malawi: 2408 Massachusetts Avenue, NW, Washington, DC 20008.

Malaysia: 2401 Massachusetts Avenue, NW, Washington, DC 20008.

Mali: 2130 R Street, NW, Washington, DC 20008.

Malta: 2017 Connecticut Avenue, NW, Washington, DC 20008.

Marshall Islands: 2433 Massachusetts Avenue, NW, Washington, DC 20008.

Mauritania: 2129 Leroy Place, NW, Washington, DC 20008.

Mauritius: 4301 Connecticut Avenue, NW, Suite 441, Washington, DC 20008.

Mexico: 1911 Pennsylvania Avenue, NW, Washington, DC 20006.

Micronesia: 1725 N Street, NW, Washington, DC 20036.

Moldova: 1511 K Street, NW, Suites 329 and 333, Washington, DC 20005.

Mongolia: 2833 M Street, NW, Washington, DC 20007.

Morocco: 1601 21st Street, NW, Washington, DC 20009.

Mozambique: 1990 M Street, NW, Suite 570, Washington, DC 20036.

Namibia: 1605 New Hampshire Avenue, NW, Washington, DC 20009.

Nepal: 2131 Leroy Place, NW, Washington, DC 20008.

Netherlands: 4200 Linnean Avenue, NW, Washington, DC 20008.

New Zealand: 37 Observatory Circle, NW, Washington, DC 20008.

Nicaragua: 1627 New Hampshire Avenue, NW, Washington, DC 20009.

Niger: 2204 R Street, NW, Washington, DC 20008.

Nigeria: 1333 16th Street, NW, Washington, DC 20036.

Norway: 2720 34th Street, NW, Washington, DC 20008.

Oman: 2535 Belmont Road, NW, Washington, DC 20008.

Pakistan: 2315 Massachusetts Avenue, NW, Washington, DC 20008.

Palau: Palau Liaison Office, 444 North Capital Street, NW, Washington, DC 20036.

Panama: 2862 McGill Terrace, NW, Washington, DC 20008.

Papua New Guinea: 1615 New Hampshire Avenue, NW, 3rd Floor, Washington, DC 20009.

Paraguay: 2400 Massachusetts Avenue, NW, Washington, DC 20008.

Peru: 1700 Massachusetts Avenue, NW, Washington, DC 20036.

Philippines: 1600 Massachusetts Avenue, NW, Washington, DC 20036.

Poland: 2640 16th Street, NW, Washington, DC 20009.

Portugal: 2125 Kalorama Road, NW, Washington, DC 20008.

Qatar: 600 New Hampshire Avenue, NW, Suite 1180, Washington, DC 20037.

Romania: 1607 23rd Street, NW, Washington, DC 20008.

Russia: 2650 Wisconsin Avenue, NW, Washington, DC 20007.

Rwanda: 1714 New Hampshire Avenue, NW, Washington, DC 20009.

Saint Kitts and Nevis: 2100 M Street, NW, Suite 608, Washington, DC 20037.

Saint Lucia: 3216 New Mexico Avenue, NW, Washington, DC 20016.

Saint Vincent and the Grenadines: 1717 Massachusetts Avenue, NW, Suite 102, Washington, DC 20036.

Sao Tome and Principe: Mission to United Nations, 122 East 42nd Street, Suite 1604, New York, NY 10168.

Saudi Arabia: 601 New Hampshire Avenue, NW, Washington, DC 20037.

Senegal: 2112 Wyoming Avenue, NW, Washington, DC 20008.

Seychelles: 820 Second Avenue, Suite 900F, New York, NY 10017.

Sierra Leone: 1701 19th Street, NW, Washington, DC 20009.

Singapore: 3501 International Place, NW, Washington, DC 20008.

Slovakia: 2201 Wisconsin Avenue, NW, Suite 380, Washington, DC 20007.

Slovenia: 1525 New Hampshire Avenue, NW, Washington, DC 20036.

South Africa: 3051 Massachusetts Avenue, NW, Washington, DC 20008.

Spain: 2375 Pennsylvania Avenue, NW, Washington, DC 20037.

Sri Lanka: 2148 Wyoming Avenue, NW, Washington, DC 20008.

Sudan: 2210 Massachusetts Avenue, NW, Washington, DC 20008.

Suriname: 4301 Connecticut Avenue, NW, Suite 108, Washington, DC 20008.

Swaziland: 3400 International Drive, NW, Washington, DC 20008.

Sweden: 1501 M Street, NW, Washington, DC 20005.

Switzerland: 2900 Cathedral Avenue, NW, Washington, DC 20008.

Syria: 2215 Wyoming Avenue, NW, Washington, DC 20008.

Tanzania: 2139 R Street, NW, Washington, DC 20008.

Thailand: 1024 Wisconsin Avenue, NW, Washington, DC 20007.

Togo: 2208 Massachusetts Avenue, NW, Washington, DC 20008.

Trinidad and Tobago: 1708 Massachusetts Avenue, NW, Washington, DC 20036.

Tunisia: 1515 Massachusetts Avenue, NW, Washington, DC 20005.

Turkey: 1714 Massachusetts Avenue, NW, Washington, DC 20036.

Turkmenistan: 1511 K Street, NW, Suite 412, Washington, DC 20005.

Uganda: 5911 16th Street, NW, Washington, DC 20011.

Ukraine: 3350 M Street, NW, Washington, DC 20007.

United Arab Emirates: 3000 K Street, NW, Suite 600, Washington, DC 20007.

United Kingdom: 3100 Massachusetts Avenue, NW, Washington, DC 20008.

Uruguay: 1918 F Street, NW, Washington, DC 20006.

Uzbekistan: 1511 K Street, NW, Suites 619 and 623, Washington, DC 20005.

Venezuela: 1099 30th Street, NW, Washington, DC 20007.

Western Samoa: 820 Second Avenue, Suite 800, New York, NY 10017.

Yemen: 2600 Virginia Avenue, NW, Suite 705, Washington, DC 20037.

Zaire: 1800 New Hampshire Avenue, NW, Washington, DC 20009.

Zambia: 2419 Massachusetts Avenue, NW, Washington, DC 20008.

Zimbabwe: 1608 New Hampshire Avenue, NW, Washington, DC 20009.

71

U.S. Embassies in Other Countries

When you can't find the information you need through a foreign embassy located in the United States (see list 70), try a U.S. embassy located in the other country. This list has the mailing addresses of U.S. embassies throughout the world. Address your letter to the Embassy of the United States of America, unless a different office is indicated (see *Cuba*, for example). When the address is a foreign location, rather than a U.S. APO number, put the country name on the last line of the address.

Albania: PSC 59, Box 100(A), APO AE 09624.

Algeria: B.P. 549, Alger-Gare 16000, Algiers.

Angola: Luanda, Department of State, Washington, DC 20521-2550 *(pouch).*

Argentina: Unit 4334, APO AA 34034.

Armenia: 18 Gen Bagramian, Yerevan.

Australia: Canberra, APO AP 96549.

Austria: Boltzmanngasse 16, A-1091, Vienna.

Azerbaijan: Azadliq Prospekti 83, Baku.

Bahamas, The: P.O. Box 9009, Miami, FL 33159.

Bahrain: Manama, FPO AE 09834-5100.

Bangladesh: G.P.O. Box 323, Dhaka 1000.

Barbados: Bridgetown, FPO AA 34055.

Belarus: Starovilenskaya 46-220002, Minsk.

Belgium: PSC 82, Box 002, APO AE 09724.

Belize: Unit 7401, APO AA 34025.

Benin: B.P. 2012, Cotonou.

Bolivia: La Paz, APO AA 34032.

Bosnia and Herzegovina: 43 Ul. Dure Dakovica, Sarajevo.

Botswana: P.O. Box 90, Gaborone.

Brazil: Unit 3500, APO AA 34030.

Brunei: Box B, APO AP 96440.

Bulgaria: Unit 1335, APO AE 09213-1335.

Burkina Faso: 01 B.P. 35, Ouagadougou.

Burma: Box B, APO AP 96546.

Burundi: B.P. 1720, Bujumbura.

Cambodia: Box P, APO AP 96546.

Cameroon: B.P. 817, Yaounde.

Canada: P.O. Box 5000, Ogdensburg, NY 13669-0430.

Cape Verde: Rue Abilio Macedo 81, C.P. 201, Praia.

Central African Republic: B.P. 924, Bangui.

Chad: B.P. 413, N'Djamena.

Chile: Santiago, APO AA 34033.

China: PSC 461, Box 50, FPO AP 96521-0002.

Colombia: Bogota, APO AA 34038.

Congo: B.P. 1015, Brazzaville.

Costa Rica: San Jose, APO AA 34020.

Croatia: Unit 1345, APO AE 09213-1345.

Cuba: U.S. Interests Section, c/o Swiss Embassy, Calzada between L and M Streets, Vedado, Havana.

Cyprus: Nicosia, FPO AE 09836.

Czech Republic: Unit 1330, APO AE 09213-1330.

Denmark: PSC 73, APO AE 09716.

Djibouti: B.P. 185, Djibouti.

Dominican Republic: Unit 5500, APO AA 34041.

Ecuador: Quito, APO AA 34039-3420.

Egypt: Unit 64900, APO AE 09839-4900.

El Salvador: Unit 3116, APO AA 34023.

Equatorial Guinea: P.O. Box 597, Malabo.

Eritrea: P.O. Box 211, Asmara.

Estonia: Kentmanni 20, Tallin EE 0001.

Ethiopia: P.O. Box 1014, Addis Ababa.

Fiji: P.O. Box 218, Suva.

Finland: Helsinki, APO AE 09723.

France: PSC 116, APO AE 09777.

Gabon: B.P. 4000, Libreville.

Gambia, The: Fajara, Kairaba Avenue, P.M.B. No. 19, Banjul.

Georgia: 25 Antoneli Street, Tbilisi 380026.

Germany: PSC 117, APO AE 09080.

Ghana: P.O. Box 194, Accra.

Greece: PSC 108, APO AE 09842.

Grenada: P.O. Box 54, Saint George's W.1.

Guatemala: Guatemala City, APO AA 34024.

Guinea: B.P. 603, Conakry.

Guinea-Bissau: C.P. 297, 1067 Codex, Bissau.

Guyana: P.O. Box 10507, Georgetown.

Haiti: P.O. Box 1761, Port-au-Prince.

Honduras: Tegucigalpa, APO AA 34022.

Hungary: Budapest, Department of State, Washington, DC 20521-5270 *(pouch)*.

Iceland: PSC 1003, Box 40, FPO AE 09728-0340.

India: Shanti Path, Chanakyapuri 110021, New Delhi.

Indonesia: Box 1, APO AP 96520.

Iraq: U.S. Interests Section, c/o Polish Embassy, P.O. Box 2447, Alwiyah, Baghdad.

Ireland: 42 Elgin Road, Ballsbridge, Dublin.

Israel: PSC 98, Box 100, APO AE 09830.

Italy: PSC 59, Box 100, APO AE 09624.

Ivory Coast: 01 B.P. 1712, Abidjan.

Jamaica: Jamaica Mutual Life Center, 3rd Floor, 2 Oxford Road, Kingston.

Japan: Unit 45004, Box 258, APO AP 96337-0001.

Jordan: Amman, APO AE 09892-0200.

Kazakhstan: 99/97 Furumanova Street, Almaty 480012.

Kenya: Unit 64100, APO AE 09831.

Korea, South: Unit 15550, APO AP 96205-0001.

Kuwait: Unit 69000, APO AE 09880-9000.

Kyrgyzstan: Erkindik Prospekt 66, Bishkek 720002.

Laos: Box V, APO AP 96546.

Latvia: PSC 78, Box R, APO AE 09723.

Lebanon: PSC 815, Box 2, FPO AE 09836-0002.

Lesotho: P.O. Box 333, Maseru 100.

Liberia: P.O. Box 10-0098, Mamba Point, Monrovia.

Lithuania: PSC 78, Box V, APO AE 09723.

Luxembourg: Unit 1410, APO AE 09132-5380.

Macedonia: U.S. Liaison Office, Skopje, Department of State, Washington, DC 20521-7120 *(pouch)*.

Madagascar: B.P. 620, Antananarivo.

Malawi: P.O. Box 30016, Lilongwe 3.

Malaysia: Kuala Lumpur, APO 96535-8152.

Mali: B.P. 34, Bamako.

Malta: P.O. Box 535, Valletta.

Marshall Islands: P.O. Box 1379, Majuro, MH 96960-1379.

Mauritania: B.P. 222, Nouakchott.

Mauritius: Port Louis, Department of State, Washington, DC 20521-2450 *(pouch).*

Mexico: P.O. Box 3087, Laredo, TX 78044-3087.

Micronesia: P.O. Box 1286, Pohnpei 96941.

Moldova: Strada Alexei Mateevich 103, Chisinau.

Mongolia: PSC 461, Box 300, FPO AP 96521-0002.

Morocco: PSC 74, Box 003, APO AE 09718.

Mozambique: P.O. Box 783, Maputo.

Namibia: Ausplan Building, 14 Lossen Street, Private Bag 12029, Ausspannplatz, Windhoek.

Nepal: Pani Pokhari, Kathmandu.

Netherlands: PSC 71, Box 1000, APO AE 09715.

New Zealand: PSC 467, Box 1, FPO AP 96531-1001.

Nicaragua: Managua, APO AA 34021.

Niger: B.P. 11201, Niamey.

Nigeria: P.O. Box 554, Lagos.

Norway: PSC 69, Box 1000, APO AE 09707.

Oman: P.O. Box 202, Code 115, Madinat Qaboos, Muscat.

Pakistan: Unit 62200, APO AE 09812-2200.

Palau: U.S. Liaison Office, P.O. Box 6028, Koror 96940.

Panama: Unit 0945, APO AA 34002.

Papua New Guinea: P.O. Box 1492, Port Moresby.

Paraguay: Unit 4711, APO AA 34036-0001.

Peru: Lima, APO AA 34031.

Philippines: Manila, APO AP 96440.

Poland: Unit 1340, APO AE 09213-1340.

Portugal: PSC 83, APO AE 09726.

Qatar: P.O. Box 2399, Doha.

Romania: Unit 1315, APO AE 09213-1315.

Russia: Moscow, APO AE 09721.

Rwanda: B.P. 28, Kigali.

Saudi Arabia: Unit 61307, APO AE 09803-1307.

Senegal: B.P. 49, Dakar.

Serbia and Montenegro: Unit 1310, APO AE 09213-1310.

Seychelles: Unit 62501, Box 148, APO AE 09815-2501.

Sierra Leone: Walpole and Siaka Stevens Streets, Freetown.

Singapore: Singapore City, FPO AP 96534.

Slovakia: Hviezdoslavovo Namestie 4, 81102 Bratislava.

Slovenia: Ljubljana, Department of State, Washington, DC 20521-7140 *(pouch)*.

South Africa: P.O. Box 9536, Pretoria 0001.

Spain: Madrid, APO AE 09642.

Sri Lanka: P.O. Box 106, Colombo.

Sudan: Khartoum, APO AE 09829.

Suriname: Paramaribo, Department of State, Washington, DC 20521-3390 *(pouch)*.

Swaziland: P.O. Box 199, Mbabane.

Sweden: Standvagen 101, S-115 89 Stockholm.

Switzerland: Jubilaeumstrasse 93, 3005 Bern.

Syria: P.O. Box 29, Damascus.

Taiwan: [unofficial contact] American Institute in Taiwan, 1700 North Moore Street, Suite 1700, Arlington, VA 22209-1996.

Tajikistan: Octyabrskaya Hotel, 105A Prospect Rudaki, Dushanbe 734001.

Tanzania: P.O. Box 9123, Dar es Salaam.

Thailand: Bangkok, APO AP 96546.

Togo: Rue Pelletier Caventou and Rue Vauban, Lome.

Trinidad and Tobago: P.O. Box 752, Port-of-Spain.

Tunisia: 144 Avenue de la Liberte, 1002 Tunis-Belvedere.

Turkey: PSC 93, Box 5000, APO AE 09823.

Turkmenistan: 9 Pushkin Street, Ashgabat.

Uganda: P.O. Box 7007, Kampala.

Ukraine: 10 Yuria Kotsyubynskoho, 254053 Kiev 53.

United Arab Emirates: Abu Dhabi, Department of State, Washington, DC 20521-6010 *(pouch)*.

United Kingdom: PSC 801, Box 40, FPO AE 09498-4040.

Uruguay: Montevido, APO AA 34035.

Uzbekistan: 82 Chilanzarskaya, Tashkent.

Venezuela: Caracas, APO AA 34037.

Vietnam: PSC 461, Box 400, FPO AP 96521-0002.

Western Samoa: P.O. Box 3430, Apia.

Yemen: P.O. Box 22347, Sanaa.

Zaire: Unit 31550, APO 09828.

Zambia: P.O. Box 31617, Lusaka.

Zimbabwe: P.O. Box 3340, Harare.

72

World Trade Center Offices in the United States

World Trade Center offices have a variety of information pertaining to trade in different regions throughout the world. Other offices located in a World Trade Center building, such as government agencies and international companies, may also have useful information. The following list includes several dozen main offices throughout the United States. Address your letters to World Trade Center, followed by the mailing address given here.

Alaska: University of Alaska, Anchorage, 421 West First Avenue, Suite 300, Anchorage, 99501.

Arizona: 201 North Central Avenue, Suite 2700, Phoenix, 85073.

California: 350 South Figueroa Street, Suite 172, Los Angeles, 90071.

Colorado: 1625 Broadway, Suite 680, Denver, 80202.

Connecticut: 177 State Street, 4th Floor, Bridgeport, 06604.

Delaware: 1207 King Street, P.O. Box 709, Wilmington, 19899.

District of Columbia: 6801 Oxon Hill Road at PortAmerica, Oxon Hill, MD 20745.

Florida: 1 World Trade Plaza, 80 Southwest 8th Street, Suite 1800, Miami, 33130.

Georgia: 303 Peachtree Street, NE, Lower Lobby 100, Atlanta, 30308.

Hawaii: 201 Merchant Street, Suite 1510, P.O. Box 2359, Honolulu, 96804.

Illinois: The Merchandise Mart, 200 World Trade Center, Suite 929, Chicago, 60654.

Indiana: 54 Monument Circle, Suite 600, Indianapolis, 46204.

Iowa: 3200 Ruan Center, 666 Grand Avenue, Des Moines, 50309.

Kansas: 350 West Douglas Avenue, Wichita, 67202.

Kentucky: 410 West Vine, Suite 290, Lexington, 40507.

Louisiana: 2 Canal Street, Suite 2900, New Orleans, 70130.

Maryland: Suite 1355, Baltimore, 21202.

Massachusetts: Executive Offices, Suite 50, Boston, 02210.

Michigan: 1251 Fort Street, Trenton, 48183.

Minnesota: 30 East 7th Street, Suite 400, Saint Paul, 55101.

Missouri: 121 South Meramec, Suite 1111, Saint Louis, 63105.

Nevada: P.O. Box 71961, Las Vegas, 89170.

New York: The Port Authority of New York & New Jersey, 1 World Trade Center, Suite 35E, New York, 10048.

North Carolina: c/o Greater Wilmington Chamber of Commerce, P.O. Box 330, Wilmington, 28402.

Ohio: 200 Tower City Center, 50 Public Square, Cleveland, 44113.

Oregon: 1 World Trade Center, 121 Southwest Salmon Street, Suite 250, Portland, 97204.

Pennsylvania: Koppers Building, Suite 2312, 436 7th Avenue, Pittsburgh, 15219.

Rhode Island: 1 West Exchange Street, Providence, 02903.

South Carolina: P.O. Box 975, Charleston, 29402.

Tennessee: 67 Madison Avenue, Suite 1004, Memphis, 38103.

Texas: 1200 Smith, Suite 700, Houston, 77002.

Virginia: Virginia Port Authority, 600 World Trade Center, Norfolk, 23510.

Washington: 1301 5th Avenue, Suite 2400, Seattle, 98101.

Wisconsin: Pfister Hotel, 424 East Wisconsin Avenue, Milwaukee, 53202.

73

State Tourism Offices in the United States

If you need general information about a state, you may find it at a state tourism office, which can provide information on anything from the range of weather and climate in the state to the type of industry and its location. (For specific information about a particular subject, such as state taxes, contact the appropriate state office or department, such as the state's Department of Revenue, usually located in the capital city.) The following list gives the address of one of the main tourism offices in each state (some states have more than one), except in Colorado, which currently has none.

Alabama: Bureau of Tourism & Travel, P.O. Box 4927, Montgomery, 36103.

Alaska: Alaska Division of Tourism, P.O. Box 110801, Juneau, 99811.

Arizona: Arizona Office of Tourism, 2702 North 3rd Street, Suite 4015, Phoenix, 85004.

Arkansas: Arkansas Department of Parks and Tourism, 1 Capitol Mall, Little Rock, 72201.

California: California Division of Tourism, P.O. Box 1499, Sacramento, 95812.

Connecticut: Tourism Promotion Service, Department of Economic Development, 865 Brook Street, Rocky Hill, 06067.

Delaware: Delaware Tourism Office, Delaware Economic Development Office, 99 Kings Highway, P.O. Box 1401, Dover, 19903.

District of Columbia: Office of Tourism & Promotion, 1212 New York Avenue, NW, #200, Washington, 20005.

Florida: Department of Commerce Visitors Inquiry, 126 Van Buren Street, Tallahassee, 32399.

Georgia: Tourist Division, P.O. Box 1776, Atlanta, 30301.

Hawaii: Hawaii Visitors Bureau, 2270 Kalakaua Avenue, Suite 801, Honolulu, 96815.

Idaho: Department of Commerce, Tourism Development, 700 West State Street, Boise, 83720.

Illinois: Illinois Bureau of Tourism, 100 West Randolph, Suite 3-400, Chicago, 60601.

Indiana: Indiana Department of Commerce, Tourism & Film Development Division, One North Capitol, Suite 700, Indianapolis, 46204.

Iowa: Iowa Department of Economic Development, Division of Tourism, 200 East Grand Avenue, Des Moines, 50309.

Kansas: Kansas Department of Commerce & Housing, Travel & Tourism Development Division, 700 Southwest Harrison Street, Suite 1300, Topeka, 66603.

Kentucky: Department of Travel Development, Department MR, P.O. Box 2011, Frankfort, 40602.

Louisiana: Office of Tourism, P.O. Box 94291, Baton Rouge, 70804.

Maine: Maine Publicity Bureau, P.O. Box 2300, Hallowell, 04347.

Maryland: Office of Tourism Development, 217 East Redwood Street, 9th Floor, Baltimore, 21202.

Massachusetts: Office of Travel and Tourism, 100 Cambridge Street, 13th Floor, Boston, 02202.

Michigan: Michigan Jobs Commission, Travel Bureau, P.O. Box 3393, Livonia, 48151.

Minnesota: Minnesota Office of Tourism, 100 Metro Square, 121 Seventh Place East, Saint Paul, 55101.

Mississippi: Department of Economic and Community Development, Tourism Development, P.O. Box 1705, Ocean Springs, 39566.

Missouri: Missouri Division of Tourism, Truman State Office Building, 301 West High Street, P.O. Box 1055, Jefferson City, 65102.

Montana: Department of Commerce, Travel Montana, P.O. Box 200533, Helena, 59620.

Nebraska: Department of Economic Development, Division of Travel and Tourism, P.O. Box 98913, Lincoln, 68509.

Nevada: Commission on Tourism, Capitol Complex, Carson City, 89710.

New Hampshire: Office of Travel and Tourism, P.O. Box 1856, Concord, 03302.

New Jersey: Division of Travel and Tourism, CN 826, Trenton, 08625.

New Mexico: New Mexico Department of Tourism, Room 751, Lamy Building, 491 Old Santa Fe Trail, Santa Fe, 87503.

New York: Division of Tourism, 1 Commerce Plaza, Albany, 12245.

North Carolina: Travel and Tourism Division, Department of Commerce, 430 North Salisbury Street, Raleigh, 27603.

North Dakota: North Dakota Tourism, 604 East Boulevard, Bismarck, 58505.

Ohio: Ohio Division of Travel and Tourism, P.O. Box 1001, Columbus, 43266.

Oklahoma: Oklahoma Tourism and Recreation Department, Literature Distribution Center, P.O. Box 60789, Oklahoma City, 73146.

Oregon: Tourism Commission, 775 Summer Street, NE, Salem, 97310.

Pennsylvania: Office of Travel & Tourism, Room 453, Forum Building, Harrisburg, 17120.

Rhode Island: Rhode Island Tourism Division, 1 West Exchange Street, Providence, 02903.

South Carolina: South Carolina Division of Tourism, Box 71, Columbia, 29202.

Tennessee: Department of Tourist Development, P.O. Box 23170, Nashville, 37202.

Texas: Travel Information Services, Texas Department of Transportation, P.O. Box 5064, Austin, 78763.

Utah: Utah Travel Council, Council Hall, Capitol Hill, Salt Lake City, 84114.

Vermont: Department of Travel and Tourism, 134 State Street, P.O. Box 1471, Montpelier, 05601.

Virginia: Virginia Division of Tourism, 901 East Byrd Street, Richmond, 23219.

Washington: Washington State Department of Community, Trade and Economic Development, 906 Columbia Street, SW, P.O. Box 48300, Olympia, 98504.

West Virginia: Division of Tourism, 2101 Washington Street East, Charleston, 25305.

Wisconsin: Travel Information, Department of Tourism, Box 7976, Madison, 53707.

Wyoming: Wyoming Division of Tourism, I-25 at College Drive, Cheyenne, 82002.

U.S. Chambers of Commerce in One Hundred of the Largest U.S. Cities

When you need city or community information, one of the most helpful of all organizations is the chamber of commerce, development board, visitors bureau, or similar organization serving a particular city or metropolitan area. If the organization doesn't have the information you need, a knowledgeable staff can usually direct you to another source. This list has addresses, arranged by state, for chambers of commerce and similar organizations in one hundred of the most populous U.S. cities.

ALABAMA

Birmingham: Chamber of Commerce, 2027 First Avenue North, 35202.

Mobile: Chamber of Commerce, P.O. Box 2187, 36652.

Montgomery: Montgomery Area Chamber of Commerce, P.O. Box 79, 36101.

ALASKA

Anchorage: Chamber of Commerce, 441 West 5th Avenue, Suite 300, 99501.

ARIZONA

Mesa: Convention and Visitor's Bureau, 120 Center, 85201.

Phoenix: Chamber of Commerce, 201 North Central Avenue, 27th Floor, 85073.

Tucson: Chamber of Commerce, P.O. Box 991, 85702.

CALIFORNIA

Anaheim: Chamber of Commerce, 100 South Anaheim Boulevard, Suite 300, 92805.

Bakersfield: Greater Bakersfield Chamber of Commerce, 1033 Truxtun Avenue, 93301.

Fremont: Chamber of Commerce, 2201 Walnut Avenue, Suite 110, 94538.

Fresno: Chamber of Commerce, 2331 Fresno Street, 93721.

Huntington Beach: Chamber of Commerce, Seacliff Office Park, 2100 Main Street, #200, Huntington Beach, 92648.

Long Beach: Chamber of Commerce, One World Trade Center, Suite 350, 90831.

Los Angeles: Chamber of Commerce, 350 South Bixel Street, P.O. Box 3696, 90051.

Oakland: Oakland Metropolitan Chamber of Commerce, 475 14th Street, 94612.

Riverside: Chamber of Commerce, 3685 Main Street, Suite 350, 92501.

Sacramento: Chamber of Commerce, 917 7th Street, 95814.

San Bernardino: San Bernardino Area Chamber of Commerce, 546 West 6th Street, P.O. Box 658, 92402.

San Diego: Greater San Diego Chamber of Commerce, 402 West Broadway, Suite 1000, 92101.

San Francisco: Convention and Visitors Bureau, 201 3rd Street, Suite 900, 94103.

San Jose: Chamber of Commerce, 180 South Market Street, 95113.

Santa Ana: Chamber of Commerce, 856 North Ross Street, P.O. Box 205, Santa Ana, 92701.

Stockton: Chamber of Commerce, 445, West Weber Avenue, Suite 220, 95203.

COLORADO

Aurora: Aurora Planning Department, 1470 South Havana Street, Room 608, 80012.

Colorado Springs: Chamber of Commerce, P.O. Box B, 80901.

Denver: Denver Metro Chamber of Commerce, 1445 Market Street, 80202.

DISTRICT OF COLUMBIA

Washington: D.C. Chamber of Commerce, 1301 Pennsylvania Avenue, NW, Suite 309, 20004.

FLORIDA

Hialeah: Hialeah-Dade Development, Inc., 501 Palm Avenue, 33010.

Jacksonville: Chamber of Commerce, 3 Independent Drive, 32202.

Miami: Metro-Dade Department of Planning, Development,

and Regulation, Research Division, 111 Northwest 1st Street, Suite 1220, 33128.

Saint Petersburg: Saint Petersburg Area Chamber of Commerce, P.O. Box 1371, 33731.

Tampa: Chamber of Commerce, 401 East Jackson Street, P.O. Box 420, 33601.

GEORGIA

Atlanta: Metro Atlanta Chamber of Commerce, 235 International Boulevard, NW, 30303.

Columbus: Chamber of Commerce, P.O. Box 1200, 31902.

HAWAII

Honolulu: Hawaii Visitors Bureau, 2270 Kalakaua Avenue, 96815.

ILLINOIS

Chicago: Chicagoland Chamber of Commerce, 1 IBM Plaza, Suite 2800, 60611.

INDIANA

Fort Wayne: Chamber of Commerce, 826 Ewing Street, 46802.

Indianapolis: Chamber of Commerce, 320 North Meridian Street, 46204.

IOWA

Des Moines: Greater Des Moines Chamber of Commerce Federation, 601 Locust Street, Suite 100, 50309.

KANSAS

Wichita: Chamber of Commerce, 350 West Douglas, 67202.

KENTUCKY

Lexington: Greater Lexington Chamber of Commerce, 330 East Main Street, 40507.

Louisville: Louisville Area Chamber of Commerce, 600 West Main Street, 40202.

LOUISIANA

Baton Rouge: Chamber of Commerce, P.O. Box 3217, 70821.

New Orleans: New Orleans Metropolitan Convention and Visitors Bureau, Inc., 1520 Sugar Bowl Drive, 70112.

Shreveport: Chamber of Commerce, P.O. Box 20074, 71120.

MARYLAND

Baltimore: Greater Baltimore Committee, 111 South Calvert Street, Suite 1500, 21202.

MASSACHUSETTS

Boston: Greater Boston Chamber of Commerce, 1 Beacon Street, 4th Floor, 02108.

MICHIGAN

Detroit: Greater Detroit Chamber of Commerce, 600 West Lafayette Boulevard, P.O. Box 33840, 48232.

Grand Rapids: Chamber of Commerce, 111 Pearl Street, NW, 49503.

MINNESOTA

Minneapolis: City of Minneapolis Office of Public Affairs, 323M City Hall, 350 South 5th Street, 55415.

Saint Paul: Saint Paul Area Chamber of Commerce, 332 Minnesota Street, Suite N-205, 55101.

MISSISSIPPI

Jackson: Metro Jackson Chamber of Commerce, P.O. Box 22548, 39225.

MISSOURI

Kansas City: Greater Kansas City Chamber of Commerce, 911 Main Street, Suite 2600, 64105.

Saint Louis: Saint Louis Community Development Agency, 330 North 15th Street, 63103.

NEBRASKA

Lincoln: Chamber of Commerce, P.O. Box 83006, 68501.

Omaha: Greater Omaha Chamber of Commerce, 1301 Harney Street, 68102.

NEVADA

Las Vegas: Chamber of Commerce, 711 East Desert Inn Road, 89109.

NEW JERSEY

Jersey City: Hudson County Chamber of Commerce, 574 Summit Avenue, Suite 404, 07306.

Newark: Regional Business Partnership, 1 Newark Center, 07102.

NEW MEXICO

Albuquerque: Convention and Visitors Bureau, P.O. Box 26866, 87125.

NEW YORK

Buffalo: Greater Buffalo Partnership, 300 Main Place Tower, 14202.

New York: Convention and Visitors Bureau, 2 Columbus Circle, 10019.

Rochester: Chamber of Commerce, 55 St. Paul Street, 14604.

Yonkers: Chamber of Commerce, 20 South Broadway, 12th Floor, 10701.

NORTH CAROLINA

Charlotte: Chamber of Commerce, P.O. Box 32785, 28232.

Greensboro: Chamber of Commerce, P.O. Box 3246, 27402.

Raleigh: Chamber of Commerce, 800 South Salisbury Street, P.O. Box 2978, 27602.

OHIO

Akron: Akron Regional Development Board, Cascade Plaza, 44308.

Cincinnati: Chamber of Commerce, 300 Carew Tower, 441 Vine Street, 45202.

Cleveland: Greater Cleveland Growth Association, 200 Tower City Center, 50 Public Square, 44113.

Columbus: Chamber of Commerce, 37 North High Street, 43215.

Dayton: Dayton Chamber of Commerce, 1 Chamber Plaza, 45402.

Toledo: Toledo Area Chamber of Commerce, 300 Madison Avenue, Suite 200, 43604.

OKLAHOMA

Oklahoma City: Chamber of Commerce, Economic Development Division, 123 Park Avenue, 73102.

Tulsa: Metropolitan Tulsa Chamber of Commerce, 616 South Boston Avenue, Suite 100, 74119.

OREGON

Portland: Portland Metropolitan Chamber of Commerce, 221 Northwest Second Avenue, 97209.

PENNSYLVANIA

Philadelphia: Office of City Representative and City Commerce Director, 1600 Arch Street, 13th Floor, 19103.

Pittsburgh: Greater Pittsburgh Convention and Visitors Bureau, 4 Gateway Center, 15222.

TENNESSEE

Memphis: Memphis Area Chamber of Commerce, 22 North Front Street, Suite 200, P.O. Box 224, 38101.

Nashville: Chamber of Commerce, 161 4th Avenue, 37219.

TEXAS

Arlington: The Arlington Chamber of Commerce, 316 Main Street, 76010.

Austin: Chamber of Commerce, P.O. Box 1967, 78767.

Corpus Christi: Greater Corpus Christi Business Alliance, P.O. Box 640, 78403.

Dallas: Greater Dallas Chamber, Information Services, 1201 Elm Street, Suite 2000, 75270.

El Paso: Greater El Paso Chamber of Commerce, 10 Civic Center Plaza, 79901.

Fort Worth: Chamber of Commerce, 777 Taylor Street, #900, 76102.

Garland: Chamber of Commerce, 914 South Garland Avenue, 75040.

Houston: Greater Houston Partnership, 1200 Smith Street, 77002.

Lubbock: Chamber of Commerce, P.O. Box 561, 79408.

San Antonio: Chamber of Commerce, 602 East Commerce, P.O. Box 1628, 78296.

VIRGINIA

Chesapeake: Hampton Roads Chamber of Commerce, 420 Bank Street, P.O. Box 327, 23501.

Hampton [Newport News]: Virginia Peninsula Chamber of Commerce, 6 Manhattan Square, P.O. Box 7269, 23666.

Norfolk: Hampton Roads Chamber of Commerce, 420 Bank Street, P.O. Box 327, 23501.

Richmond: Chamber of Commerce, P.O. Box 12280, 23241.

Virginia Beach: Virginia Beach Department of Economic Development, One Columbus Center, Suite 300, 23462.

WASHINGTON

Seattle: Greater Seattle Chamber of Commerce, 1301 5th Avenue, Suite 2400, 98101.

Spokane: Chamber of Commerce, 1020 West Riverside Avenue, P.O. Box 2147, 99210.

Tacoma: Chamber of Commerce, P.O. Box 1933, 98401.

WISCONSIN

Madison: Greater Madison Chamber of Commerce, P.O. Box 71, 53701.

Milwaukee: Metropolitan Milwaukee Association of Commerce, 756 North Milwaukee Street, 53202.

75

Major Independent and Governmental Agencies and Other Organizations

Numerous governmental and other organizations exist for a variety of purposes and deal with a wide range of subjects, from environmental protection to transportation safety to patents and trademarks. Writers who need information on a specific topic may be able to find an agency that specializes in that topic. The following are some of the agencies and other organizations that deal with many areas of interest to business writers.

Administrative Conference of the United States, 2120 L Street, NW, Suite 500, Washington, DC 20037.

Bureau of Economic Analysis, Department of Commerce, 1441 L Street, NW, Washington, DC 20230.

Bureau of Export Administration, Department of Commerce, P.O. Box 273, Washington, DC 20044.

Bureau of the Census, Department of Commerce, 4700 Silver Hill Road, Suitland, MD 20746.

Commodities Futures Trading Commission, 2033 K Street, NW, Washington, DC 20581.

Consumer Product Safety Commission, East West Towers, 4330 East West Highway, Bethesda, MD 20814.

Economic Development Administration, Department of Commerce, 14th Street and Constitution Avenue, NW, Washington, DC 20230.

Employment and Training Administration, Department of Labor, 200 Constitution Avenue, NW, Washington, DC 20210.

Employment Standards Administration, Department of Labor, 200 Constitution Avenue, NW, Washington, DC 20210.

Environmental Protection Agency, 401 M Street, SW, Washington, DC 20460.

Equal Employment Opportunity Commission, Office of Communications and Legislative Affairs, 1801 L Street, NW, Washington, DC 20507.

Export-Import Bank of the United States, 811 Vermont Avenue, NW, Washington, DC 20571.

Federal Communications Commission, 1919 M Street, NW, Washington, DC 20554.

Federal Deposit Insurance Corporation, 550 17th Street, NW, Washington, DC 20429.

Federal Energy Regulatory Commission, 941 North Capitol Street, NE, Washington, DC 20426.

Federal Labor Relations Authority, 607 14th Street, NW, Washington, DC 20424.

Federal Maritime Commission, 800 North Capitol Street, NW, Washington, DC 20573.

Federal Mediation and Conciliation Service, 2100 K Street, NW, Washington, DC 20427.

Federal Reserve System, 20th and C Streets, NW, Washington, DC 20551.

Federal Trade Commission, 6th Street and Pennsylvania Avenue, NW, Washington, DC 20580.

General Accounting Office, 441 G Street, NW, Washington, DC 20548.

General Services Administration, 18th and F Streets, NW, Washington, DC 20405.

Government Printing Office, North Capitol & H Streets, NW, Washington, DC 20401.

Immigration and Naturalization Service, U.S. Department of Justice, 425 I Street, NW, Room 7116, Washington, DC 20536.

Internal Revenue Service, Department of the Treasury, 1111 Constitution Avenue, NW, Washington, DC 20224.

Legal Services Corporation, 750 First Street, NE, Washington, DC 20002.

Library of Congress, 10 First Street, SE, Washington, DC 20540.

Merit Systems Protection Board, 1120 Vermont Avenue, NW, Washington, DC 20419.

National Commission on Libraries and Information Science, 1110 Vermont Avenue, NW, Suite 820, Washington, DC 20005.

National Labor Relations Board, 1099 14th Street, NW, Washington, DC 20570.

National Mediation Board, 1301 K Street, NW, Suite 250, Washington, DC 20572.

National Transportation Safety Board, 490 L'Enfant Plaza, SW, Washington, DC 20594.

Occupational Safety and Health Administration, 200 Constitution Avenue, NW, Washington, DC 20210.

Occupational Safety and Health Review Commission, 1120 20th Street, NW, Washington, DC 20036.

Office for Civil Rights, Department of Health and Human Services, 330 Independence Avenue, SW, Washington, DC 20201.

Office of Technology Assessment, 600 Pennsylvania Avenue, SE, Washington, DC 20510.

Office of the United States Trade Representative, 600 17th Street, NW, Washington, DC 20506.

Patent and Trademark Office, Department of Commerce, Washington, DC 20231.

Securities and Exchange Commission, 450 5th Street, NW, Washington, DC 20549.

Small Business Administration, 409 3rd Street, SW, Washington, DC 20416.

Social Security Administration, Department of Health and Human Services, 6401 Security Boulevard, Baltimore, MD 21235.

Trade and Development Agency, State Annex 16, Room 309, Washington, DC 20523.

Trade Regulation Enforcement, Federal Trade Commission, Enforcement Division, 6th Street and Pennsylvania Avenue, NW, Washington, DC 20580.

U.S. Agency for International Development, 320 21st Street, NW, Washington, DC 20523.

U.S. Commission on Civil Rights, 624 9th Street, NW, Washington, DC 20425.

U.S. Customs Service, Department of the Treasury, 1301 Constitution Avenue, NW, Washington, DC 20229.

U.S. Information Agency, 301 Fourth Street, SW, Washington, DC 20547.

U.S. International Trade Commission, 500 E Street, NW, Washington, DC 20436.

U.S. Postal Service, 475 L'Enfant Plaza, SW, Washington, DC 20260.

U.S. Trade Commission, 500 E Street, SW, Washington, DC 20436.

76

Important U.S. Associations and Societies

Thousands of private, often nonprofit, associations and societies serve millions of members across the United States. These organizations were founded to provide information, education, and other resources to their members. Typically, an association or society devotes itself to a specific subject, such as chemical manufacturing or direct-mail marketing. Because there are so many of these groups specializing in a wide range of subjects, writers often can find valuable, authoritative information—from either the headquarters office or one of the group's members—that isn't available elsewhere. The following is a small sample of associations and societies that may have useful information for business writers (for a complete list, consult *Gale's Encyclopedia of Associations,* available in most library reference rooms).

Aerospace Industries Association of America, 1250 Eye Street, NW, Washington, DC 20005.

Air and Waste Management Association, One Gateway Center, Pittsburgh, PA 15222.

Air Transport Association of America, 1301 Pennsylvania Avenue, NW, Suite 1100, Washington, DC 20004.

American Arbitration Association, 140 West 51st Street, New York, NY 10020.

American Association of Colleges and Universities, 1818 R Street, NW, Washington, DC 20009.

American Automobile Association, 1000 AAA Drive, Heathrow, FL 32746.

American Bankers Association, 1120 Connecticut Avenue, NW, Washington, DC 20036.

American Booksellers Association, 828 South Broadway, Tarrytown, NY 10591.

American Business Clubs, 3315 North Main Street, High Point, NC 27265.

American Business Press, 675 Third Avenue, Suite 415, New York, NY 10017.

American Business Women's Association, 9100 Ward Parkway, P.O. Box 8728, Kansas City, MO 64114.

American Chemical Society, 1155 16th Street, NW, Washington, DC 20036.

American Civil Liberties Union, 132 West 43rd Street, New York, NY 10036.

American Economics Association, 2014 Broadway, Suite 305, Nashville, TN 37203.

American Federation of Television and Radio Artists, 260 Madison Avenue, 7th Floor, New York, NY 10016.

American Gas Association, 1515 Wilson Boulevard, Arlington, VA 22209.

American Hotel and Motel Association, 1201 New York Avenue, NW, Washington, DC 20005.

American Institute of Architects, 1735 New York Avenue, NW, Washington, DC 20006.

American Institute of Biological Sciences, 730 11th Street, NW, Washington, DC 20001.

American Institute of Certified Public Accountants, 1211 Avenue of the Americas, New York, NY 10036.

American Institute of Chemical Engineers, 345 East 47th Street, New York, NY 10017.

American Insurance Association, 1130 Connecticut Avenue, NW, Suite 1000, Washington, DC 20036.

American Iron and Steel Institute, 1101 17th Street, NW, Suite 1300, Washington, DC 20036.

American Library Association, 50 East Huron Street, Chicago, IL 60611.

American Management Association, 135 West 50th Street, New York, NY 10020.

American Marketing Association, 250 South Wacker Drive, Chicago, IL 60606.

American Mathematical Society, 201 Charles Street, Providence, RI 02904.

American Petroleum Institute, 1220 L Street, NW, Washington, DC 20005.

American Society for Industrial Security, 1655 North Fort Myer Drive, Suite 1200, Arlington, VA 22209.

American Society for Personnel Administration, 606 North Washington Street, Alexandria, VA 22314.

American Society for Quality Control, 611 East Wisconsin Avenue, Milwaukee, WI 53201.

American Society of Association Executives, 1575 I Street, NW, Washington, DC 20005.

American Society of Civil Engineers, 345 East 47th Street, New York, NY 10017.

American Society of International Law, 2223 Massachusetts Avenue, NW, Washington, DC 20008.

American Society of Journalists and Authors, 1501 Broadway, Suite 302, New York, NY 10036.

American Society of Mechanical Engineers, 345 East 47th Street, New York, NY 10017.

American Society of Travel Agents, 1101 King Street, Alexandria, VA 22314.

American Stock Exchange, 86 Trinity Place, New York, NY 10006.

American Translators Association, 1800 Diagonal Road, Suite 220, Alexandria, VA 22314.

Associated Press, 50 Rockefeller Plaza, New York, NY 10020.

Association for Computing Machinery, 1515 Broadway, 17th Floor, New York, NY 10036.

Association for Information and Image Management, 1100 Wayne Avenue, Suite 1100, Silver Spring, MD 20910.

Association for Investment Management and Research, 5 Boar's Head Lane, Charlottesville, VA 22901.

Association for Systems Management, P.O. Box 38370, Cleveland, OH 44138.

Association of American Inventors, 2020 Pennsylvania Avenue, N.W., Washington, DC 20006.

Association of American Publishers, Inc., 71 5th Avenue, New York, NY 10003.

Association of American Universities, One Dupont Circle, Suite 730, Washington, DC 20036.

Association of Authors Representatives, 10 Astor Place, 3rd Floor, New York, NY 10003.

Association of Business Writers of America, Inc., 1450 South Havana Street, Suite 424, Aurora, CO 80012.

Association of Desk-Top Publishers, 3401-A800 Adams Way, San Diego, CA 92116.

Association of Direct Market Agencies, 60 East 42nd Street, Suite 1841, New York, NY 10165.

Association of Management Consulting Firms, The, 521 5th Avenue, 35th Floor, New York, NY 10175.

Association of National Advertisers, 155 East 44th Street, New York, NY 10017.

Association of Professional Translators, 3 Mellon Bank Center, Room BF50, Pittsburgh, PA 15259.

Association of Records Managers and Administrators, 4200 Somerset Drive, Suite 215, Prairie Village, KS 66208.

Authors League of America, 234 West 44th Street, New York, NY 10036.

Bibliographical Society of America, P.O. Box 397, Grand Central Station, New York, NY 10163.

Business Marketing Association, 150 North Wacker Drive, Suite 1760, Chicago, IL 60606.

Chamber of Commerce of the U.S.A., 1615 H Street, NW, Washington, DC 20062.

Chemical Manufacturers Association, 1300 Wilson Boulevard, Arlington, VA 22202.

Construction Industry Manufacturers Association, 111 East Wisconsin Avenue, Milwaukee, Wisconsin 53202.

Consumer Federation of America, 1424 16th Street, NW, #604, Washington, DC 20036.

Council of Better Business Bureaus, 4200 Wilson Boulevard, Suite 800, Arlington, VA 22203.

Council of Consulting Organizations, 521 5th Avenue, New York, NY 10175.

Digital Printing and Imaging Association, 10015 Main Street, Fairfax, VA 22031.

Direct Marketing Association, Inc., 1120 Avenue of the Americas, New York, NY 10036.

Electronic Industries Association, 2001 Pennsylvania Avenue, Washington, DC 20006.

Environmental Information Association, 1777 Northeast Expressway, Suite 150, Atlanta, GA 30329.

Federal Bar Association, 1815 H Street, NW, Washington, DC 20006.

Financial Analysts Federation, 5 Boar's Head Lane, Charlottesville, VA 22903.

Freelance Editorial Association, P.O. Box 380835, Cambridge, MA 02238.

General Contractors of America, 1957 E Street, NW, Washington, DC 20006.

Geological Society of America, 3300 Penrose Place, P.O. Box 9140, Boulder, CO 80301.

Industrial Designers Society of America, 1142 East Walker Road, Great Falls, VA 22066.

Industrial Health Foundation, 34 Penn Circle West, Pittsburgh, PA 15206.

Information Industry Association, 1625 Massachusetts Avenue, NW, Suite 700, Washington, DC 20036.

Institute for Certification of Computer Professionals, 2200 East Devon Avenue, Suite 247, Des Plaines, IL 60018.

International Association of Business Communicators, One Hallidie Plaza, Suite 600, San Francisco, CA 94102.

International City/County Management Association, 777 North Capitol Street, NW, Suite 500, Washington, DC 20002.

International Credit Association, 243 North Lindbergh Boulevard, Saint Louis, MO 63147.

International Intercultural Programs, 220 East 42nd Street, New York, NY 10017.

International Real Estate Institute, 8383 East Evans Road, Scottsdale, AZ 85260.

International Trademark Association, 1133 Avenue of the Americas, New York, NY 10036.

International Training in Communication, 2519 Woodland Drive, Anaheim, CA 92801.

Kiwanis International, 3636 Woodview Trace, Indianapolis, IN 46268.

Magazine Publishers of America, 919 Third Avenue, New York, NY 10022.

Metric Association, 10245 Andasol Avenue, Northridge, CA 91325.

National Academy of Engineering, 2101 Constitution Avenue, NW, Washington, DC 20418.

National Academy of Sciences, 2101 Constitution Avenue, NW, Washington, DC 20418.

National Association of Business and Educational Radio, 1501 Duke Street, Alexandria, VA 22314.

National Association of Desktop Publishers, 460 Old Boston Street, Topsfield, MA 01983.

National Association of Home Builders, 1201 15th Street, NW, Washington, DC 20005.

National Association of Investors Corporation, 711 West Thirteen Mile Road, Madison Heights, MI 48068.

National Association of Manufacturers, 1331 Pennsylvania Avenue, NW, Suite 1500 North Tower, Washington, DC 20004.

National Association of Parliamentarians, 213 South Main Street, Independence, MO 64050.

National Business Education Association, 1906 Association Drive, Reston, VA 22091.

National Cooperative Business Association, 1401 New York Avenue, NW, Suite 1100, Washington, DC 20005.

National Education Association, 1201 16th Street, NW, Washington, DC 20036.

National Electrical Manufacturers Association, 2101 L Street, NW, Washington, DC 20037.

National Foreign Trade Council, Inc., 1625 K Street, NW, Washington, DC 20006.

National Grocers Association, 1825 Samuel Morse Drive, Reston, VA 22090.

National League of Cities, 1301 Pennsylvania Avenue, NW, Washington, DC 20004.

National Recycling Coalition, 1727 King Street, Suite 105, Alexandria, VA 22514.

National Safety Council, 1121 Spring Lake Drive, Itasca, IL 60143.

National Society of Professional Engineers, 1420 King Street, Alexandria, VA 22314.

National Taxpayers Union, 108 North Alfred Street, Alexandria, VA 22314.

National Urban League, 500 East 62nd Street, New York, NY 10022.

National Writers Association, 1450 South Havana, Suite 424, Aurora, CO 80012.

National Writers Union, 113 University Place, 6th Floor, New York, NY 10003.

New York Stock Exchange, 11 Wall Street, New York, NY 10005.

Newspaper Association of America, The Newspaper Center, 11600 Sunrise Valley Drive, Reston, VA 22091.

Personal Communication Industry Association, 500 Montgomery Street, Suite 700, Alexandria, VA 22314.

Photographic Society of America, 3000 United Founders Boulevard, #103, Oklahoma City, OK 73112.

Printing Industries of America, 100 Dangerfield Road, Alexandria, VA 22314.

Professional Photographers of America, 57 Forsyth Street, NW, Suite 1600, Atlanta, GA 30303.

Securities Industry Association, 120 Broadway, New York, NY 10271.

Society for Human Resource Management, 606 North Washington Street, Alexandria, VA 22314.

Society of Actuaries, 475 North Martingale Road, Suite 800, Schaumburg, IL 60173.

Society of American Business Editors and Writers, c/o Janine Latus-Musick, University of Missouri, School of Journalism, 76 Gannett Hall, Columbia, MO 65211.

Society of Illustrators, Inc., 128 East 63rd Street, New York, NY 10021.

Society of Manufacturing Engineers, One SME Drive, Dearborn, MI 48121.

Society of Professional Journalists, 16 South Jackson Street, Greencastle, IN 46135.

Society of the Plastics Industry, 1275 K Street, NW, Suite 400, Washington, DC 20005.

Speech Communication Association, 5105 Backlick Road, Annandale, VA 22003.

Technical Association of the Pulp and Paper Industry, 15 Technology Parkway, S/Atlanta, Norcross, GA 30092.

U.S. Chamber of Commerce, 1615 H Street, NW, Washington, DC 20062.

U.S. English, 818 Connecticut Avenue, NW, Suite 200, Washington, DC 20006.

United Press International, 1400 I Street, NW, Washington, DC 20005.

Women in Communications, Inc., 2101 Wilson Boulevard, Suite 417, Arlington, VA 22201.

77

Large-Circulation Public Libraries in Major U.S. Cities

Sometimes a small local or company library isn't adequate for a writer who needs the more extensive resources of a high-volume, large-circulation library. This list has more than eighty such large public libraries located in major cities throughout the United States. Addresses are organized by state.

ALABAMA

Birmingham: Birmingham Public Library, 2100 Park Place, 35203.

ARIZONA

Phoenix: Maricopa County Library District, 17811 North 32nd Street, 85032.

Tucson: Tucson Public Library, 101 North Stone Avenue, 85701.

CALIFORNIA

Long Beach: Long Beach Public Library and Information Center, 101 Pacific Avenue, 90822.

Los Angeles: Los Angeles Public Library, 630 West 5th Street, 90071.

Sacramento: Sacramento Public Library, 828 I Street, 95814.

San Diego: San Diego County Library System, 5555 Overland Avenue, Building 15, 92123.

San Diego: San Diego Public Library, 820 E Street, 92101.

San Francisco: San Francisco Public Library, 100 Larkin Street, 94102.

San Jose: San Jose Public Library, 180 West San Carlos Street, 95113.

COLORADO

Denver: Denver Public Library, 10 West 14th Avenue, 80204.

DISTRICT OF COLUMBIA

Washington: Library of Congress, 10 1st Street, SE, 20540.

FLORIDA

Jacksonville: Jacksonville Public Library, 122 North Ocean Street, 32202.

Miami: Miami-Dade Public Library, 101 West Flagler Street, 33130.

Saint Petersburg: Saint Petersburg Public Library, 3745 9th Avenue North, 33713.

Tampa: Tampa-Hillsborough County Public Library, 900 North Ashley Drive, 33602.

GEORGIA

Atlanta: Atlanta-Fulton Public Library, 1 Margaret Mitchell Square, NW, 30303.

HAWAII

Honolulu: Hawaii State Public Library, 478 South King Street, 96813.

ILLINOIS

Chicago: Chicago Public Library, 400 South State Street, 60605.

INDIANA

Evansville: Evansville-Vanderburgh County Public Library, 22 Southeast 5th Street, 47708.

Fort Wayne: Allen County Public Library, P.O. Box 2270, Fort Wayne, 46801.

Indianapolis: Indianapolis-Marion County Public Library, P.O. Box 211, 46206.

IOWA

Des Moines: Des Moines Public Library, 100 Locust, 50309.

KANSAS

Wichita: Wichita Public Library, 223 South Main Street, 67202.

KENTUCKY

Louisville: Louisville Free Public Library, 301 York Street, 40203.

LOUISIANA

New Orleans: New Orleans Public Library, 219 Loyola Avenue, 70140.

MARYLAND

Annapolis: Anne Arundel County Public Library, 5 Harry S. Truman Parkway, 21401.

Baltimore: Baltimore County Public Library, 320 York Road, Towson, 21204.

MASSACHUSETTS

Boston: Boston Public Library, 666 Boylston Street, 02117.

Springfield: Springfield City Library, 220 State Street, 01103.

Worcester: Central Massachusetts Regional Library System, 3 Salem Square, 01608.

MICHIGAN

Detroit: Detroit Public Library, 5201 Woodward Avenue, 48202.

Grand Rapids: Grand Rapids Public Library, 60 Library Plaza, NE, 49503.

MINNESOTA

Minneapolis: Minneapolis Public Library, 300 Nicollet Mall, 55401.

Saint Paul: Saint Paul Public Library, 90 4th Street West, 55102.

MISSISSIPPI

Jackson: Jackson-Hinds Library System, 300 North State Street, 39201.

MISSOURI

Independence: Mid-Continent Public Library, 15616 East 24 Highway, 64050.

Kansas City: Kansas City Public Library, 311 East 12th Street, 64106.

Saint Louis: Saint Louis County Library, 1640 South Lindbergh Boulevard, 63131.

Saint Louis: Saint Louis Public Library, 1301 Olive Street, 63103.

NEBRASKA

Lincoln: Lincoln City Libraries, 136 South 14th Street, 68508.

Omaha: Omaha Public Library, 215 South 15th Street, 68102.

NEW JERSEY

Newark: Newark Public Library, 5 Washington Street, 07101.

NEW MEXICO

Albuquerque: Albuquerque Public Library, 501 Copper Avenue, NW, 87102.

NEW YORK

Brooklyn: Brooklyn Public Library, Grand Army Plaza, 11238.

Buffalo: Buffalo and Erie County Public Library, Lafayette Square, 14203.

Jamaica: Queensborough Public Library, 89-11 Merrick Boulevard, 11432.

New York City: New York Public Library, 5th Avenue and 42nd Street, 10018.

Rochester: Rochester Public Library, 115 South Avenue, 14604.

NORTH CAROLINA

Charlotte: Charlotte and Mecklenburg County Public Library, 310 North Tryon Street, 28202.

Winston-Salem: Forsyth County Public Library, 660 West 5th Street, 27101.

OHIO

Akron: Akron-Summit County Public Library, 55 South Main Street, 44326.

Cincinnati: Cincinnati and Hamilton County Public Library, 800 Vine Street, 45202.

Cleveland: Cleveland Public Library, 325 Superior Avenue East, 44114.

Columbus: Columbus Metropolitan Library, 96 South Grant Avenue, 43215.

Dayton: Dayton and Montgomery County Public Library, 215 East 3rd Street, 45402.

Youngstown: Public Library of Youngstown and Mahoning County, 305 Wick Avenue, 44503.

OKLAHOMA

Oklahoma City: Metropolitan Library of Oklahoma City, 131 Dean A. McGee Avenue, 73102.

Tulsa: Tulsa City-County Library, 400 Civic Center, 74103.

OREGON

Portland: Multnomah County Library, 1407 Southwest 4th Avenue, 97205.

PENNSYLVANIA

Erie: Erie County Library System, 27 South Park Row, 16501.

Philadelphia: Philadelphia Free Library, 1901 Vine Street, Logan Square, 19103.

Pittsburgh: Carnegie Library of Pittsburgh, 4400 Forbes Avenue, 15213.

RHODE ISLAND

Providence: Providence Public Library, 225 Washington Street, 02903.

SOUTH CAROLINA

Greenville: Greenville County Library, 300 College Street, 29601.

TENNESSEE

Knoxville: Knox County Public Library System, 500 West Church Avenue, 37902.

Memphis: Memphis-Shelby County Public Library and Information Center, 1850 Peabody Avenue, 38104.

Nashville: West Ben Public Library of Nashville and Davidson County, 225 Polk Avenue, 37203.

TEXAS

Austin: Austin Public Library, P.O. Box 2287, 78768.

Dallas: J. Eric Johnson Public Library, 1515 Young Street, 75201.

El Paso: El Paso Public Library, 501 North Oregon Street, 79901.

Fort Worth: Fort Worth Public Library, 300 Taylor Street, 76102.

Houston: Houston Public Library, 500 Mckinney Street, 77002.

San Antonio: San Antonio Public Library, 600 Soledad Street, 78205.

UTAH

Salt Lake City: Salt Lake City Library System, 2197 East 7000 South, 84121.

VIRGINIA

Fairfax: Fairfax County Public Library, 13135 Lee Jackson Memorial Highway, Suite 301, 22033.

Norfolk: Norfolk Public Library, 301 East City Hall Avenue, 23510.

Richmond: Richmond Public Library, 101 East Franklin Street, 23219.

WASHINGTON

Seattle: Seattle Public Library, 1000 4th Avenue, 98104.

WEST VIRGINIA

Charleston: Kanawha County Public Library, 123 Capital Street, 25301.

WISCONSIN

Madison: Madison Public Library, 201 West Mifflin Street, 53703.

Milwaukee: Milwaukee Public Library, 814 West Wisconsin Avenue, 53233.

78

U.S. Government
Printing Office Branch Bookstores

Like regular commercial bookstores, government bookstores offer another useful research outlet for writers. The U.S. Government Printing Office in Washington, D.C., operates nearly two dozen branch bookstores across the United States. The following list gives the addresses of the bookstores arranged by state.

ALABAMA

Birmingham: 2021 3rd Avenue, North, O'Neill Building, 35203.

CALIFORNIA

Los Angeles: 505 South Flower Street, ARCO Plaza, Level C, 90071.

San Francisco: 303 2nd Street, Marathon Plaza, Room 141-S, 94107.

COLORADO

Denver: 1961 Stout Street, Rogers Federal Building, Room 117, 80294.

Pueblo: 201 West 8th Street, Norwest Bank Building, 81003.

DISTRICT OF COLUMBIA

Washington: 710 North Capitol Street, SW, 20401.

FLORIDA

Jacksonville: 100 West Bay Street, Suite 100, 32202.

GEORGIA

Atlanta: 5999 Peachtree Street, NE, 30309.

ILLINOIS

Chicago: 401 South State Street, 1 Congress Center, Suite 124, 60605.

MARYLAND

Laurel: 86660 Cherry Lane, 20707.

MASSACHUSETTS

Boston: 10 Causeway Street, Room 169, 02222.

MICHIGAN

Detroit: 477 Michigan Avenue, Federal Building, Suite 160, 48226.

MISSOURI

Kansas City: 5600 East Bannister Road, Room 120, 64137.

NEW YORK

New York: 26 Federal Plaza, Room 110, 10278.

OHIO

Cleveland: 1240 East 9th Street, Federal Building, Room 1653, 44199.

Columbus: 200 North High Street, Room 207, 43215.

OREGON

Portland: 1305 Southwest lst Avenue, 97201.

PENNSYLVANIA

Philadelphia: 100 North 17th Street, Morris Building, 19103.

Pittsburgh: 1000 Liberty Avenue, Federal Building, Room 118, 15222.

TEXAS

Dallas: 1100 Commerce Street, Cabell Federal Building, Room 100, 75242.

Houston: 801 Travis Street, Suite 120, 77002.

WASHINGTON

Seattle: 915 2nd Avenue, Jackson Federal Building, Room 194, 98174.

WISCONSIN

Milwaukee: 310 West Wisconsin Avenue, Federal Plaza, Room 150, 53202.

79

Useful Business Databases

Various organizations maintain large collections of data on specific subjects, such as computer products. This information is frequently available to the public through the Internet; through an on-line subscriber service, such as CompuServe (see the next list); or by purchase of a CD-ROM containing the collection of data. The following databases are useful for writers. Contact the supplier to find out more about content and how the data are provided, such as by subscription or by purchase of a CD-ROM, and to learn about the charges and access requirements.

ASBA Exchange, American Small Business Association, P.O. Box 612663, Dallas, TX 75216.

Books in Print Online, R. R. Bowker Co., 245 West 17th Street, New York, NY 10011.

Bowker's International Serials Database, R. R. Bowker Co., 245 West 17th Street, New York, NY 10011.

Business Periodicals Index, H. W. Wilson Co., 950 University Avenue, Bronx, NY 10452.

Business Software Database, Information Sources, Inc., 1173 Colusa Avenue, P.O. Box 7848, Berkeley, CA 94707.

Business Week, McGraw-Hill, Inc., 1221 Avenue of the Americas, New York, NY 10020.

BYTE, McGraw-Hill, Inc., 1 Phoenix Mill Lane, Peterborough, NH 03458.

Career Information Service, 1787 Agate Street, Eugene, OR 97403.

CD-ROM Databases, Worldwide Videotex, P.O. Box 138, Babson Park Branch, Boston, MA 02157.

Computer Products Directory, P.O. Box 439, Collingdale, PA 19073.

Database Directory, Knowledge Industry Publications, Inc., 701 Westchester Avenue, White Plains, NY 10604.

DIAL-A-FAX Directory Assistance, DIAL-A-FAX Directories Corporation, 1761 West Hillsboro Boulevard, Suite 204, Deerfield Beach, FL 33442.

DIALOG BLUESHEETS, DIALOG Information Services, Inc., 3460 Hillview Avenue, Palo Alto, CA 94304.

Dow Jones Business and Financial Report, Dow Jones & Co., Inc., P.O. Box 300, Princeton, NJ 08540.

Editors Only, P.O. Box 175, Litchfield, CT 06759.

Encyclopedia of Associations, Gale Research, Inc., 835 Penobscot Building, Detroit, MI 48226.

Home/Office Small Business RoundTable, GE Information Services, 401 North Washington Boulevard, Rockville, MD 20850.

Illustrated Handbook of Desktop Publishing, Highlighted Data, P.O. Box 17229, Washington Dulles International Airport, Washington, DC 20041.

Journal of Commerce, Journal of Commerce, Inc., 110 Wall Street, New York, NY 10005.

LEXIS International Trade Library, Mead Data Central, Inc., 9393 Springboro Parkway, P.O. Box 933, Dayton, OH 45401.

Management Matters, Merton Allen Associates, P.O. Box 15640, Plantation, FL 33318.

PR and Marketing Forum, CompuServe Information Service,

5000 Arlington Centre Boulevard, P.O. Box 20212, Columbus, OH 43220.

Software Directory, The, Menu Publishing, Mayview Road at Park Drive, P.O. Box MENU, Pittsburgh, PA 15241.

The Small Business Tax Review, Hooksett Publishing, Inc., P.O. Box 895, Melville, NY 11747.

TRW Updated Credit Profile, TRW Credit Data Division, 505 City Parkway West, Orange, CA 92668.

Writer's Electronic Bulletin Board, P.O. Box 1069, Branson, MO 65616.

80

Selected Internet Service Providers

An increasing number of organizations are offering access to the Internet. Some of the providers, such as CompuServe, America Online, and Prodigy, also offer other information to their network subscribers. Before selecting a service provider or changing providers, users often find it helpful to request current information from several organizations to compare charges, degree of access (full or partial), and other available benefits and services. The following list of selected service providers is a small sample of the increasing Internet access options.

a2i Communications, 1211 Park Avenue, #202, San Jose, CA 95126.

Advanced Network & Services, Inc. (ANS), ANS CO+RE Systems, Inc., 2901 Hubbard, Ann Arbor, MI 48105.

America Online, 8619 Westwood Center Drive, Vienna, VA 22182.

CompuServe Information System, 5000 Arlington Center Boulevard, P.O. Box 20212, Columbus, OH 43220.

Delphi, 1030 Massachusetts Avenue, Cambridge, MA 02138.

eWorld, Apple Computer, 20525 Mariani Avenue, MS 36BC, Cupertino, CA 95014.

GEnie, General Electric, 45 West Gude Drive, Rockville, MD 20850.

MCI Mail, 1133 19th Street, NW, 7th Floor, Washington, DC 20036.

Netcom Online Communications Services, 3031 Tisch Way, San Jose, CA 95117.

Panix Public Access Unix, 15 West 18th Street, 5th Floor, New York, NY 10011.

Performance Systems International (PSI), 510 Huntmor Park Drive, Herndon, VA 22070.

Prodigy, 445 Hamilton Avenue, White Plains, NY 10601.

SPRINTLINK, Sprint, 13221 Woodland Park Road, Herndon, VA 22071.

U.S. Internet, 1127 North Broadway, Knoxville, TN 37917.

UUNET Technologies, 33060 Williams Drive, Fairfax, VA 22031.

World, The, Software Tool & Die, 1330 Beacon Street, Brookline, MA 02146.

INDEX

a2i Communications (Internet service provider), 318
Abbreviations
  in documents, 11–12
  in E-mail, 24
  E-mail emoticons, 224–27
  information technology, 227–41
  in international messages, 22
  for Internet phrases, 222–24
Accents, 179
Accuracy
  of business letters, 14
  in E-mail, 24
  of messages, 9–10
  of statistics, 10–11
Acronyms, 11, 227
Active voice, 15, 31, 133, 138, 141
Active words, 37–42
Acute accents, 179
Addresses, 12
Adjective pronouns, 133
Adjectives, 15, 133, 134
  and adverbs, 31
  comparative and superlative degrees of, 141, 234
  and comparisons, 31, 162–63
  and infinitives, 137
  as modifiers, 137
  relative, 140
Advanced Network & Services, Inc. (Internet service provider), 318
Adverbs, 133
  and adjectives, 31

comparative and superlative degrees of, 141, 234
  and infinitives, 137
  as modifiers, 137
  relative, 140
Agreement, 133
Aircraft names, 183
America Online (Internet service provider), 318
Analyzing readers, 4–5, 8, 29
Anecdotes, 18
Anger, 15, 16, 23
Anglicized foreign words, 179–81
Antecedents, 134, 139, 140
Apologizing, 15
Apostrophes, 177
Appearance of documents, 8
Appositives, 134
Articles, 134
ASBA Exchange (database), 316
Asking favors, 3
Associations and societies in U.S., 296–305
Attitude change, 3
Automated postal sorting, 12
Auxiliary verbs, 134, 139

Bad–news messages, 15, 19–20, 86
Behavior change, 3
Bias
  in language, 13, 27, 100–102, 104–12
  personal, 9
Bias of readers, 5

ABOUT THE AUTHOR

Mary A. DeVries is the author of dozens of business and reference books, including two other books of lists—*The Complete Word Book* and *The Professional Secretary's Book of Lists and Tips*—and numerous books about writing and word usage, such as the *Practical Writer's Guide, Guide to Better Business Writing,* and *Business Thesaurus.*